Becoming a Borderland

Transition in Northeastern India

Series Editor: Sumi Krishna, Independent scholar, Bangalore

The uniquely diverse landscapes, societies and cultures of northeastern India, forged through complex bio-geographic and socio-political forces, are now facing rapid transition. This series focuses on the processes and practices that have shaped, and are shaping, the peoples' identities, outlook, institutions, and economy. Eschewing the homogenising term 'North East', which was imposed on the region in a particular political context half a century ago, the series title refers to the 'northeastern' region to more accurately reflect its heterogeneity. Seeking to explore how the 'mainstream' and the 'margins' impact each other, the series will foreground both historical and contemporary research on the region including the Eastern Himalaya, the adjoining hills and valleys, the states of Arunachal Pradesh, Assam, Manipur, Meghalaya, Mizoram, Nagaland, Sikkim and Tripura. It will publish original, reflective studies that draw upon different disciplines and approaches, and combine empirical and theoretical insights to make scholarship accessible for general readers and to help deepen the understanding of academics, policy-makers and practitioners.

Also in this Series

Education and Society in a Changing Mizoram: The Practice of Pedagogy
Lakshmi Bhatia
ISBN 978-0-415-58920-8

Unfolding Crisis in Assam's Tea Plantations: Employment and Occupational Mobility
Deepak K. Mishra, Vandana Upadhyay and **Atul Sarma**
ISBN 978-0-415-52308-0

Agriculture and a Changing Environment in Northeastern India
Editor: Sumi Krishna
ISBN 978-0-415-63289-8

Conflict and Reconciliation: The Politics of Ethnicity in Assam
Uddipana Goswami
ISBN 978-0-415-71113-5

Northeastern India and its Neighbours: Negotiating Security and Development
Rakhee Bhattacharya
ISBN 978-1-138-79533-4

Colonialism and Resistance: Society and State in Manipur
Editors: Arambam Noni and **Kangujam Sanatomba**
ISBN 978-1-138-79553-2

Becoming a Borderland

*The Politics of Space and Identity
in Colonial Northeastern India*

Sanghamitra Misra

Routledge
Taylor & Francis Group
LONDON NEW YORK NEW DELHI

First published 2011 in India
by Routledge
912 Tolstoy House, 15–17 Tolstoy Marg, Connaught Place,
New Delhi 110 001

Simultaneously published in the UK
by Routledge
2 Park Square, Milton Park, Abingdon, OX14 4RN

Routledge is an imprint of the Taylor & Francis Group, an informa business

© 2011 Sanghamitra Misra

Paperback edition published 2015

Typeset by
Glyph Graphics Private Limited
23, Khosla Complex
Vasundhara Enclave
Delhi 110 096

British Library Cataloguing-in-Publication Data
A catalogue record of this book is available from the British Library

ISBN 978-1-138-84745-3

Contents

Tables

Abbreviations

ALCP	Assam Legislative Council Proceedings
APAI	Assam Police Abstract of Intelligence
ASF	Assam Secretariat Files
ASP	Assam Secretariat Proceedings
BTA	Bengal Tenancy Act
DHAS	Department of Historical and Antiquarian Studies
GP	Goalpara Papers
GTA	Goalpara Tenancy Act
HPP	Home Political Proceedings
NAI	National Archives of India
OIOC	Oriental and India Office Collection
PHA	Political History of Assam

Acknowledgements

This book has emerged out of research done for a doctoral dissertation at the School of Oriental and African Studies (SOAS), London. Over the years, it has accumulated many debts and it is my pleasure to be able to record them. I thank the Commonwealth Trust for funding my research for a Ph.D. degree. For additional financial support, I thank The Harold Hyam Wingate Foundation, the SOAS fieldwork grant and the Indian Council of Social Science Research. A British Academy — AHRC-ESRC Visiting Fellowship — made further research and a finalisation of the manuscript possible. I thank the Economic and Social Research Council for this and the SOAS for institutional support.

My deepest debt is to Peter Robb, who has been the most committed and untiring reader of this manuscript, right from its inception as a doctoral dissertation. Peter carefully and patiently read the countless drafts that were thrust upon him, improving them through his insights and comments. His affection and generosity has been a source of sustained support. For sharpening many of the arguments of this book through his own engagements with histories of margins and for being such a wonderful teacher of history, I thank Neeladri Bhattacharya. I thank Sabyasachi Bhattacharya for his suggestions which helped frame many questions at an initial stage of research. Willem van Schendel's commitment to research on borderlands has always been a source of much inspiration and I am grateful for his interest in my work. I am indebted to Birendranath Datta for sharing his extensive knowledge of Assam's history and for giving so generously of his time. In the many evenings spent discussing Goalpara's history with him and Eva Datta at their place in Guwahati, I learnt to love Goalpara as they did. Gautam Bhadra's suggestions helped clarify many ideas at an early stage of writing and I am grateful to him for this. For their comments on various parts of my work, I warmly thank Shubho Basu, Avril Powell, Indrani Chatterjee, Sanjib Baruah and David Ludden. For his intellectual companionship and friendship, I thank Bodhisattva Kar.

For their hospitality and kindness during my fieldwork, I am grateful to Sukanta Chaudhuri and Supriya Chaudhuri. I am especially indebted to Tripathnath Chakravarty and his family for welcoming me into their home at Dhubri and helping me with my research. A considerable part of my archival notes were made at Ajit Baruah's place in Dhubri who gave me access to his personal collection of papers and I am extremely grateful for his generosity. Arupjyoti Saikia added to my research with a range of primary material and I thank him for his help.

Various chapters and sections of this book have benefited from being presented at some recent conferences. A Sephis workshop on 'Challenging the Master Narrative' at Cebu, Philippines, added significantly to the arguments in this book. For their interventions and insights at the workshop, I thank Mamadou Diouf, Willem van Schendel, Andres Barba, Michel Baud and Jorge Pavez. A conference organised by the Asian Borderlands Network at Guwahati helped open up new possibilities and connections in my research. For the immensely valuable discussions and comments at the conference on 'Writing the Northeast' at the Jawaharlal Nehru University, New Delhi, which enriched this work, I thank the participants and organisers. Parts of this work were also revised when presented at a panel at the 2009 World Economic History Congress at Utrecht.

For their help with finding material, my sincere thanks to Mr Baishya at the Assam State Archives, Guwahati; the staff at the Oriental and India Office Collections, British Library, London; the National Library, Kolkata; the West Bengal State Archives, Kolkata; the SOAS Library, London; the Nehru Memorial Museum and Library, New Delhi; the Collectorate and Police Archives at Dhubri; the Library at Centre for Studies in Social Sciences, Kolkata; the Sahitya Sabha Library, Guwahati; the Department of Historical and Antiquarian Studies, Guwahati; and the Dibrugarh University Library.

To Sumi Krishna for her interest in the project and coaxing me on towards necessary deadlines, my warm thanks. I thank the editorial team at Routledge India for their patience in accommodating my various requests.

To Yenkhom Jilangamba, Lipokmar Dzuvichu, John Thomas and other fellow travellers, my gratitude for shared political and academic concerns and for giving this work the sense of a collective project. I thank Elizabeth Robb for a warmth and concern that was mine for the asking, every time. For their affection and support, I thank Harriet and Marshal Horne, Neeraj Malik and Javed Malick, Monica Fagioli, Sayako Kanda, Anthony Gorman, Pradeep Narayanan, Veronica Castro, Leela Sami, Njane Mugambe, Takeshi Nagata, Tanweer Fazal, John Parker, Talat Ahmed and Navnita Behera. I thank Sakkar Tejani and Shabnum Tejani for giving me a home in London and for willingly putting up with my frequent intrusions into it. Bhavana Krishnamoorthy's friendship and arguments meant more than she would have acknowledged and in her absence, I am left to imagine what her criticisms would have been.

For the warmth of familial support and for her encouragement, I thank Jaya Singh. For being my friend and sharing my life across distances for years, and for many conversations that hopefully reflect in this work, I thank Rochelle Pinto. My grandparents provided me with a home in Guwahati for many years. For as long as I can remember, my brother, Arindam, has always been more confident about my work than I have ever been. My parents, Tilottoma and Udayon Misra, have followed the course of this book with enthusiasm and also with an increasing impatience. Their engagement with its concerns makes the book as much theirs as mine. For innumerable close readings, comments and for her help with the translations, a special word of thanks for my mother.

Goalpara and its surrounding regions in the late nineteenth century

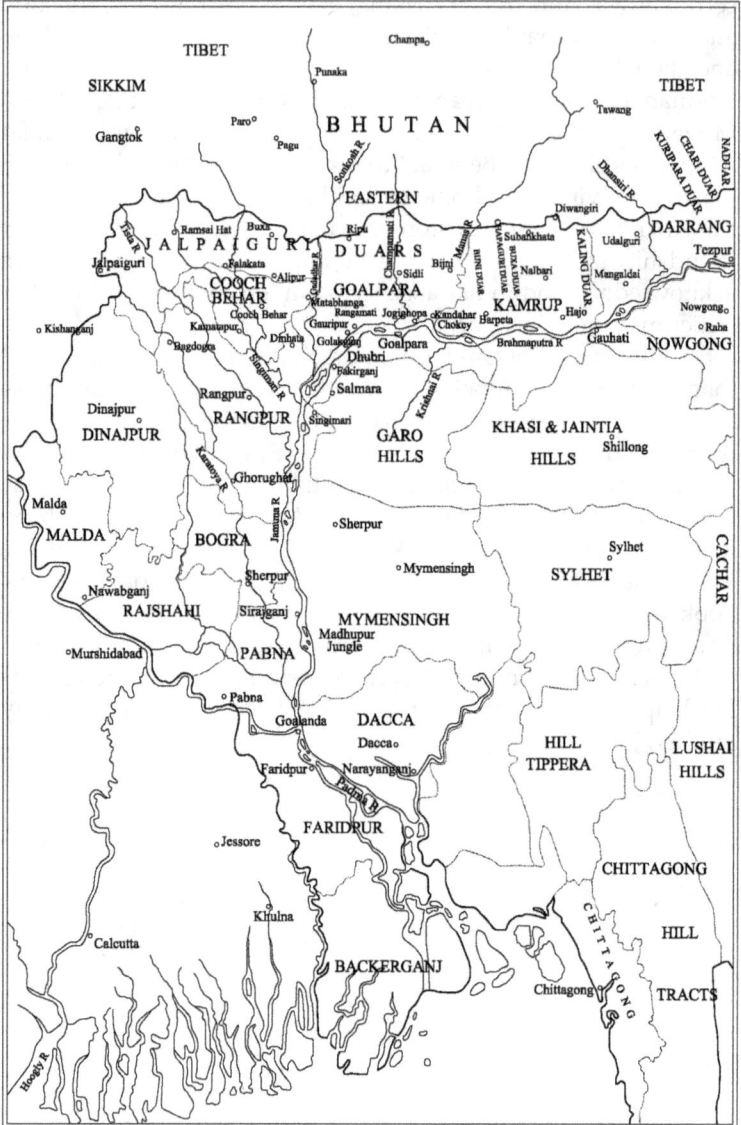

Source: Prepared by the author.

Introduction

❂

Becoming a Borderland tells the story of the ways in which political conquest and economic domination forcibly and irrevocably alters pre-existing orders of space in parts of eastern and northeastern India. It investigates how, through the control and exploitation of the economy by a violent colonial state, another spatial imagination and order entrenches itself in the region, only to continue in different forms as a legacy that the post-colonial state inherits. The story begins in the period of the late Mughal imperium when the region of Goalpara and its surrounds — the Eastern Duars, Cooch Behar, the southern foothills of Bhutan, the northeastern borders of Bengal — constituted for the Mughal empire an anomalous zone on its borders, with a political economy that was oriented towards the northern regions of Bhutan, Tibet and Lhasa. The book then takes the reader across a span of a critical century and a half in the history of this region to narrate its dramatic and irreversible transformation under colonial conquest and rule and subsequent contestations over cultural nationalism. The founding of colonial rule resulted in a fundamental change in the manner in which political and economic space came to be imagined and apportioned, creating a fragmented zone of dependent and independent polities and bounded political units of the British Empire, and a circumscribed borderland district of Goalpara with a fractured administrative history and political economy.[1] Under colonialism, Goalpara was reduced to both an economic hinterland of the colonial market and into a culturally peripheral space. Colonial policies fractured the region into 'many borderlands', fraught by contesting narratives and counter-narratives often pertaining to cultural identity. These tensions over appropriations of history and public space were articulated forcefully, forming the local politics of identity in Goalpara, which also fundamentally affected the trajectories of the neighbouring nationalisms of Assam and Bengal. The book grounds the nature of these political and cultural formations in the changing regimes of law and land use under colonialism.

My initial forays into research in this area were to study a brief period of dramatic economic change that had been triggered by an unprecedented migration of cultivators from Eastern Bengal into the western borders of the colonial province of Assam in the early twentieth century. What had until then been a region with large stretches of uninhabited lands and sparse population was within the span of a mere decade transformed into a space of extensive mobility and sharp increases in population; the 'waste-lands' and marshes now became well-cultivated fields of paddy and jute. These were changes propelled by the demands of capital, market and a revenue-extracting state which assiduously encouraged large groups of people to settle and cultivate these tracts of land. That the frontiers of cultivation had been reached by the last decades of the nineteenth century in adjacent northern and eastern Bengal, creating a situation of growing saturation of available cultivable land (Bose 1986; Eaton 1993), clearly influenced colonial policies on land and migration in Assam. The resultant migration northeastward towards what were identified as some of the most fertile remaining agricultural frontiers of South Asia, i.e., Goalpara and western Assam, was a spectacular phenomenon, initially just in terms of its numbers and then because of the immense changes effected in patterns of land use, their differential impact on divergent social groups and on local organisational politics. These are themes that have been discussed to an extent in available historical works on Goalpara (Guha 1974, 1977, 2000; Barman 1994). However, as this book argues, the migration of land-hungry and skilled cultivators — products of modern regimes of property and familiar with the world of legal titles — in large numbers into a region with very different notions of landholding and property rights, has a crucial significance of an altogether different order. The conditions of land acquisition and land appropriation that the migration produced altered radically and forever the classification and division of space in the region of Goalpara and the surrounding areas of western Assam.

Contemporary historical literature refuses to sufficiently illustrate these fundamental issues, preferring instead to confine the history of Goalpara and its surrounds to their characterisation as static 'historical frontiers', and later, as 'borderlands of heart-lands'. In this manner, the larger histories and intertwinings of capital, conquest, trade, and culture that Goalpara testifies to from as early as the late eighteenth century are erased. In the documents of the colonial archive, the region is categorised as a 'frontier' on the subcontinental mainstream; and this concept of a 'frontier' is extended to include social norms, speech practices, notions of political power, agrarian production, marketing networks, and ecosystems. This view from the record room framed the region as a zone of even greater liminality and exaggerated indeterminate boundaries than was usual for officials conquering and administering polities in northeastern India.

This is a representation that uncannily returns in the postcolonial histories of the nations that Goalpara and its surrounds spill into, where its history surfaces only as fragments, as the stories of the borders of 'heartlands', or as the histories of the fringes of nation states. In the few historical works in which parts of this region feature, the region is a 'frontier', albeit of various kinds, to be subsumed into larger spaces of the Mughal and colonial empire and then of the nation. Richard Eaton's work (1993) on the spread of Islam into Bengal, with its focus on the eastern 'frontiers', covers a part of the region that the work studies and hence is a good example to begin with. Eaton has several references in his book to the polity of Cooch Behar, an area that he identifies only as being located in the 'remotest frontiers of imperial expansion' (Eaton 1993: 157). The presence of vast marshlands and dense forests, and the absence of a powerful state that could resist the advancing Mughal army ensured that 'in the east, the agricultural and political frontiers collapsed into one' (ibid.) with a third frontier, the cultural frontier of Islam, also blending into it. The description of the eastern polity of Cooch Behar, along with the region of Kamrup, is as a 'frontier' of various kinds for the civilisation that was Bengal and this is reiterated through the book. More recently, Joya Chatterjee, writing on the arbitrariness of the process that was the Partition of India, makes an equally arbitrary categorisation of the societies and polities on the borders of Bengal:

> For much of its medieval history, Bengal remained a marcher region over which the empires of the north had at best an uncertain control, and culturally it retained many of the characteristics of a

frontier zone, between the settled agrarian society of the Gangetic plains and the nomadic cultivators, hunters and gatherers of India's northeast (Chatterjee 2007: 6).

This 'core' centric imagination, with its view from mainland India and from the heartlands of Bengal, and its willingness to allow an unproblematised overlap of the borders of historical research with those of the contemporary nation state is reflected in Swaraj Basu's history of an identity movement among the Rajbansis, a community that inhabited parts of north Bengal, eastern Bihar and Goalpara.[2] Basu acknowledges that enquiries into differences in the societal structures between the community living in Goalpara and in Bengal could lend greater complexity to the narrative. Neither this nor the fact that the movement had a significant origin and presence in the area tempts the author, however, to cross the borders of his research into adjacent Goalpara. The trend is resonated in histories of Bhutan. Leo Rose's study (1977) projects the contemporary identity of Bhutan as a sovereign, independent nation, into the colonial and even the pre-colonial period. Aspects of shared histories and elements of overlapping sovereignty and territoriality are impossible to recover when interactions between Bhutan, the Duar area and polities such as Bijni and Sidli are introduced under the heading of 'foreign relations' (Rose 1977: Ch. 2).[3] Without the exploration of pre-colonial forms of power and space in the region, shared sovereignty can only appear to be a 'curious form of joint administration', between political units that are, in Rose's representation, 'similar to contemporary ones'. And his text becomes yet another strategy for an anachronistic construction of the nation. Little wonder then that 'it is still extraordinary that we still find it difficult to count histories that do not belong to a contemporary nation' (Duara 1995: 3)

Evidently, the agenda for histories of these countries as well as those of northeastern Bengal and regions further east in the colonial period continue to be set by the empirical and theoretical preoccupations of historians who are reluctant not just to think outside of the boundaries of the modern nation state but also outside of the colonial spatial order. An obvious underlying argument in all of this is a revisiting of the much critiqued, tenacious connection between history and the nation. Nationalist histories in India, while being 'agendas for power' in their own right, also consistently met the new nation's demands for a homogenising historical narrative, such as could subsume smaller, errant histories in the very act of resisting colonialism. The process of subsumption is reproduced, and within the 'regional histories', the story of a regional nationalism represses alternative narratives about spaces made illegitimate by the triumphant story of the colonial spatial order that finds its legacy ironically claimed by the nation state. Within an Indian nationalist geography that protects the Gangetic basin as its sacred historical core, Assam remains an eastern frontier in perpetuity and any evidence that might suggest otherwise is met with intense political anxiety. In Assam's own nationalist narratives, these frameworks of dominance and appropriation tirelessly re-emerge to marginalise its perceived borderlands (Goalpara).

And scholars of South Asia are apparently not alone in this. Northeastern India is a historically liminal frontier zone for South East Asian Studies as well. Historians of South East Asia might see Java as 'free of the burden of being a civilization ... a crossroads that draws upon, transforms and reworks currents coming from China, Champa, India, Iraq and even the Netherlands' (Subrahmanyam 2005: 6) but in the works of scholars working on Thailand, Indonesia and Vietnam, areas such as Northeastern India, Yunan, Sri Lanka, Madagascar, and New Guinea continue to be represented as 'marches, the borderlands that separate the region from other world regions' (van Schendel 2002a: 650–51). There is a return to the civilisational narrative here which is but a regurgitation of the narrative of the nation state, warping social space and inscribing boundaries around national cultures.[4] The arguments of this book are a critique of this persistence of elements of the civilisational narrative, in works of history on northeastern India. Despite the processes of state formation — conflated in these histories with the value of 'civilisation' — in certain parts of the region under study (Cooch Behar, Bhutan), they remained outside of the 'civilisational' cores of neighbouring Assam and Bengal, except when the narratives of later cultural nationalism demanded that the peripheries be identified as repositories of civilisational antiquity. Even this act of inclusion into the national pasts of cores condemned this region to the inferior temporality of a space that consisted of fragments of ancient histories of various nations. That these border areas lacked a certain geographical compactness (the privilege of neighbouring Bengal, for example) and were marked by the difficult terrain of the Himalayas, the Tibetan plateau and dense forests at the foothills, all of which made the region appear like a conglomerate of separate physical entities, only reaffirmed its historical peripheralisation.[5]

How, then, does one write the history of spaces that have until now appeared only as disconnected fragments of national borders in dominant histories? These are issues that have exercised historians writing on the northeast in recent times whose exasperation with unimaginative colonial cartographic projects that fixed political boundaries in a terrain of unusual topographical fluidity and human mobility has been accompanied by pleas for a more 'flexible geography'.[6] The practices of the postcolonial state, too, demonstrate an inability to escape the continuing hold of the colonial spatial order, the persistent resonance of which continue to determine political mobilisations around ideas of ethnicity, territorial rights and indigeneity in contemporary northeastern India (Baruah 2008).[7] A way out of this morass in thought could be to see the region not just in terms of its connections with the immediate locale, but also with the histories of other larger spaces which are concomitantly historicised — in this case, Goalpara and the apparently more stable spaces of 'Assam' and 'Bengal' of the nineteenth century.[8] If it makes little sense to talk of Southeast Asia in this period as if it were isolated from the Indian world, it makes equally little, if not less, sense to write a history of these borderlands by cutting it off at the borders of the Indian state when so much of it was about the myriad cultural and economic connections with places that included Bhutan, Tibet, Nepal, Bengal, and Assam.[9] Apart from doing away with the pressure of researching well-defined convenient geographical units of analysis, such an approach contains the possibilities of defying civilisational constants as well as the confines of national geography. What one writes instead is a history of connections that offers other spatial imaginations and spatial histories for northeastern India. Such a history iterates the significance of social places that existed in various complex webs of exchange and memories of those places that refused to disappear under the onslaught of colonial modernity and even survived to subvert it. It reiterates the location of Goalpara within an intricate network of trade flows that encompassed the spaces of many contemporary nation states, and its subsequent subjugation under British rule to the fundamental processes in histories of empires and settlement: land acquisition, sedenterisation, regulation and control of labour, the disciplining and reorientation of routes of migration and trade. In other words, other connected histories.

The emerging field of Zomia studies might be relevant to the above concerns interested as it is in a critique of histories written from 'heartlands' and also because of its powerful indictment of 'Area studies' and state-centred views of the world.[10] Willem van Schendel proposes the use of the term 'Zomia'[11] for a vast borderland region of Asia, in which

> shared ideas, related lifeways, and long-standing cultural ties (much like larger civilizational spaces) are manifold. They include language affinities (for example, Tibeto-Burman languages), religious commonalities (for example, community religions and, among the universalistic religions, Buddhism and Christianity), cultural traits (for example, kinship systems, ethnic scatter zones), ancient trade networks, and ecological conditions (for example, mountain agriculture) (van Schendel 2002a: 654).

While Zomia in the past was at the centre of processes of state formation, in contemporary times van Schendel sees its prime political characteristic as that of being 'relegated to the margins of ten valley-dominated states with which it has antagonistic relationships' (ibid.). Zomia's political marginalisation and a reiteration of its significance as 'one of the largest remaining non-state spaces in the world' has more recently returned as key themes in James Scott's work (2009) on the history of upland Southeast Asia. The founding of agrarian states, the politics of settling, disciplining and regulating labour for the production of surplus, and the persistent escape from the state by those who choose an 'ungoverned' way of life are among the many strands that Scott weaves together in his compelling narrative that sweeps across the highlands of south and southeast Asia from pre-colonial to contemporary times.

Yet, it is significant that neither van Schendel's essay nor Scott's *The Art of Not Being Governed* think it necessary to sufficiently focus on or draw out the implications from the scale and objectives of British or French imperialism in these highlands. There are some allusions to the subsuming reach of the colonial and post-colonial state in Scott (2009),[12] but no detailed elucidation of the calibration of power and violence in these modern states or of the coercive nature of state-driven capitalism. That the struggle for the protection of indigenous people in the present century (Scott's 'last enclosure') which opens a critical space for resistance against the machinations of the modern state, and the intrusion of capital into the life of the inhabitants of resource-rich global peripheries, is unprecedented in the history of resistance to the state and market is not recognised by these scholars of Zomia. On the contrary, Scott proceeds to reify the state in history:

> [T]he signal, distinguishing trait of Zomia, vis-à-vis the lowland regions it borders, is that it is relatively stateless ... the hill populations of Zomia have actively resisted incorporation into the framework of the classical state, the colonial state, and the independent nation-state (Scott 2009: 19).

That no single nation state can claim the history that *Becoming a Borderland* writes would seem to make it coeval with the concerns of Zomia studies — the physical area that it covers includes the overlapping margins of at least three nation states, and if differing notions of space such as this work explores, particularly sacred topographies are used, its scope extends further to include parts of the highlands of Tibet, China and Nepal. But here the parallels end. For this book refuses to exonerate the colonial state from its fundamental role in determining the *nomos* — the spatial order and orientation — of this part of eastern India as of every other part of the conquered world: 'The nomos of a tribe, its order and orientation, by which it becomes historically settled, turns a part of the earth into a force field, becomes visible in the appropriation of land' (Schmitt 2006: 71). Approaching the history of a 'peripheral' region through the constitutive act of spatial ordering violently enforced by the colonial state, the book will retrieve some of the splendid resistance and negotiation of the local peoples to the consolidation of the state and market, in the form of a movement for a Goalparia identity. But in the main, the book is an investigation into the ways in which a certain form of political power — British imperialism — violently acquires and then exploits resources, subordinates and reorients local and regional markets, and imposes new regimes of property and oppressive systems of revenue and tax collection to maintain and further its rule. It is about comprehending the relationship between the economy, economic 'growth', and political power and authority, and their production of the space of a borderland/nation state.

Put another way, the book follows the despondent trail of the 'region's' induced subjugation, fragmentation and appropriation under colonialism and of its reappropriation, yet again, and erasure and reinscription into the grand narratives of the postcolonial histories of several nations as new spaces.[13]

The period from the late eighteenth to the early nineteenth century is a good place to begin this story. A scattered collection of sources (*sanads*, travelogues from Mughal expeditions, early colonial travel and ethnographic writings and private manuscripts, records from the colonial archive) reveals elements of pre-colonial polities, their spatial orders and networks of trade and migration. This is the terrain of the two initial chapters of the book. The first chapter explores how the region that became the colonial district of Goalpara, and adjacent parts of northeastern Bengal appear in these sources — much like it does in Eaton's work, for example — as the last zones of Mughal rule, as a terrain with an inhospitable climate and dense forests, a 'frontier outpost' through the period of late Mughal rule, with its chieftains scattered over the largely unconquered countryside, tied in loose tributary relationships with local Mughal officials. The *Baharastan-i-Gayabi*,[14] an account written in Persian by a commander of a Mughal expedition in this region in the mid-seventeenth century, records in detail the several rebellions by local chieftains, Koch cultivators and Mughal officials who had been appointed to regulate revenue administration in the area, details of which are interspersed with accounts of the difficulties of military expeditions in the forested tracts of what was perceived as a frontier region of the Mughal empire. These are images that colonial records and accounts reiterate. The most exhaustive of these accounts were those of Francis Buchanan Hamilton, who wrote:

> During the Mogul rule, the Nawab resided at Rangamatti with some troops; but it seemed to have been the wish of the Moghul government to encourage the growth of forests and reeds and which might serve as a check to the incursions of the Assamese and nothing was required of the chiefs descended from Parikshit nor from the zamindars from the hilly country except a tribute so nominal. The petty chiefs who remained nominally under the authority of the Nawab of Rangamatti would have been entirely uninterrupted in cutting each other's throats, and in reducing the country to a desert.[15]

The extension of Mughal rule into the region effected changes in the local political economy through a transformation of patterns of revenue settlement, and as the book discusses in its first chapter, this was evident in the extension of the margins of agriculture and of peasantisation as also in the sustained peasant rebellions against difficult revenue demands by local chieftains. A trend within the historiography from northeastern India has been to attribute the failure of the Mughal imperium to adequately incorporate this part of eastern India into its administrative structures, to the unfamiliarity of this difficult environmental terrain. By turning the historical gaze to local structures of power and authority instead, the book suggests important inquiries into the ways in which states are shaped and produced in negotiation with local communities. The first chapter also lays out many bases of the pre-colonial connected histories that are the core of the book — shared cultural, economic and social characteristics such as hill agriculture and physical mobility — between the different social groups of Mughal Goalpara and its surrounds.

The late eighteenth century in this part of eastern India was not about the extension of political frontiers of the late Mughals alone. It was significant also for the complex workings of local power and hierarchy that continued to be produced in the various shared spaces that marked the region, enabled and sustained by its connections with Bhutan, Tibet, Cooch Behar, and other surrounding areas. The second chapter explores how, towards the northern parts, examples of these interdependencies translated into ideas of overlapping territoriality and sovereignty for the Rajas of Bijni, Sidli and Cooch Behar and for the Dharma Raja of Bhutan. The practice of overlapping sovereignties extended across the physical space of the Tibetan plateau, including the Dalai Lama, the Ahom king and the Raja of Bhutan within it. Evidently, then, the histories of hill and valley societies are hardly hermetically sealed and lowland cultures and hill polities can only be read together, whether in their oppositional or reciprocal relationships. This allows for the book to make reflexive connections between the histories of western Assam, northern Bengal, Bhutan, Tibet, and Bangladesh. Several of the fairs in the region of the Eastern Duars appear to have been part of a larger sacred topographical space, with descriptions of the nature of trading in the Duar area suggesting that this region was perceived as part of the religious space of the sacred sovereign realm of the Bhutan monarch.

In the pre-colonial and sometimes continuing into the early colonial period, the several circuits of trade, pilgrimage and migration routes that criss-crossed Bhutan, Tibet, Cooch Behar, Rangpur (of which Goalpara formed a part), and the Duars or the foothills of the Himalayas provided an enduring base for a connected history of the western parts of northeastern India. Some of the shared histories of the communities from the region are investigated in the second chapter of the book which finds a mixed bag of practices that are marked by their itinerant ways of being. Traders in horses and salt from Bengal and Bhutan, besides trading in a long list of other profitable items, journeyed into Tibet and Assam, meeting along the way Tibetan lamas travelling to collect tributes for the Dalai Lama of Lhasa and Bhutanese officials travelling to pay their tribute at the Duar fairs to the Towang Raja, a tributary of Lhasa. Along with the more contingent and common strategies of shifting cultivators fleeing oppressive taxation regimes and escaping to the Bhutan foothills, and elephant catchers migrating for the winter season to the plains of Assam, these could be considered as part of a 'circulatory regime'[16] that included local ideas of state-making and accompanying notions of sacred topography and overlapping sovereignties. The chapter indicates the difficulties of conceptualising the relations between authority, politico-administrative boundary making, and trade, across the pre-colonial and colonial period. It understands sovereignty as constituting an 'economic' control and symbolic expanse that often far extended the territorial limits of administrative power — the trade in commodities of high value but low volume (yak tails, rhino horns) being an example of such a reach of the state. Pre-colonial history was not all about 'fuzziness' and fluidity, and there are several examples of material fixity, the structures of power and social hierarchies. The book argues that in a lateral analysis of the region, the period emerges as one when its links with the imagined core of Indian history were less significant than of those with other areas. These were clearly 'frontiers' only in the civilisational narrative from 'India'.

The second chapter, as other parts of the book, is also about the early interests and conquests of the East India Company in the region; the Company was involved in the local political terrain, demonstrating a steady clarity of purpose, establishing its authority and power through a protracted process ultimately dependent on military strength. Behind the mask of an apparent inchoate

Company rule and its negotiations over private and commercial trading rights, the foundations of firm land revenue settlements were being laid, as well as that of a grid for the access to and regulation of the other resources of the land. A coercive reorientation of trading practices in the hills to meet the demands of a colonial expansion elsewhere in the empire was simultaneously being put into place. The persistent and sustained violence of British conquest through the forced entry of the colonial market by the third quarter of the century acquired and regulated labour for increased revenue. The effects of these processes are almost immediately visible in the phenomenon of forced migration and demographic change in the region. The actual transformation of a variegated local ecology into the ordered worlds of jute and paddy fields and the classification of land into forests, riverine areas, commons, and wastes, is both enabled and confirmed by cartographic procedures. Colonialism emerges as a powerful disjuncture in the history of the region, enforcing a new and irreversible *nomos* on the regional political economy.

As the third chapter of the work discusses, the aggressive sedenterisation through the 'colonisation of wastelands' scheme, the extension of colonial legality and the migration of over a million cultivators from the bordering districts of eastern Bengal into Goalpara (and also Cooch Behar) over just two decades of the twentieth century dramatically altered the demographic composition of the region. More importantly, these changes added substantially to the economic surplus demanded by the colonial state. It was the role of the colonial market, however, in the production of these borderlands that offers more substantive insights into the ways in which territory, economy and culture came to be imagined in this region through colonial conquest. From the mid-nineteenth century onwards, excessive taxation at colonial custom houses inevitably forced changes in trading practices, initiating a process that was to end with the integration of Goalpara and the Duar region into the trading networks of eastern India, particularly that of the province of Bengal. This reorientation of a vibrant pre-colonial world of trade would result in a gradual reduction and the eventual disappearance of a most visible element in the political economy of the region: the seasonal trade with Bhutan, Tibet and the Garo Hills, carried on in several weekly markets and fairs along the many mountain passes of the Duars and the southern hills.

In several parts of the world, the restructuring of local spaces was almost irreconcilably linked to a larger process of creating homogenised global spaces forged by new sets of connections. In this part of the globe, colonisation fragmented the region into unambiguous, compact political units; for instance, the coming into being of Bhutan. By the last decades of the nineteenth century, the colonial state organised a spatial order that was characterised by its frozen parts. A large portion of what later formed the district of Goalpara was already subsumed by the East India Company in the late eighteenth century. According to the terms of a treaty between the ruler of Cooch Behar and the East India Company in 1772, the former became a protectorate of the Company Government. The hilly Eastern Duars continued to be controlled by the Bhutan monarch until 1866, when they were 'annexed' to the colonial empire in India. This made Bhutan a separate, independent polity. The Garo Hills were formed into a separate district by 1874, an enforced hill–plain dichotomy being the underlining notion of the bulky files of the colonial archive. The painstaking and complicated process of fixing territories with political boundaries that were previously continually negotiable, had begun simultaneously,[17] although the overlapping sovereignties of Bhutan, Bijni, Cooch Behar, and smaller chieftainships (such as the Baikunthapur zamindar) would continue to be a source of considerable anxiety for colonial officials through much of the nineteenth century. Nevertheless, an ideology of a unified territorialised entity was being enforced — to be later claimed selectively by local collectivities — and stitched to an emerging entity called India. For administrative units within this entity, spaces such as Bhutan, Tibet, Nepal, and all the other places in between were firmly external to the new topography. Since there were no overlaps in territoriality possible within a colonial spatial order, Cooch Behar, Goalpara and the Garo Hills as the products of a 'cookie cutter' administrative imagination were political units that could exist henceforth only as parts of this colonially constituted territory. That initial nationalist imaginings in colonial South Asia were 'crystallised around the notion of a territorially delimited economic collective, a national economy in the 1870s and 1880s' (Goswami 1998: 611) only added to this production of a nation space.

The remaining chapters of the book search for the cultural expressions — of these changes in political-economy — in the emerging public spaces in Goalpara and Assam, and in the many competing claims on these spaces. These were most evident in the assertive politics of language and the writing of history, both of the colonial and of the traditional elite. In the 1920s and 1930s, these were processes that transformed Goalpara and the regions around it into a politically and culturally charged space, engendering a powerful politics of identity. Documenting the intersections between economy (land), culture and politics, the fourth and fifth chapters of the book investigate the embeddedness of language and linguistic identity in the continuously shifting terrain of local political economy.[18] The narrative weaves together the objective 'reality' of the several significant material and cultural pre-colonial connections discussed in the preceding chapters, with the memory of these as they were later reproduced in various practices from the region. The colonial production of space was resisted, appropriated and circumvented by various groups of the region in the language of culture and linguistic identity because interventions in the deeper structures of political-economy (land, commerce, revenue) were foreclosed. Certain inhabitants of the borderland were clearly at a greater material advantage in the use of ideological resources that could resist the spatial strategies of the colonial state and of the nation. And in this region, it was the zamindars, other sections of the traditional landed elite, chieftains of polities such as Bijni and Sidli, and members of the new middle class who were better enabled to access local history and the state.

In the early decades of the twentieth century, some members of this local elite reinvented themselves by attempting to appropriate the languages of colonialism.[19] Through their writings and practices, the regional elite produced the idea of a 'Goalparia', a spatialised conception of a borderland cultural collective that had at its core a narrative of apparently irreducible cultural and historical differences with the new and hegemonic nationalist 'Assamese' and 'Bengali' identities. The fourth and fifth chapters of the book discuss the processes that went into the making of this borderland identity in the early decades of the twentieth century: the more obvious territorialisation of space and identity and a sense of an unruptured historical continuity for the borderland — that defied colonial–administrative divisions — drew upon a collective memory of a shared identity of the region. Debates around the production of linguistic identity and difference, and the determination of linguistic hierarchies, were privileged media in the imagination of a borderland identity. This is the subject of the fourth chapter of the book. This chapter details the contestations around the fixing of the language of the borderland, drawing attention to the many interconnections between the discursive and the political-economy aspects that this process of ascription entailed. It brings these concerns to focus around the articulation of Rajbanshi, the speech practice of several districts of eastern and northern Bengal and of communities living in the Duar region and in the western borders of Assam, as the language of the region by the local elite.

The writing of counter narratives from the region during this period, produced in contestation with the hegemonic master narratives of Assamese and Bengali nationalisms, which represented 'cultural frontiers' like this borderland as 'repositories of ancient culture and history' and hence as a ready resource to bolster the project of cultural nationalism, is the subject of the fifth chapter of the book. The chapter explores the ways in the counter narratives from Goalpara drew substantially from the notion of a shared historical experience of borderland people that was distinct from that of both Assam and Bengal. It also studies practices that were remarkable in their extensive use of the ideological resource of memories of pre-colonial historical connections of the region. Subverting and destabilising colonial projects that sought to extensively restructure and homogenise local spatial organisation, particularly ideas of political space as well as cultural difference and identity in a region that had been constituted as a historically peripheralised borderland of the empire in India, these memories contested and reconfigured prevalent economic practices, local politics of identity, production of linguistic difference, and historical imagination. It is the heterogeneity of these practices and the contested terrain that they inhabited in the nineteenth and early twentieth century that the book hopes to explore.

✳

Notes

1. Between 1765 and 1822, following the imposition of the East India Company's rule in Bengal, the Permanently Settled parts of Goalpara were included within the district of Rangpur. In 1822, Goalpara was formed into a separate district of Northeast Rangpur, also in Bengal.

In 1826, the year of the beginning of formal colonial intervention in Assam, Northeast Rangpur was separated from Bengal and included within the Assam Valley Division. In 1867, Northeast Rangpur became a part of the newly formed Chief Commissionership of Cooch Behar. The following year, it was placed under the jurisdiction of the Judicial Commissioner of Assam. In 1874, Goalpara was included as a district under the new Province of Assam but was transferred to Bengal after the Partition of 1905. In 1912, Goalpara was once again included within the administration of Assam.

2. These included the districts of Rangpur, Cooch Behar, Jalpaiguri, Dinajpur, Malda, and Darjeeling in north Bengal, Purnea in Bihar, and Goalpara in Assam (Basu 2003: 27).

3. 'Foreign Relations: Neutralizing the External Environment' (Rose 1977: Ch. 2). Nagendra Singh (1978) discusses Bhutan's various historical connections with the polities in its south, including Cooch Behar and Assam, again in a manner that writes for the nation and does not admit fuzziness of any kind, particularly in matters of sovereignty and territoriality.

4. And it is an important indictment of the civilisational discourse, which 'survives despite our awareness that people have been moving, for millennia, back and forth across this semi-permeable membrane between the "civilized" and the "uncivilized" or the "not-yet-civilized" … despite the perennial existence of societies that occupy an intermediate position socially and culturally between the two presumed spheres … despite massive evidence of cultural borrowing and exchange in both directions … despite the complementarity that makes the two spheres a single economic unit' (Scott 2009: 99).

5. Writing on an area contiguous to this region, Willem van Schendel describes these as 'places that disappear into the folds of the map … regions which are victims of cartographic surgery … routinely sliced into pieces by the makers of regional maps, a treatment never meted out to heartlands such as the Ganges valley' (2002a: 652).

6. Laying out the ways in which national geography controls spatial imagination, 'and conveys a specific location, identity and meaning', Ludden makes a plea for locating the history of Assam within a more 'flexible geography' that would trace 'mobile and overlapping elements in human history in the valleys and mountains around the Brahmaputra and Barak rivers'. Assam occupies a borderland of Asian drainage systems and hence 'the Brahmaputra … is the easternmost river of Southasia, but it is also the westernmost in East Asia. In this context, India's Northeast is commonly found on maps of East Asia. Assam and the rest of the Northeast, as well as the adjacent Chittagong Hill Tracts in Bangladesh, can subsequently be seen as a western region of East Asia, an eastern region of Southasia, and as a

region where South and East Asia overlap. It is this overlapping that is impossible to accommodate on national maps; it thus effectively disappears from the public conscious' (Ludden 2005: 3).

7. As an antidote to the stranglehold of this colonial spatial imagination, Sanjib Baruah recommends the recognition of local cultural dynamics and strategies of spaces, 'the pre-colonial networks, resource use and property regimes did not neatly stop at the colonial border between the hills and the plains', and their persistence into contemporary times (Baruah 2008: 17).

8. Only once the British conquered Assam in 1826 did the area obtain — for the first time in its history — a firm regional identity as a part of Indian imperial geography. Until 1874, British Assam was part of a novel imperial territory called 'Bengal', which included West Bengal, Bihar, Orissa, Jharkhand, Northeast India, and present-day Bangladesh. British Assam always included the Brahmaputra and Barak river valleys, as well as the Surma–Kushiara river basin of Sylhet. After 1860, the tea industry spread across hills around these rivers and enhanced control of the administrative unity of Sylhet and Assam (Ludden 2005: 4).

9. See the rich work on connected histories pioneered by Sanjay Subrahmanyam which envisages a 'world of interactions' that enables issues of space to be looked at flexibly and in a temporally dynamic fashion' (Subrahmanyam 2005: 3): 'we are obliged more and less constantly to rethink our notions of frontiers and circuits, to redraw maps that emerge from the problematics we wish to study rather than invent problematics to fit our pre-existent cartographies' (ibid.: 4). These are insights that this book will borrow from in order to reconstruct the history of this northeastern borderland in the years preceding, as well as in the initial decades of, British rule.

10. '[Q]uartered and rendered peripheral by … strong communities of area specialists of East, Southeast, South and Central Asia' (van Schendel 2002a: 647), van Schendel argues, the production of knowledge about Zomia slowed down, affected by the academic politics of scale that create and sustain area studies.

11. Zomia is a term used in several Tibeto-Burman languages spoken in the Indo-Bangladesh-Burma border area for people living in the hills. 'Zo' is a relational term, meaning 'remote' and hence carries the connotation of living in the hills; 'mi' means 'people' (Scott 2009: 16).

12. 'Only the modern state, in both its colonial and independent guises, has the resources to realize a project of rule that was a mere glint in the eye of its precolonial ancestor; namely to bring the non-state people to heel' (Scott 2009: 4).

13. There has been for some time now an emerging and growing body of borderland studies that are recovering histories both outside and

beyond the nation while raising related questions about the structuring of colonial knowledge and the historicity of spaces. The impact of the imposition of a hegemonic discourse of space and power by the colonial state and the accompanying erasure of local, more fluid spatial practices in areas which then came to constitute 'border areas' has been the focus of several colonial histories. Rich reflections of these historical processes include (Nugent and Asiwaju 1996) and (Wilson and Donnan 1998). Such research offers an important alternate conceptual location for scholars looking across Asian borders.

14. An important source of information for the period of Mughal rule in Goalpara is the *Baharastan-i-Gayabi*, a Persian chronicle written by Mirza Nathan, a Mughal general who accompanied the Mughal army on its expeditions to eastern parts of the kingdom during the seventeenth century. The chronicle has been translated and published in two volumes. See Borah (1936).

15. 'General View of the History of Rangpur', in Account of the District or Zila of Rangpur, Mss Eur D 74: The Buchanan Hamilton Manuscripts, OIOC.

16. I borrow this phrase from Markovits et al. (2003). Circulation, according to the authors, 'is different from simple mobility, in as much as it implies a double movement of going forth and coming back, which can be repeated indefinitely. In circulating, things, men and notions transform themselves. Circulation is therefore a value loaded term which implies an incremental aspect and not the simple reproduction across space of already formed structures and notions. The totality of circulations occurring in a given society and their outcomes could be viewed as defining a "circulatory regime", susceptible to change over time' (ibid.: 3).

17. Letter from Major James Rennell, with one sketch map, dated December 1767, of Rangpur, Cooch Behar and Bhutan, Mss Eur F218/103, OIOC.

18. Despite the abundance of work on language and linguistic identity in colonial India, it is unfortunate that these important connections between land and culture are missed or ignored in much of this literature.

19. Here this work differs from studies on the nature of local authority of agrarian powers in South Asia which have often focused on their declining financial fortunes in the eighteenth and nineteenth centuries. See Tambs-Lyche's work (1997) on Kathiawar, and John McLane's work (1993) which focuses on the continuing relevance of kinship in the local imagination of Burdwan in Bengal.

1

❂

The Political Economy of State-making in a Pre-colonial 'Frontier'

Goalpara, along with Cooch Behar, and the later colonial districts of Dinajpur, Rangpur and Jalpaiguri, was part of the medieval Koch kingdom which at its height in the sixteenth century encompassed large parts of western Assam and northern Bengal. The fragmentation of the Koch kingdom was followed by about two centuries of Mughal rule. The Mughals failed to establish effective control, particularly over the eastern portions of the annexed territory but the western portion, including Goalpara, remained at least under nominal Mughal rule until its occupation by the East India company in 1765 (Barman 1994: 2). As in several other parts of India, in this region too, the decline of the Mughal state in the last decades of the eighteenth century and the fragmentation of its eastern acquisitions were accompanied by the emergence of several petty principalities.[1]

This chapter looks at the negotiated character of state formation during the Mughal imperium in this part of eastern and northeastern India. It emphasises the critical ties that these processes shared with the environment, evident in the strategic use made by the local chiefs and peasant groups of the varied terrain of the region — the dense tropical forests, the alluvial plains of the Karatoya, Manas and the Godadhor, and the Garo Hills — in their several sometimes coherent and sometimes more fragmented struggles against the Mughal state. In its analyses of the effects of the state on patterns of mobility and sedenterisation, the chapter gestures towards the emergence of conceptual realms among communities based on shared ethnicities and territoriality as also their potential inclusion into wider networks of trade and other connectivities. It therefore anticipates an encounter between colonial and indigenous forms of space and power, to be underscored powerfully with the entry of the Company Raj and the colonial state, which is the theme of the next chapter.

The Political and Ecological Landscape of a Frontier Place

The accounts of Francis Buchanan Hamilton, who visited Goalpara in the early decades of the nineteenth century, dates the earliest Mughal invasions of the region to around 1603 or 'to two years after the death of Akbar'.[2] Buchanan comments on the 'desire of encroachment that induced the Moslems, in the reign of Aurangzeb, to invade Assam, the limits of which were then very narrow'.[3] The annexation of Assam would have meant an expansion of the Mughal territories beyond the river Manas but was resisted by the Ahom army.[4] The resultant battles between the Ahoms, the dynasty that ruled over large parts of eastern Brahmaputra valley, and the Mughal army have been chronicled by several writers, including the anonymous chronicler of the *Padshah Buranji* (Bhuyan 1947).[5]

A signifi cant source for the period under study and presumably written between 1719 and 1731 in the Ahom court, the *Padshah Buranji* details the long and indecisive struggle by Mughal commanders including Jai Singh, Ram Singh and Mir Jumla for the control of the Ahom kingdom. The battle between Jai Singh and the Rajas of Cooch Behar, who had asserted their independence from the Mughals, is the subject of the seventh chapter, which also has references to the role of the king of Cooch Behar in the conflict (ibid.: 119). The text tells the story in much detail, of the frequent forced retreats of the Mughals, and the signing of the final treaty, whereby the Mughals agreed to maintain the ruler of Cooch Behar, a border state lying to the west of the river Sonkosh, as a tributary.

Mughal political interest in the Koch kingdom and in the kingdom of Assam that bordered it, has been explained by scholars as, 'the very essence of the existence' of empires and kingdoms, 'which saw themselves as continually expanding to become universal empires' (Embree 1977: 258). Within this theory of the pattern of expansion, the 'frontier' would have emerged as a temporary halt, 'the vanguard of a forward-moving culture' and excluded from the permanent pattern of Mughal administrative control. Thus, 'from the beginning of Mughal power in India under Babar in 1526 to its furthest expansion under Aurangzeb it was always an empire of expansion ... in fact, expansion eastward to Bengal and southward to the Deccan kingdoms was an irresistible challenge for an ambitious ruler' (ibid.: 263).

This expansive imperium was not characterised necessarily by shifting and permeable physical boundaries, where the 'frontier was never regarded as a fixed limit', marking instead 'the outer limits of Mughal administrative control which could expand and contract, depending upon the abilities and resources of a ruler at a particular time' (ibid.: 262).[6] Rather, the experience of the Mughal and Koch kingdoms indicate the existence of political territories that were defined with precision rather than fluidity. For the Mughals, the boundaries were often natural markers such as rivers (the Manas as the boundary between Ahom and Mughal territory) and *chowkis* or outposts such as the one at Rangpur.[7] The Upper Brahmaputra Valley and the Nawab of Bengal's territory formed the surrounding perennial or nuclear areas with the hills of the Bhutan kingdom to the north, the Sonkosh to the west and the Manas to the east forming the boundaries around. For the Koch kingdom, there are references to the demarcation of the boundaries of the empire by the Koch kings. Ralph Fitch, a merchant from London who visited the court of the Koch king, Maharaja Naranarayan, in the middle of the sixteenth century and offered details about the life of the people of Cooch Behar, alluded to 'the sharp pointed cones' which although were more likely to be used for defence, also served the purpose of marking the boundaries of the Koch Empire (Ryley 1899: 112).[8]

Fixed political boundaries however were not always conterminous (a corollary of the nature of political power) with the limits of political power. Rather, the nature of political power could lend itself to considerable 'imprecision', its sociology dependent on the relationships of reciprocity and fealty between people, not merely on a rigid definition of territorial boundaries. The region in the pre-colonial period, had 'in a real sense ... no political frontiers at all with the Power of one ruler gradually fading into the distance and merging imperceptibly with the ascending Power of a neighbouring sovereign' (Anderson 1990: 41).[9] The complex negotiations over power between the Mughal state and local chiefs, underscored in the methods of revenue and tribute collection, makes this more apparent.

Available sources such as the *Baharastan-I-Gayabi*,[10] and Abdul Hamid Lahori's *Padshah Namah*[11] suggest that Mughal imperial authority viewed Rangamati (of which Goalpara was a part) as the military and political frontier of their territories in Bengal and excluded this border area from regular imperial patterns of administrative control and revenue administration. For the Mughal state, this would have established a relationship which allowed the chieftains to pay only a nominal tribute while assuring them a degree of autonomy in return for providing a measure of frontier defence at minimal expense to the Mughal treasury. That the region had a difficult geographical terrain and environmental conditions further justified this arrangement. The *Baharastan-I-Gayabi* records in great detail the several rebellions by local chieftains, Koch cultivators and Mughal officials who had been appointed to regulate revenue administration in the area. These details are interspersed with accounts of the difficulties of military expeditions in the forested tracts of a frontier region. The inclusion of hilly, forested areas such as the Garo Hills within the jurisdiction of the Rangamati thana implied that 'officers of police and of justice (had) little influence ... especially considering the difficulty with which the forests and thickets of reeds had to be penetrated'.[12]

This discomfort of the Mughal imperium with what was obviously an unfamiliar geographical and political landscape, contrasted with the settled villages of parts of neighbouring eastern Bengal and their emerging systems of governance, found a strong resonance in the colonial descriptions of Mughal rule in the region. William Hunter noted that one of the duties of the Muhammadan military officials in charge of Rangamati and Goalpara was to encourage the growth of jungle and reeds as a protection against the inroads of the Assamese (Hunter 1887: 113). Writing about the 'frontier zamindars' of Goalpara of the Mughal period, the then political agent, David Scott, described them as 'lords of the marches',[13] 'indolent, incapable and devoid of any principles', characteristics that he attributed to the 'legacy

of the Mughal state [during the rule of which] both petty revo-
lutions or plans for usurpation were common'.[14] His criticism
of this 'legacy' led him to warn that 'rights exercised freely and
abusively by the Mughal agents in Goalpara could not be grafted
upon the Company's system of the Government, which denied
such powers rigidly even to its confidential servants'.[15] The Duar
region and northeastern Bengal in early colonial ethnographies
is described as being a region, 'the petty chiefs of which would
have continued entirely uninterrupted in cutting each other's
throats and in reducing the country to a desert, were it not for the
Company's gigantic power which put a stop to all petty attacks,'[16]
an obvious anxiety to underline the effectiveness and paternalism
of the state that had replaced Mughal rule in this 'unstable frontier polity' being visible here.

The colonial archives acknowledge, albeit reluctantly, the
presence of a more complex and diverse set of strategies of state
formation in the region. And accounts of peasant rebellions and
complex pre-Mughal land tenure systems in Persian documents
are powerful corroborative evidence of these formations, as the
next section of this chapter will argue. The pre-colonial period
emerges from these sources as being equally about the encounter of the Mughal state with local strategies of state formation
that included regional chiefdoms, clan chieftaincies and their
kinship ties, and their accompanying notions of power. Mughal
state-making then also becomes a study in local hierarchies and
interdependencies, a base for the larger connected histories that
are explored in the next chapter.[17]

When the region of Goalpara, Cooch Behar and parts of the
Duars was brought under the expanding Mughal empire through
a series of military expeditions, several local Rajas, chieftains and
nobles, conceded defeat and accepted ranks of subservience. The
Rajas of Bijni and Sidli were two such significant local powers:
'both the Rajas had been subject to the Mughals, who could not
possibly have passed into Assam and back without subjecting
them'.[18] The Raja of Bijni, in particular, claimed that his family
had long been territorial chieftains or Rajas in these parts and
had once held all the territory from the middle of Rangpur to the
middle of Kamrup.[19] A petition from the Raja to the East India
Company in the last decades of the eighteenth century stated
that while 'in the course of time we lost all, except the land now

in our possession, and had to seek the protection of the Mughal Government, but on coming under their jurisdiction, we had to pay not rent but a tribute of elephants for the lands of Habraghat, Khauntaghat and Bijnee'.[20] Although in later times, the Bijni Raja's claim to being a 'privileged tributary' was to be questioned by the colonial state which categorised his estate as an 'ordinary zamindari' estate, there was a recognition that 'under the Nawab Nazim of Dacca the ancestors of the petitioner's family had held Bijnee for many years before the Company assumed the Moffusil administration of Bengal in 1765'.[21] Both the Rajas were rendered tributaries and 'mal and fauzdarry was levied in the usual manner'.[22] The zamindar of the Karaibari estate, similarly, was a small chieftain of the region bordering the Garo hills whose acceptance of Mughal suzerainty established a political relationship which allowed for the payment of a tribute in elephants to the Mughal state rather than revenue from the land.

The rest of Goalpara's zamindars were part of a local gentry who were recognised as zamindars by Mughal *sanads* and gradually appropriated hereditary rights in land to emerge as powerful lords by the early decades of the eighteenth century. After the annexation of Goalpara to the Company's territories in the latter part of the century, officials noted that 'the several states on the northeast frontier of the Bengal province have never undergone a regular survey, nor have the internal resources been the subject of official scrutiny during the Mughal government; some of them were made subject to the provision of elephants with which this particular tract was abounded; the internal management of all was left almost entirely to the hereditary chiefs found in possession of the estates, who were thus treated rather as tributaries than subjects'.[23]

A few of them, like the zamindar of Gauripur, had their origins as 'primarily tax gatherers, rather than as a taxpayer (and were) … paid for their services through the *nankar* or allowance' (Habib 1999: 217). However, unlike the rest of Mughal India, the zamindars of the region of eastern Bengal, including Goalpara, had the land revenue fixed for long, unspecified periods and taken in fixed amounts which gave it the appearance of a tribute rather than that of rent. The earliest of the imperial sanads was probably issued by the Emperor Jahangir in 1606 to Kabindra Patra, who is identifi ed as the ancestor of the Gauripur zamindar by the colonial ethnographer, Francis Buchanan, and by officials of the Gauripur estate. Documents from the estate elucidate the greatness of Kabindra Patra, who rose from the position of a qanungo under the Mughal state.[24] The zamindar of the neighbouring Mechpara estate was a choudhari who occupied a crucial position in revenue administration and also received a nankar for his services to the Mughal state. Buchanan Hamilton identifies him as a local chieftain who paid a nominal share of the revenue of Mechpara estate to the Mughal *faujdar* at Rangamati.

The relations between the Mughal state and the local powers were however not marked by vulnerability and submission alone. Instead, these relations were rendered more complex, most significantly by the tactical use made by local chiefs and Rajas of the unfamiliarity of the Mughals with the local environmental and physical terrain. Many of the alliances that were made had as an important component, the implicit acknowledgment by the state of the critical importance of local knowledge. To begin with, this was apparent in the nature of negotiated political obligations and rights that termed the Rajas of Bijni, Sidli and Karaibari as *peshkashi* zamindars, separate and distinct from the other zamindars. This categorisation gave them considerable military power and autonomy in issues connected to the political and administrative affairs of their estates apart from being a confirmation of their traditional titles by the emperor. Peishkashi zamindars of the Bijni and Sidli estates also exercised a substantial degree of judicial authority under both the Mughal state and later, during the rule of the East India Company.[25] The following note in some early colonial correspondence on the problems of governance in the zamindari tracts of Goalpara and Garo Hills highlights these 'very ambiguous boundaries of the different contiguous powers' during the Mughal period, in an attempt at 'unravelling the clue of their rival pretensions':

> The policy of the Moghul Govt with respect to the zamindars on the frontier was widely different from that pursued by them in the interior of their provinces. The subjection of the former was of a feudal nature. They held their zamindaris on the tenure of representing falcons or elephants, or some other mark of dependence, and sometimes on the payment of tribute. But the internal government of these zamindaris was left to these hereditary chieftains,

who were considered rather as tributaries than subjects. Such is the account given by Sisson of the tenure and situation of great zamindaris on the northeastern limits of the Bengal territory, and we are satisfied it applied equally to other parts of our border possessions, particularly in the mountainous and jungly country. A considerable amount of independence was conceded to these zamindaris which were not allowed to others. They were also treated not as subjects but as feudatories, entitled to the protection of the paramount state on the simple obligation of paying a moderate tribute, preserving the line of boundary. Our records throughout the whole period of our connection with Indian territory ... bear witness to this arrangement as a great, pervading principle of Moghul dynasty, the best, most sure, durable protection for the interior of such a continental empire.[26]

The peshkash and the rent paid by the zamindars and hereditary chiefs empire was frequently irregular, with the obligation of these chieftains to hand over the surplus being largely dependent on the nature of the Mughal state's authority in the region. This characteristic was even more pronounced at the turn of the eighteenth century when the extent of the state's internal influence and, that of the arable economy were constantly in a state of flux in other parts of the empire as well (Bayly 1999: 31). Through much of the period of its rule in the region, however, the Mughal state benefited from the autonomy exercised by the zamindars in Goalpara as it ensured the state a share of the surplus of a divergent economy.

A substantial part of the income of the state acquired through the local Rajas and zamindars during this period consisted of non-agricultural dues. Much of the peshkash paid to the Mughal state consisted of forest produce, local products including cotton or elephants,[27] with the zamindars drawing upon both settled agricultural activity and the resources of the large, predominantly uncultivated stretches within their zamindaris to generate surplus. Although agricultural dues formed a substantial part of the income of the zamindar of Gauripur, the principal emoluments of the Kalumalupara zamindar were derived from custom houses and from duties levied on the cotton brought in by the Garos for sale, while 'a share of everything sold in the market and duties levied on the produce of wastes' formed an important part of the zamindari income of the estate of Mechpara.[28] 'Anciently, the main reliance of the frontier zamindars were on their *sairat* duties and not upon land tax'.[29]

For the chiefs, their resourcefulness and knowledge of the local terrain meant that many of them could levy tribute on areas that were beyond the boundaries of the Mughal state. The forests were the key base for tribute collection. The cotton grown in the Garo hills, along with elephants and *ahgur*, a precious wood, formed an important part of the peshkash paid to the Mughal faujdar at Rangamati who confirmed the zamindars in their lordships (Mackenzie 1884: 245). The relationship between the Garos and the surrounding agricultural plains was a study in community interaction, stretching back to the period of Koch rule. The late eighteenth century saw this interaction continuing to sustain the zamindari network of tribute and trade.[30] Simultaneously, there was an extension of the limits of settled cultivation under zamindars who occupied the Garo areas in order to increase the production of cotton.

The relationship of these communities with the zamindars was a part of the process whereby groups such as the Garos gradually acquired an important role in the regional economy in the Mughal period. The following extract from an early colonial account reflects this: 'Notwithstanding the numerous instances of ill treatment, and the constant succession of fraud and falsehood, the necessity with which the Garos labour under to procure salt and iron, the luxury of eating beef, fish, and other animal foods, that their mountains produce but scantily, and the desire of receiving brass rings and other finery in return for the cotton they rear in the hills, compelled them to deal with the Bengalese and the trade, in this district at least, was entirely carried on at markets held near the frontier. To these markets, when on tolerable terms with the zamindar, the Garos repaired once a week during the dry season ... almost the only article they brought for sale was the cotton in the seed' (M'Cosh 1837: 65).

That the knowledge of local resources of the local powers was frequently combined with shared kinship ties with the peasantry only added to the process of increasing consolidation of the interests of these notables. Surplus extraction was frequently based on kinship ties between the cultivators, and the zamindars and local chiefs. The 'ties of blood' between the zamindars of the estates bordering the Garo hills was a powerful connection that partially explained their ability to not just levy taxes on the Garo haats, and raid their villages, but also to enforce claims to a shared sovereignty with local Garo chieftains.[31] The Kachari community, which was scattered over parts of Goalpara and the neighbouring Kamrup district, continued to retain assert kinship ties with their deposed ruler and contributed fixed amounts of their income as a mark of their continued loyalty. Several of the peasant rebellions described above too were from villages with shared kinship ties. There are references in the *Baharastan-I-Gayabi* to protests by villages composed entirely of Koch peasants and led by Koch landlords against changes in the form of land revenue payment by the Mughal state (Borah 1936: 403).

These rebellions underlined yet again the contested nature of Mughal imperium in this part of eastern India. They also told stories of the boldness of 'frontier chieftains' and communities which refused to accept defeat in the hands of what was clearly a superior agrarian power and instead used their knowledge of the forests, rivers and seasons, of kinship bonds, and varied subsistence patterns to not just temporarily incapacitate the enemy but even inflict decisive defeats. The next section explores some such stories of resistance.

A Troubled Story of Agrarianisation

The persistence of peripatetic communities, the reliance on the forest for the payment of tribute and the relative autonomy of local powers from the core of the Mughal state does not reduce in anyway, however, the significance of agrarianisation in the Mughal imperium. The prioritisation of sedenterisation in the seventeenth and eighteenth century meant that the extension of Mughal rule into parts of Cooch Behar and Goalpara ensured their inclusion into the political economy of the empire as well. There was a visible pushing forward of the margins of agriculture and a consolidation of peasant society during this period. Following from this, as in other parts of the empire, was the idea of 'a civilized society (as) one (that was) primarily engaged in agriculture' (Singh 1995: 21) 'societies which were predominantly non-agricultural in nature (being) viewed as primitive and as a threat to settled agrarian areas where Mughal land revenue regulations were methodically applied' (ibid.: 30).

According to Mughal accounts and early colonial writings, the introduction of the Mughal pattern of revenue administration in Goalpara began with the defeat of the Koch king Parikshit in 1603.

This was followed by the appointment of a Mughal faujdar at Rangamati thana, and the subsequent reorganisation of the country of Koch Hajo by the revenue official, Ibrahim Karori. During the initial years of its rule, the revenues for the Mughal state were collected directly from the cultivators by the *karori*, a salaried official, who visited villages and determined the land revenue to be paid. To facilitate the collection of revenue by the karoris the country was divided into *sarkars*, which in turn were divided into parganas and taluks.[32]

However, it was evident from early on that for obtaining a share in the revenue of an economy such as Koch Hajo, the Mughal state would have to rely heavily on intermediaries and also adapt to a range of revenue extraction methods. The collection of this revenue was therefore also assigned to a class of *ijaradars* in the first decades of Mughal rule. The *Baharastan-I-Gayabi* records the appointment of various revenue offi cers and the pattern of revenue collection in Koch territory: 'Abdus Salam, who was appointed as the commander of the army at Kuch appointed in different parts of the city and in the vicinity of the river Rangamati, his own and his brother's offi cers and ordered Mirza Hasan, the Diwan and the Bakshi, to arrange for the collection of revenue in the parganas and other places. The Mirza, due to his great experience, divided the parganas of the Kuch territory into twenty well defined circles. Some of the lands were assigned to the imperial karoris and the faujdars to realise the revenue. Some of the land was given to mustajirs [revenue farmers] by taking the kabuliyat [the deed of acceptance] from them for those parganas' (Borah 1936: 273).

Clearly then, Mughal rule was building on the sedenterisation of peasant society that had taken place under the preceding Koch dynasty and other local powers. Buchanan suggests that several of the 'scattered, settled villages in the region between the Sonkosh and the Manas rivers, surrounded as usual by gardens, reeds, forests and fields and each may have contained some shops'[33] had their origins in the pre-Mughal period. There is evidence that some of these villages were dominated by a single caste, which in the case of the settled villages was mostly the Rajbanshi Koch community who customarily paid revenue in labour (Bhadra 1984: 481). The evidence of settled villages in these writings is also accompanied by comments on the nature of taxation in the

Mughal period in colonial records, frequently determined by measuring the land in terms of 'so much per plough' or, in places of shifting cultivation, by 'so much per the dao or the bill hook or by the kodal or hoe'.[34]

Several of these settled villages were under a system of revenue administration called the *paik* system, which was prevalent in most parts of the Koch and the neighbouring Ahom kingdom. 'The king afterwards held a census and created the paiks ... he made four people equivalent to a gote [a unit] of paiks' (Goswami 1917: 55) states an eighteenth century chronicle from the region of Darrang about the Koch king Naranarayan. Under this system, paiks or armed retainers were given arable land free of revenue charges in return for their manning the border regions.[35] Commenting on the nature of the pre-Mughal revenue administration, the contemporary chronicle, the *Fathiya-I-Ibriya* of Shihabuddin Talish, a traveller who accompanied the Mughal commander Mir Jumla, noted that 'to collect revenue from the peasant of these areas is not the rule. From every house, one person in every three was brought for services to the king.'[36] Lahori's *Padshah Namah* observed that the paiks were given jagirs by the order of the king and were employed in the capturing and driving of elephants, apart from cultivation.[37] Their grantees included weavers, blacksmiths and messengers.[38]

The changes effected in this land revenue administration by Mughal commanders included the taxing of *paikan* land that had hitherto been exempt from assessment and had therefore important implications for the existing patterns of power and authority in the region. There are instances of negotiation of the state with local powers and cultivators over revenue demands, as when a collector of the Ghurla pargana was dismissed on account of peasant protests. The appointment of the new collector had as a condition, his written agreement to 'perform the assigned duties diligently in such a manner that the cultivable land should increase, and he would not oppress anyone' (Eaton 1993: 158) as well as the peasant's written approval of his nominee.[39]

Negotiation did not in any way however, preclude more violent forms of peasant protest against the Mughal state as the rich body of evidence of numerous peasant rebellions across the seventeenth and early eighteenth century suggests. Evidently, the state was not responsive enough to the peasant's experience of the new forms of surplus extraction, for during the same period as the petitioning by the Ghurla peasants (1664) the countryside of the erstwhile Koch kingdom and its surrounds broke into a series of sustained rebellions.

There is rich historical evidence of these rebellions in the form of contemporary political chronicles and travel accounts. A significant factor behind these rebellions, which emerge as a persistent feature of Mughal rule in the region, was the reluctance of the cultivators and some of the landed classes to accommodate a centralised fiscal system based on rent collection through payment in cash or crops. Instead, they favoured the previous revenue organisation reliant on labour service and decentralised local powers. Thus the *Baharastan-I-Gayabi* notes that 'after the departure of Raja Lakshminarayan (the former Koch king) Mir Safi introduced a number of changes in the revenue assessment of all the parganas of Jahangirbad'.[40] The allowances made in the form of salaries for the paiks were also charged to revenue assessment. The *Gayabi* continues: 'Owing to his lack of intelligence, he [Mir Safi] did not pay any heed to the discord in the region and the sedition of the cultivators ... one portion of the parganas was handed over to the karoris and another portion to the mustajirs. When the mustajirs after a slight increase in assessment brought the parganas under their own possession and thought of increasing it to their own benefit, it created causes of discontent among the ri'aya' (Borah 1936: 288–89).

This discontent of the cultivators was to snowball into a much larger rebellion in the Putimari area of the Khuntaghat pargana. Khuntaghat was a part of the estate of the Raja of Bijni. The perceived humiliation of local rulers was critical in ensuring the support of the other local powers in this rebellion: 'The Mughals had promised to maintain the dignity of the king of Kuch Behar, Lakhminarayan and Parikshitnarayan, the king of Kamrup. But the latter was placed under the surveillance and later deported to the court of the Mughal emperor. This action roused the nobles and exacerbated tensions, leading to the outbreak of the rebellion in Khuntaghat' (Bhadra 1984). In an appropriate illustration of the pre-colonial state as a 'radically seasonal phenomenon' (Scot 2009: 61), the ryots timed their refusal to pay revenue with the onset of the rainy season, a difficult period for Mughal expeditions into forested tracts of territory. Beginning as a minor protest against the treatment meted out to the deposed Koch king, Lakshminarayan, the rebellion soon turned violent. The Koch peasants killed several mustajirs and karoris whom they charged with illegal extraction of revenue (Borah 1936: 288–89). They also extended the rebel territory close to the Mughal headquarters of Rangamati, captured the fort at Jahangirabad, and fortifi ed the residence of the king, Parikshit (ibid.: 290–352). Mughal writers describe the Khuntaghat rebellion as 'a serious uprising of the enemy' in which boats from neighbouring villages were used 'to rush upon the fort of the enemy' (ibid.: 354). It kept the Mughal army in a state of siege for days when 'not even a straw was available for the horses, not to speak of grains' (ibid.: 302).[41]

Resistance to Mughal systems of revenue extraction continued through this period, visible in the zones of mobility that marked the pre-colonial. Cultivators migrating from the plains of Rangpur to the Duar foothills were fleeing difficult tax regimes and retaining a distance from the state.[42] The *Baharastan-I-Gayabi* has references to peasant resistance to payment of land taxes, led by rebels such as Sanatan, Parshuram and Naba (ibid.: 641–48). That an 'overwhelming concern for obtaining and holding population at the core is shot through every aspect of pre-colonial statecraft' (Scott 2009: 67) was evident in the attempts by the Mughal state to contain these fleeing cultivators. In 1699, the emperor Jahangir issued a *badshahi parwana* that forbid the cultivators of the Mechapara pargana from deserting their lands. Another sanad issued by the Mughal state in 1683 authorised the qanungo of Mechpara, Debiprasad Barua, to persist with the collection of nankar from the peasants who had fl ed to the Parbatjoar estate to escape taxes and had continued with their cultivation in the area (Sanyal 1965: 137–38). Conditions in the Parbatjoar estate mentioned above could not have been very congenial either, as only six of its forty manors were inhabited in the late eighteenth century. The proprietor attributed this desolation chiefly to the occasional claims made by the Barua on these lands.[43] That there was a low population density and there were large extents of available arable land would have helped. Along with spatial mobility, these acted as serious constraints on the effective power of the Mughal state as well as that of local chiefs.

Khuntaghat emerged as a key site of peasant resistance in the region, wherein in the middle of the seventeenth century, a Koch chieftain, Sanatan, organised several thousand Koch cultivators and staged an insurrection at Dhamdhama. The message from the Mughal commander to Sanatan, which has been reproduced by the author of the *Baharastan-I-Gayabi*, Mirza Nathan, was indicative of the challenges faced by the Mughal officials in the collection of revenue even within the political confines of the Mughal empire. Referring to the rebel leader's opposition to Ibrahim Karori, the local revenue official, the Mughal commander 'admonished' Sanatan with the following message: 'It has been reported that Shaykh Ibrahim Karori has treated you with violence and oppression. The object of our appointment to Kamrup with all the officers is that we shall appoint another Karori if the present incumbent is found oppressing the ryots. If any trouble has been created by the ryots, we shall punish them for their impertinence so that they may not be able to display any desire for such unbecoming acts in the future' (Borah 1936: 370).

Sanatan's reply rejected the terms of peace offered and dwelt instead on the 'oppressions penetrated in this country' by the Mughal revenue officials, in particular by Ibrahim Karori: 'Now the ryots do not possess the power and ability to turn their attention to the payment of revenues. How can I be pacified by Your Excellency's arrival? Two of our noble Rajas accepted imperial vassalage and gave lakhs and crores. What benefit have they derived that I may consider as an advantage? I will agree to the terms on condition that: Ibrahim Karori must be severely punished; remission of our revenues should be made for a whole year; the imperial army should withdraw from Ghilanay and the allowance of the paiks should be given direct and not made an addition to revenues due to government' (ibid.: 370). The text goes on to record the continued resistance by Sanatan, the support he received from the people in the form of provisions, and his final escape to Jutia, a fortress in the midst of forests. Sanatan's reply is significant because it clearly articulates a preference for the pre-Mughal economic relations that were altered by the Mughal regime. His remarks about the injustice faced by the deposed Koch kings also suggest the existence of strong kinship ties within the Koch community in that period. Santan's sentiments were obviously reciprocated by the Koch nobles because a Mughal chief observed: 'Due to the circulation in the territory of Kuch of the news of the arrest of the Rajas, some of the Kuch chiefs in order to wipe off their *badnami*, raised an insurrection' (Bhadra 1984: 487).

At around the same time as Sanatan's rebellion, there was another uprising in the Khuntaghat area, termed as the *Hathikheda* (*The Capture of Elephants*) rebellion in the *Gayabi*. The rebellion began with the refusal of several *gharuwari paiks* (auxiliary footmen) to help capture elephants for their Mughal commanders, and their subsequent death in the hands of the Mughal official, Baqir Khan (Borah 1936: 638–39). Qulij Khan, the commander, 'sent his officer with a force of six to seven hundred cavalry, and one thousand match-lock men over and above the regiment which was at Ghilanay (but) he failed to suppress the rebellion' (ibid.: 641). Instead, the rebels marched from Khuntaghat to Jahingirabad or Ghilanay. 'The whole family of Qulij Khan has been imprisoned and Jahangirbad has been raided and occupied by the rebels', (ibid.: 640) stated a letter to Islam Khan, the Mughal offi cer in charge of the expeditions against *bhati*, or the region of Koch Behar and western Assam, including Goalpara. Baqir Khan was caught alive and killed, along with a large number of Mughal soldiers, and all the elephants of the Mughal government were confiscated. 'They proclaimed a headman of the elephant drivers as their king, rose in open revolt and created an amazing situation', remarks Nathan in his concluding section on the *Hathikheda* rebellion (ibid.).

Resistance to payment of surplus and hostility towards Mughal revenue officials characterised another peasant rebellion in the area, this time in the pargana of Bhitarband and Bahirband, situated in the vicinity of the fort of Dhubri, 'the foremost of all the forts in the Koch territory' (ibid.: 231). Mirza Nathan ordered his forces to raid the regions of Bhitarban and Bahirban and to bring the ryots under control, failing which they were to bring them as captives and drive them away from their lands (ibid.). Resistance to taxation was evidently met by harsh measures for the text goes on to recount how 'the Mirza went with his imperial colleagues and did not allow the natives any respite even to drink water for a period of four days and nights. He brought many of them as captives and seized an innumerable number of cattle; and his companions seized many beasts of burden' (ibid.: 233). Shortly after the Bhitarband rebellion, the cultivators of Khatribag which was the jagir of Mirza Nathan, having taken advantage of the floods, stopped their payment of revenue but were subdued with the aid of local zamindars.

These rebellions were accompanied by that of Ibrahim Karori himself. He had 'misappropriated more than 70,000 rupees of the imperial revenues and made a great waste ... led astray an army of more than 3,000 people with him and instigated a force of the Kuch regiment against Mirza Salih Arghun', the commander of a Mughal expedition into Koch Hajo. The state appears to have faced similar situations in other parts of the empire as well, which finally led to the winding up of the 'Karori experiment' (Habib 1999: 229). The rebellion of Ibrahim Karori appears to have been reflective of larger processes that were at work in the late seventeenth century, a period during which the system of assignments of revenue on which the Mughal nobles had subsisted had begun to break down.[44]

Against this background, the replacement of salaried officials of the state like the karoris, and the ijaradars, with regional chieftains must have appeared to be a favourable compromise for the Mughal state. This would have been particularly true on account of the ability of the these regional notables to extract surplus from an area that included a spread of mixed economies of settled cultivation as well as shifting and foraging ones. As an example of this shift, the *Baharastan-I-Gayabi* details the reliance of Islam Khan, the Mughal commander, on Raja Pratapditya, in his task of 'punishing the people of Koch Vihar'. 'Islam Khan, for the sake of drawing the attention of the other zamindars and also in consideration of the high positions held by the aforesaid Raja Pratapaditya among the Zamindars of Bengal, bestowed honours upon him beyond measure, and consoled and encouraged him. On the first day he was presented with a horse, a grand robe of honour and a bejewelled sword-belt, and thus he was converted into a loyal officer' (Borah 1936: 27). By the beginning of the eighteenth century, the attempts had proved temporary, to reinstate descendants of former Koch rulers such as Chandranarayan over the region of Koch Hajo in return for a nominal peshkash or tribute to the Mughal state. The system of surplus collection was now firmly in the hands of local chieftains and notables who had replaced the ijaradars and karoris and whose obligation to hand over part of the proceeds was often conveniently forgotten when empires collapsed.[45]

With increasing zamindari intervention in the processes of agricultural production, the stage appears to have been set for a growing stratification within local rural society. The elements of fluidity within the pre-colonial that were discussed earlier in the chapter did not preclude the presence of hierarchies and differences. Rather, contemporary sources suggest the existence of a complex social order where apart from the cultivating classes, there was also the emergence of other classes including the *sukhwas*, who had no possessions and lived merely in service without being employed in manual labour, and the *khawas*, who were artists and traders as well. Buchanan writes that Mughal chronicles record the existence of both domestic and field serfdom in Goalpara, particularly in the eastern parts of the region, bordering the Ahom kingdom.[46] 'The turbulent chiefs of the east are desirous of keeping slaves, as they are more ready than free men to perform acts of violence[47] ... such slaves were well treated and promoted to offices of considerable importance in the management of their master's affairs'.[48]

Indicative also of rural hierachisation was the significant role played by the zamindars in the religious and cultural life of this society and of their control over the diverse local resources under the Mughal state. The local zamindars now collected a large variety of abwabs or cesses. These included the *thulijat*, which was levied on timber stacked on the banks of rivers, the *chulunta masool*, which was levied on timber floating down the rivers, and the *rusi* and *bastoo salami*, which were taxes collected from cultivators to cover the expenses of land measurement and assessment but credited to the general income of the zamindar. There were also tolls on canoes and on traders in the several village haats or local markets.[49]

Towards the latter half of the eighteenth century, when the decline of the Mughal state made it possible for these regional notables to seize greater privileges, there is evidence of taxes such as the *marcha*, paid to the zamindar by a bride on the occasion of a marriage ceremony among the cultivators on his estate. This tax was described by colonial administrators as 'a long established practice which the people are so accustomed to that they deem it a part of their marriage expenses'.[50] Other similar taxes which reflected the increasing assumption of the role of the local gentry by the zamindars included the *tohoori* or *parbuni*, a tax levied at the time of the annual Durga Puja and fi xed at 'pice or so on each rupee of the rental'.[51]

Origin legends and their claims to superior genealogies conferred necessary legitimacy on the power of local chiefs, zamindars, and their kin groups. Produced primarily to bolster the legends of conquest' that were so necessary for the affirmation of the warrior status of landlords and local chiefs, these myths illustrated their claims of having won their power by conquering or expelling wild tribes. As an example, the descendants of the estate of Mechpara traced their genealogy from Bhagadatta, the legendary king of Kamrup. Later interpretations attributed their origin to the Rabha tribe.[52] A different version of this origin legend related a history of conflict between the Garos, who were believed to have been the original inhabitants of the region, and the ancestors of the present occupants who belonged to the Pala dynasty of Bengal (Barman 1994: 59). The estate of Kalumalupara was believed to have been 'first occupied by a tribe of fishermen, who were called Chondals, and belonged to an impure tribe, who were defeated and the area occupied by the descendants of one Vishwanath Choudhuri'.[53]

With vast stretches of uncultivated tracts and the role of zamindars as settlers of these making such acquisitions of legitimacy indispensable for ensuring a steady supply of land revenue,[54] the origin myths reflected the transition to agrarianisation of social groups and their accompanying discomfort with their peripatetic pasts. For the zamindars of Goalpara and northeastern Bengal, the denial of such ties was also the beginning of a process that brought them closer to similar imaginings of space and power in eastern India. But that was a later process, for these parts of eastern India during the Mughal period, despite an increasing peasantisation, continued to have several elements of a more liquid landscape. The extension of cultivation and the emergence of social groups separated by their economic interests were not necessarily indicative of the diversity of the environment and of the types of subsistence strategies that were practiced. There remained several groups which did not make a clear transition to settled life and persisted with their non-sedentary ways while continuing to be an integral part of the regional political economy.[55] Mughal accounts of expeditions into Goalpara comment on the existence of an abundance of uncultivated forested stretches on the fringes of settled agricultural land. The accounts of local resistance and rebellion were accompanied by descriptions of the fortresses of regional chieftains, which were almost always located in dense forests that often took the Mughal army several days to clear (Borah 1936: 461). Early colonial travellers and ethnographers also described the greater part of Goalpara's hills as 'covered with forests' and 'the whole country overwhelmed and overgrown by thickets of reeds'. These writings dwell at length on the 'waste-lands which were as varied in kind as the cultivated areas'.[56]

There are indications too of a diminishing of the forest cover with the extension of cultivation. Methods were suggested for the clearing of these jungles, seen as a clear threat to the spread of an agrarian order. In late Mughal Goalpara the forest had advanced into zamindari estates, several of which were described as 'exceedingly ill cultivated, the farmers uncommonly poor and unskilled in agriculture'.[57] The descriptions of the estate of Parbatjoar, consisting of a 'very wild tract of land with some fine level land which had settled cultivation',[58] was true for several other zamindari estates as well. Mechpara in the pre-colonial period was divided into a hilly, forested and uncultivated area and an area with permanent villages where taxes could be fixed by the plough, while the possibilities of cultivation of vast stretches of fertile land in the estate of Kalumalupara were frustrated by its 'impure tribes'.[59]

Accounts of the period speak of groups of nomads and settled cultivators, each with distinct life ways, who lived lives of mutual dependence with several areas of shared economy and culture. Living on the fringes of the agrarian order, these communities at times could not be made to conform consistently even to a loosely defined political and economic relationship with either the Mughal state or its intermediaries. The state's policies of sedenterisation succeeded in binding people to permanent settlements, but often only for brief periods. The Meches, the Rabhas and the Bodos were among the several communities in Mughal Goalpara who lived in these forested areas and whose sense of community identity was located in the choices that they made regarding their economic and cultural practices. Each of these communities had large groups of shifting or *jhum* cultivators within them who also practised other forms of non-sedentary cultivation such as hoe or *baku* cultivation. Colonial records suggest that large stretches of land in late Mughal Goalpara were cultivated by clearing fresh ground and were taxed by the Mughal state according to the land cleared by the kodal or the hoe as against the plough which was the unit of measurement elsewhere in the region. In his notes titled 'On the hoe cultivation carried on by rude tribes', Buchanan estimated the amount of land under this cultivation in the Ronggpur district at 17,760 'Calcutta bighas', a large part of which was within the area that later formed the district of Goalpara. Although requiring greater labour, hoe cultivation could prove to be as productive per acre as sedentary cultivation with the plough.[60] As in other forms of non-sedentary cultivation the same field was cultivated for two or three years at a stretch until it was exhausted and then allowed a fallow period of four to five years.

The practice of particular subsistence patterns however were not reasons for excluding other forms of production. Shifting or jhum cultivation and timber felling, settled agriculture and hunting and foraging techniques were practised alternately, frequently within the same community. In most zamindari estates during this period, even settled cultivators appear to have built their huts in 'a scattered manner, surrounded by a few plantains and bamboo trees ... the reason for this nakedness being the fact that people do not live long in one place; whenever the ground was exhausted by repeated crops and required weeding, they go to a place which has had four or five years of rest'.[61] The Rajbanshis, a part of the larger Koch community, which had a long tradition of plough cultivation, and from which the majority of settled agriculturists were drawn, frequently resorted to shifting cultivation for growing crops such as mustard and gram despite their village centred and rule-bound agrarian order.[62] The agrarian locations of certain areas suggest a constant state of flux, along with their human occupants. Hoe cultivators also lived in 'fixed, settled villages, with houses and gardens, and moved only when there were disturbances from the Bengalese'.[63] And several settled villages practised mixed cultivation, gathering and foraging to supplement their income during the lean seasons. The Rajbanshis included groups such as the Pani Koch within their community, who 'lived amidst the woods and frequently changed their abode to cultivate land ... almost entirely by the hoe' through the Mughal period.

The Rabhas had the Pati Rabhas and the Rongdaniya Rabhas, the former having made the transition to a more sedentary form of plough cultivation while the latter continued with the hoe and a more peripatetic life.[64] In a negation of the familiar linear civilisational narrative of social evolution that had foraging, swidden and plough cultivation on a temporal scale, living at the peripheries of the state and of settled agrarian societies appears to have been a deliberate choice for several of these communities. 'Neither the composition nor the location of a particular community was fixed. Land was cleared for agriculture but land became covered with jungles ... herdsmen settled to till or to tax the tillers but cultivators shifted to herding; swidden cultivators took to the plough but ploughmen fled to the forests' (Guha 1999: 29).

These were therefore not archaic communities, leading and preserving their ways of life in isolation. Rather, it is necessary to recognise the fluid character of these groups, the absence of rigid dividing lines between the static agrarian and the mobile hoe cultivator, and the integration of all of these in various ways into the regional political economy, as they produced cotton, timber and other products marketed initially in local fairs and then gradually, in the trading networks that crisscrossed this region and the southern Himalayas, Bhutan, Tibet and China. Though the expanding Mughal imperium's ideology of agrarianisation was to permanently change local practices, communities were being constituted and reconstituted during the period with the region being still characterised by cultures of mobility and interdependencies, by notions of space and authority very different from the ones that were to follow under the colonial state. The gradual erasure and marginalisation of these practices with the beginning of colonial intervention as well a simultaneous persistence that allowed them to reconfigure sites of colonial power is among the key concerns of the next chapter.

✳

Notes

1. The Eastern Duars, a large tract of hilly country, was ruled by several chieftains of the Bhutan monarch who were accorded the status of

tributaries of the king of Bhutan until its annexation by the British in 1865. Thus, even after Goalpara was formed into a colonial district in 1822, its northern hills remained under the administration of the Bhutan monarch while the rest of it continued to be a part of the colonial territory of Bengal and administered by the East India Company.

2. The Buchanan Hamilton Papers, Mss. Eur. D 75, 'The Account of the District or of Ronggopur Zila, Book I', p. 147, OIOC, London.

3. Ibid., p. 147.

4. This successful resistance to the Mughals was the cause for some enduring colonial representations of Assam and the Assamese including that of Francis Buchanan's: 'the people of Assam were fierce in their independence, invigorated by a nourishing diet and strong drink, ... their princes still retain their energy of mind ... not sunk under the enervating and unceasing ceremonies of the Hindu doctrines' (The Buchanan Hamilton Papers, Book I, p. 147).

5. In his introduction to the translation, Bhuyan notes that, in keeping with the tradition of all medieval Assamese chronicles, the author of the *Padshah Buranji* remains anonymous. Bhuyan placed the composition of the chronicle between 1719 and 1731.

6. Embree sees such political boundaries as a feature of the Mughal state that made contraction and expansion of imperial authority possible (Ibid.: 262)

7. 'Jai Singha halted at Patna and sent out messages to the Rajas of Cooch Behar and Dacca ... part of the nine principalities of the Mughals in eastern India. On receiving the message, the Raja of Koch Behar brought valuable presents to the emperor and Nawab Galir Beg was dispatched to settle the boundaries between the two territories' (Ibid.: 120).

8. 'Firm political boundaries were comprehensible to pre-colonial rulers and people but these were only formally activated in times of need or sacred action' (Bayly 1998: 19).

9. Anderson writes in the context of the traditional Javanese state which appears to have had a less precise sense of territoriality than the region discussed here. In a now much quoted passage, Anderson described the relationship between power and territories: 'The territorial extension of the state is always in flux; it varies according to the amount of power concentrated at the center ... the kingdoms were regarded not as having fixed and charted limits, but rather flexible, fluctuating perimeters' (Ibid.).

10. An important source for the period of Mughal rule in Goalpara is the *Baharastan-I-Gayabi*, a Persian chronicle written by Mirza Nathan, a Mughal general who accompanied the Mughal army on its expeditions to eastern parts of the kingdom during the reign of seventeenth

century. The chronicle has been translated and published in two volumes as Borah 1936.

11. Abdul Hamid Lahori's *Padshah Namah*, edited by Maulavi Kabiruddin and Maulavi Abdur Rahim was a chronicle from the reign of Shah Jahan's reign. Completed in 1648, it is an important source of information for the period.

12. The Buchanan Hamilton Papers, Book I, p. 95.

13. Letter from David Scott to W.B. Bayley, 27 September 1819, Bengal Criminal and Judicial Consultations, File no. 88, December 1821, West Bengal State Archives, Kolkata.

14. Ibid.

15. Another colonial official, Francis Jenkins, who undertook a survey of Goalpara between 1831 and 1832 traced the roots of the 'distracted state of the country to the low rates of rent paid by the zamindars on account of their being in a frontier region', (Francis Jenkins to Captain Reynolds, 31 August 1838, 'Bengal Criminal and Judicial Consultations', File no. 90, December 1841).

16. The Buchanan Hamilton Papers, Book I, p. 148; Buchanan also noted that this area was likely to have had 'only occasional visits from the Mughal chiefs ruled as it was by petty chiefs, who remained nominally under the authority of the Nawab of Rangamatti through much of the seventeenth and eighteenth centuries' (ibid.).

17. For relationships between the Mughal state and local powers and their significance for histories of state making in India, see Guha (1999); Skaria (1999); Singh (1995).

18. Letter from J.C. Haughton, Commissioner of the Cooch Behar Division, to the Secretary to the Government of Bengal, 3 April 1867, Goalpara Papers, henceforth GP, State Archives, Guwahati, File no. 7, 1866–70. The bulky offi cial correspondence from this period on the rights and the changing status of these local powers during the pre-colonial period, are an important source for understanding these polities.

19. Petition mentioned in the correspondence between J. C. Haughton, Commissioner of the Cooch Behar Division, to the Secretary to the Government of Bengal, 3 April 1867, GP, File no. 7, 1866–70.

20. Ibid., p. 6.

21. Correspondence between J. C. Haughton, Commissioner of the Cooch Behar Division, to the Secretary to the Government of Bengal, 3 April 1867, GP, File no. 7, 1866–70.

22. Letter from J. C. Haughton, Commissioner of the Cooch Behar Division, to the Secretary to the Government of Bengal, 3 April 1867, GP, File no. 7, 1866–70.

23. Papers relating to Bijnee, the Cooch Behar Commissioner's Office, File no. 1, 1866–68, State State Archives, Guwahati.

24. 'His wise statesmanship and guidance ... made him a favorite of the Emperor Jahangir who decorated him as a Raja and granted sanads for several Lakherajs' and his successors, who later had their head quarters at Rangammati, were all subsequently known as Rajas' (Papers of the Gauripur Estate, GP, File no. 197, 1929).
25. Correspondence regarding Bijni and Sidli, GP, File no. 7, 1866–70.
26. Extract Judicial Letter to Bengal, 2 February 1819, Board's Collection, 1818–20, OIOC, London.
27. Translation of questions put to the Qanungo of Rangamati by the Collector of Rangpur, regarding elephants, and the answers of the Qanungo: 'The question was put to Boolchund Qanungo of the Rangamatty District. In what condition was it necessary for the zamindars of Bijni and Bideagong to deliver elephants for the Company? What number are to be delivered and in what condition? He answered: 'The Khedas in the Taluks of Bijni and Bidiagong were established when the country was held under the Government of the Kings (Mughals) and the ready money revenue being discontinued, the zamindars received a deduction according to the number of elephants which they delivered into the stalls appointed for their reception, receipts being granted for them. From the beginning of 1182 until the present time, a deduction has been annually granted. The zamindar of Bijni ought to deliver annually 68 elephants and each elephant valued at ... making a total of 5,998 ... The zamindar of Bidiagong ought to deliver 40 elephants' (Bengal District Records: Rangpur, Vol. 6, 1786-87, Letters Issued, Published at the Bengal Secretariat Record Room, Calcutta, 1928).
28. The Buchanan Hamilton Papers, Mrs. Eur. D 75, OIOC, London, Book IV, pp. 177–80.
29. Letter from the Commissioner to the Cooch Behar Division to the Secretary to the Government of Bengal, 3 April 1867, GP, File no. 7.
30. There was an extension of the limits of settled cultivation under zamindars who occupied Garo areas in order to increase the production of cotton. By the first decades of the 19th century, although a large section of the Garo people continued to live in the hilly areas and practice non-sedentary forms of cultivation, others within the community 'paid a regular rent, used the plough, and cultivated with fully as much care as any of the neighbouring Bengalese' (John M'Cosh, quoted in Martin 1976: 690).
31. Extract Judicial Letter to Bengal, 2 February 1819, Board's Collection, 1818–20, OIOC, London.
32. 'During the Raja's [Parikshit's] reign', notes the author of the *Padshah Buranji*, 'there were only gaons or villages and no parganas. Sheikh Ibrahim introduced the pargana system and the whole area was designated as Villayat Cooch Hajo which was divided into four sarkars and several parganas under a Kanungo' (Bhuyan 1947: 190).

33. The Buchanan Hamilton Papers, Mss. Eur. D 74, Book II, p. 270, OIOC, London.

34. GP, File no. 7, 1866–70; Offi cials of the East India Company who were engaged in standardising land measurements in the nineteenth century characterised this mode of assessment as 'adapted to a zamindar or a ijaradar [which could not] be well worked by Government agency, because the Agent in the charge of the village has to watch the number of ploughs that are actually employed in the field and this is inquisitional and puts too much in the hands of a Choudhury' (GP, File no. 113, 1873).

35. It is likely that the grants of land under Koch rule consisted of approximately 12 bighas for each soldier (Choudhury 1936: 12).

36. *Fathiya-I-Ibriya,* Mss. Sarkar Collection, No. 77ff. 57a (Bhadra 1984: 482).

37. Abdul Hamid Lahori, *Padshah Namah,* edited by Maulavi Kabiruddin and Maulavi Abdur Rahim, p. 71 (Bhadra 1984: 480).

38. Ibid.

39. 'We the peasants of pargana Khorla (Ghurla) state that we were being ruined due to the oppressions of Pashupati. Therefore, quite willingly and totally on our own accord, we accept the appointment of Bulchand for which Suraj Chand qanungo has furnished *hazir-zamin* (surety) on his behalf. We undertake that when he obtains the *sanad* of *chaudhuri,* we will pay the revenues as before', quoted from Jafri (1989: 280) in Eaton (1993: 158).

40. Jahangirbad, also known as Ghilanaya, was an important centre of administration under both the Koch and the Mughal rulers and is situated a few miles away from Dhubri, the present headquarters of Goalpara district.

41. The text quotes Mirza Yusuf Barlas, the thanadar of Dakhinkul in southern Kamrup during the Khuntaghat rebellion: 'The enemy is driving us from place to place. They have not stopped chasing us and we have been driven back to the bank of the Brahmaputra. For the third day we are encamped on the sandy plains and we are besieged by the enemy' (Borah 1936: 302).

42. Such zones of mobility were defining elements of the spatial history of this part of Asia in the eighteenth and nineteenth centuries. As an example, writing on the cultivators in pre-colonial and colonial Burma and Java, M. Adas notes that there was a frequent transference of allegiance to different rulers, particularly during periods of increased demands of taxes, in areas of low population density and with expanses of cultivable but inhabited land. Adas terms such migrations, 'avoidance protests' (Adas 1981: 219).

43. The Buchanan Hamilton Manuscripts, Book IV, p. 176.

44. C. A. Bayly describes a similar situation in other parts of the Mughal empire during this period: 'Too many new nobles were absorbed into the system as Aurangzeb made his conquests in the south and tried to placate its indigenous nobility. Local revolts cut into the rents and custom dues on which the nobles lived, while the imperial treasury became less and less able to pay cash salaries' (Bayly 1988: 9).

45. For an analysis of Mughal policies of incorporating local rajas and the latter's efforts to retain legitimacy, frequently by upholding the ritual and social order, in Bengal, see John R. McLane, *Land and Kingship in 18th Century Bengal* (1993). McLane argues that the 'imperial institutions of the Mughal and the Company states met the landed rural hierarchies in the pivotal role of the zamindar [who were] subordinate but vital partners ... in governing the scattered villages' (Ibid.: p. 12).

46. The Buchanan Hamilton Papers, Book I, p. 20.

47. Ibid.

48. Ibid., p. 21; correspondence between offi cials in the early years of Company Raj estimated the number of slaves under the Rani of Bijnee at 14,000, 'employed partly as domestic servants and partly as cultivators of soil' (Letter from Hugh Baillie to John Shore, 31 May 1788, in Papers relating to Bijnee, Cooch Behar Commissioner's Office, 1866–68), State Archives, Guwahati.

49. GP, File no. 28, 1872–73.

50. Letter from the Deputy Commissioner of Goalpara to the Commissioner of Cooch Behar Division, 15 July 1872, GP, File no. 28, 1872–73.

51. Ibid., p. 8.

52. The Buchanan Hamilton Papers, Book I, p. 181.

53. Ibid., p. 177.

54. Richard Fox makes a similar suggestion in his study of the institution of the lineage in the eighteenth century United Provinces when he argues that the origin myths were frequently used by 'the elite of the stratified lineage' to sustain the authority acquired by them through political and military pioneering on the margins of state political authority (Fox 1971: 49).

55. Of relevance here is C. A. Bayly's description of the late Mughal period as consisting of frontier societies where 'the internal extent of the state's influence and of the arable economy with its more hierarchical landed society was constantly in flux' (Bayly 1988: 31) and Chetan Singh's comments on the existence of 'fiercely autarchic tribes which lay even further from the Mughal system', and of communities which 'combined a sense of social or communal cohesion that was characteristically different from the differentiated village communities of core Mughal areas' (Singh 1995: 30).

56. James Rennell, November 1765, from an extract from the *Memoirs of the Asiatic Society of Bengal,* Volume III, No. 3, pp. 95–248, 1910 November 1765 published as Appendix 1 in Hirst and Smart (1917).
57. The Buchanan Hamilton Papers, Book IV, p. 176.
58. Ibid.
59. The Buchanan Hamilton Papers, Book IV, pp. 179-80. Travelling through the region in the first decade of the 19th century, Francis Buchanan still found 'thick forests dividing cultivated land, parts of which had been destroyed by the cultivation of the rude tribes' (The Buchanan Hamilton Papers, Book I, p. 276).
60. 'Each man assisted by his wife cultivates as much as a man with a plough and two oxen, that is about 15 bighas or five acres … the men cut and hoe and the women burn the bushes, break the cods, sow the seeds' (Ibid.: 265).
61. Letter from J.C. Geddes, Officiating Commissioner to the eastern Duars, to Lieutenant-Colonel Hopkinson, Agent of the Governor General, North-Eastern Frontier, 11 July 1865, correspondence regarding Bijni and Sidli, 1866–70, State Archives, Guwahati.
62. The community persisted with this technique until the second half of the nineteenth century when there was the advent of Muslim settlers from Bengal, 'who were more accustomed to a settled life than the tenants [of the zamindari estates] who had long been the habit of skulking from wood to wood' (The Buchanan Hamilton Papers, Book IV, p. 220.)
63. The Buchanan Hamilton Papers, Book IV, p. 220.
64. Ibid., p. 546.

2

✿

Practices of Sovereignty, Practices of the Market and Early Colonialism

This chapter studies some of the early interventions of the East India Company and of the nineteenth century colonial state, with occasional necessary retreats into the late eighteenth, in the political economy of Goalpara and its surrounding regions. In particular, it stresses on the contesting spatial practices that these interventions generated and their ties with the production of economically unified, bounded territorialised units of the colonial state. The first section looks at southern Goalpara, the valleys of the Godadhor and the Brahmaputra, and its transition into colonial rule: the introduction of revenue settlements based on notions of private property in land, consolidation of settled cultivating classes and the subsequent emergence of many of the features of nineteenth century agrarian society. The second section looks at the northern region, comprising of the Eastern Duars inclining upwards towards the Bhutan kingdom and parts of Tibet, differentiated from the south by the absence of a permanent settlement of land revenue in the nineteenth century as also by greater instances of shared resources among its communities. In this region, there was an encounter between colonial and local notions of space and power, as colonial institutions and ideologies of governance met the hierarchised realms of shared sovereignty of Goalpara's zamindars, the Bhutan monarch, the Dalai Lama of Tibet, the Ahom ruler and various autonomous tributaries. These were also significant sites for the recovery of local and connected pre-colonial histories. The section that follows resonates these concerns, as it suggests that weekly markets, fairs and the more permanent marketplaces were among some of the most visible sites for cultural and political interaction between communities and rulers apart from being important transmitters of authority. In conclusion, the chapter analyses the entry of the colonial state into local marketing practices and its effect on the culture of trading in the region, including the re-orientation of existing trading connections and their integration into other networks of eastern India.

An Expanding Agrarian Order

In the period after the accession of the East India Company to the Diwani of Bengal in 1765, most of the region that would later form the colonial district of Goalpara came under the administration of the Company as a part of the Rangpur district. Between 1765 and 1793, the economic imperatives of the Company saw the introduction of a series of measures in Rangpur for the collection of revenue. This included the farming system of 1772 that sold revenue collection rights to local chieftains for a period of five years, replaced by a system of annual settlements in 1778. The Company's 'more absolutist approach (as compared to the Mughals) towards the collection of revenue ... did not dramatically alter the amount of revenue actually raised (b)ut they did change the way revenue was collected' (Wilson 2005: 104) evoking several instances of resistance from the cultivators, the most sustained and violent of which was the Rangpur *dhing* of 1783.[1] In the part of Rangpur which comprised of the zamindari estates of Goalpara, however, the availability of large stretches of uninhabited land and the sparse population allowed for the region to be treated as a transitional, frontier area of the Company's territories in eastern India. Although it was to see an aggressive reclamation of 'waste' and forest land under colonial rule, in the late eighteenth century Goalpara's zamindars were governed by policies of 'administrative exception' (Sivaramakrishnan 1996: 264) that continued to characterise them as Mughal border chieftains, paying a nominal tribute to the state (Laine 1917: 2).

This situation of exceptionalism persisted into the period after the introduction of the permanent settlement of land revenue as well. Conforming to what was the existing practice of a rather tenuous hold of the Mughal state and then of the East India Company over the local powers of the region, the extension of colonial revenue administration into southern Goalpara was not preceded by the topographical and revenue surveys that marked other territories that were part of Company rule. 'It is on record that neither during the Mughal government nor at any period anterior to the settlement were internal revenues made the subject of official scrutiny' (Mills 1854: Gowalpara).[2] Despite the commutation of rent to money after the settlement, in several of the zamindari estates the practice of payment of revenue in the forms of tribute paid to the Mughals, continued. Surveying northeastern Rangpur which comprised of Goalpara, in the early decades of the nineteenth century, Francis Buchanan observed that in the parganas of Khuntaghat and Howraghat that were 'in the estates of the Bijni Raja, one half of the rent is paid in coarse cloth woven by the women of his tenantry[3] and in 1,400 mon of dried fish ... caught at the Tobarang lake'.[4] These modes of payment in kind, using various articles drawn from the ecological resources of the region, were regarded as continuities from the period of Mughal rule when 'the Peshkash for the Khuntaghat and the Howraghat parganas of the Bijni estate was fixed at 5,998 Narayani rupees but the tribute was soon commuted to 68 elephants for the faujdar at the headquarters of Rangammaty'.[5]

The ambitions and the capacities of the colonial government, however, far exceeded those of its predecessors, and the scale of change initiated in the rural economy of southern Goalpara from the early nineteenth century onwards constituted a decisive shift towards a village-centred peasant agriculture. The dominant vision was one of agrarianisation initiated by the zamindars whose control over local peasant communities was hoped would extend over the thick forested areas of the region as well. The explicit purpose of the consolidation of the rural gentry was to re-direct the interests and energies of the local chieftains from local warfare to agrarian management and investment, assuring both stability and a steady flow of revenue. Unlike the rest of the Brahmaputra Valley, the practice of leasing out land to men with capital to organise reclamation had been resorted to by zamindars in the permanently settled estates of Goalpara from the early nineteenth century onwards.

The availability of vast stretches of uncultivated land in Goalpara and its surrounding areas through the nineteenth century, however, remained a major preoccupation in the correspondence between colonial officials, and in surveys and ethnographic accounts prior to the settlement of large stretches on land by cultivators from eastern Bengal in the last decades of that century. In his elaborate notes, Buchanan offered possible reasons for the movement of peasants: the land on both the eastern and western sides of the Brahmaputra and Sonkosh rivers, though extremely fertile, was prone to inundation. In fact, 'of all the level land east from the Brahmaputra and Sonkosh river, it is only Parbatjoar and part of Khuntaghat and Mechpara that contain any considerable portions, except mountains, that are exempted from inundation':

> The lowlands exempt from inundation are of two kinds. The first is very level and fit for cultivation of transplanted rice. The best of this is placed immediately among the hills, and especially near the Garo mountains, where it is watered by fine springs and little rivulets and has a very rich soil. They have neat gardens where they have a few fruit trees and sugarcane; also cultivate higher fields and produce rice, mustard, and wheat. Those villages that occupy the inundated areas, move from one place to another once in three years and cultivate fresh land until it is exhausted. These have little or no garden land; these villages look miserable.[6]

Thus, even in low lying areas around the river valleys, where varieties of rice were grown, the cultivators shifted their villages every five to six years. In the hilly areas, when the forests had been cleared for cultivation, the cultivators settled for a period of three years at the most, practicing hoe cultivation, after which they left it fallow again for two to three years. These conditions persisted through much of the colonial period.

That the region was known for its slow growth in population would have added to the official anxiety about 'insufficient cultivation'. The first official census was taken in 1872, but there were earlier attempts at estimating the population of the region, mostly using plough shares in the manner of Buchanan. Writing in the middle of the nineteenth century, Moffat Mills, a colonial official, expressed anxiety that something in the district was unfavourable to a rapid expansion of population (Allen 1906: 33). Mills would have found support for his observations in an account dating back to 1714, in the description of the Father Fransisco Troyand's visit to Goalpara by his companion Father Claudius Anthony Barbier.

In his notes, Barbier had noted that Rangamati, the Mughal pargana of which Goalpara formed a part, was known for its unhealthiness,[7] and referred to a common Bengali parable: 'that of two persons, who go to Rangamati, there is always one who remains there'.[8] The problem was evidently serious enough for Francis Buchanan to devote an entire document to it. In his notes on the *Population of Goalpara and the Causes which Operate on its Increase or Diminution,* Buchanan discussed the lack of energy and activity evident among the people of the Rangpur district as a whole and then offered an estimate of the proportion of some of the chief causes that could operate as a check on the population of Goalpara. Dismissing factors including early marriages as negligible checks on the population growth, Buchanan identified disease and fever as the grand check and the large stretches of uncultivated and forested land in the region as the principal cause of this fever.[9]

The offer of a variety of leases by the colonial state to encourage cultivation, without the cultivators incurring any liability through enhanced assessment in the region therefore has to be seen against this background. Most leases of land in the zamindari estates during this period were granted in perpetuity to the occupants who paid a minimal customary *nirikh* to the landlord and enjoyed permanent occupancy rights after an initial period of three years. Buchanan noted that the several leases that were granted during this period 'were apparently for the benefit of the cultivator ... to secure him in the possession of the lands for a certain time at a lower rent than the maximum to encourage him to bring wastelands under cultivation'.[10] In the absence of regular revenue surveys, the integration of local groups into the agrarian order has to be assessed primarily from the surveys of Buchanan and from a few scattered colonial reports. Since settled cultivation depended on the use of ploughs drawn by bullocks, the number of ploughs in the possession of each peasant family was considered a reliable indication of the ability of different communities to sustain independent production. Buchanan's estimate of the settled agrarian population in southern Goalpara at 162,000, with the number of ploughs at 32,400 suggests that the valley between the Sonkosh and the Manas rivers had come to support a large settled population by the early nineteenth century.[11] Colonial records from this period estimated the area of cultivated land at 677 square miles as against a total area of 4,104 square miles, though forest areas and wastelands continued to occupy 3,427 square miles in the district (Mills 1854: Appendix 4). By the turn of the century these figures had risen sufficiently for the population of southern Goalpara to be described by William Hunter as 'primarily agriculturists' (Hunter 1879: 74), 'a peasantry that could be relied upon to cling to their holdings like the Hindu peasants of other districts ... with plenty of orchards and bamboos topes to bind them to their homesteads, and no fear of them moving suddenly and capriciously'.[12]

These *projas* or under-tenants were drawn predominantly from the Rajbanshi community, which had been increasingly settling to agriculture even at the inception of the colonial regime, and by now had emerged as the dominant agricultural caste in large parts of eastern Bengal and Goalpara. Several other communities, including the Kacharis who in the 1840s were said to be practising 'a desultory nature of cultivation ... with little affection for the soil they cultivate' (Hodgson, quoted in Dalton 1872: 84), and continuing to live on the margins of settled life, were being described by colonial officials in the last decade of the century as a 'remarkably fine peasantry with a very superior cultivation of the permanent kind' (Jenkins quoted in Sanyal 1973: 9). Hunter's account from this period, too, has a similar description of the Kacharis as 'a purely agricultural group, who, with a few exceptions, live by the produce of the land' (Hunter 1879: 37). By the first decades of the nineteenth century, although a large section of the Garo people continued to live in the hilly areas and practice non-sedentary forms of cultivation, others within the community 'paid a regular rent, used the plough, and cultivated with fully as much care as any of the neighbouring Bengalese' (M'Cosh, quoted in Martin 1976: 690).

In the more prosperous estates such as Gauripur and Karaibari, control over the production process from the early decades of the nineteenth century onwards was being increasingly appropriated by a class of cultivators, the *jotedars*, drawn primarily from the Rajbanshi community. From Buchanan's account, it is obvious that they were drawn from the Brahmin and Kayastha castes as well and that 'they retained only a little land in their possession, just enough to supply their numerous families with food and this they cultivated by means of those who receive a share of the crop ... [T]he remainder they let at rack rent to under tenants and with the money given by these, pay their rent and purchase what luxuries they require'.[13] Buchanan also mentions a gradual expansion of the class, which came to include several Muslim farmers and clerics as its members.[14] In the pattern of landownership that emerged in this period in the region, the jotedars controlled large stretches of land, frequently acting as creditors for the cultivators and for an emerging class of landless labourers. Associated with this system was an informal and imprecise style of estate management wherein the jotedar:

> obtained permission from the Raja to settle and break up land; sometimes a specified quantity, but practically... took up as much as he liked, for where land abounds and ryots are few, the land is of no value. He at first with his own family and a ryot or two, cultivates what is sufficient only for their joint maintenance; by degrees, however, poor men collect around him, getting permission to cultivate and use his seed, on condition of receiving half his crop. The entire *jote* is estimated rudely, not according to the number of ploughs but by an imaginary standard called the plough. No measurement takes place. The plough of land on the border has been found to fluctuate between five and hundred bighas.[15]

In the villages of southern Goalpara and Rangpur the jotedar was therefore more than an inferior landholder under the zamindar, renting out land to under-tenants and share-croppers. Buchanan found the bigger jotedars gradually becoming a rural elite and acquiring a social status that corresponded closely to that enjoyed by the zamindars.

> In general they are well behaved men, superior by much both in manners and education ... and many of them live much better than landlords of the first families and the largest estates in the district. It is true that they do not have the same train of idle followers and flatterers, but this means that they retain their understandings and necessity of application to business sharpens their wit ... so that they manage their affairs with economy and their houses, diet and clothing are at least equal to those of the landlords and many of them can afford to ride on a horse or keep a palanquin.[16]

The *dewaniya* system, a village political device peculiar to North Bengal (Ray 1975: 190) and prevalent in the district of Goalpara as well, reflected this position of the jotedar and his control over the process of surplus collection and distribution. The dewaniya was usually a small jotedar. Under this system, he was tied in a relationship with the ordinary cultivator or the *chengra*, and played the role of an agent or go-between, between him and the zamindar's agents or the officials of the colonial state. The chengras were described by Buchanan as 'the most timid creatures imaginable ... being totally illiterate and afraid to speak even to the village clerk'.[17] The dewaniya's control over the production and distribution processes was bolstered by his dominant role in the social life of the village.[18] The jotedars may have begun as cultivators who enabled the zamindar to colonise the wastelands of his estate at minimum risk and expense, while deriving a considerable profit by subletting his surplus lands to under-tenants, but were increasingly occupying a more important position within Goalpara's rural society.

Despite the emergence of a stratified agrarian structure, the triumph of the agrarian order however was yet to be evident in most of this part of eastern India during the nineteenth century. Forests and settled agricultural areas, for instance, were far from being geographically distinct regions in the Goalpara of this period. Instead the former continued to be an important source of political and economic resource both for local powers and for the ordinary peasant, with control over and knowledge of this strategic domain ... [being seen as] a tradable resource in the regional and political arena (Guha 1999: 199). The country was described in 1765 by surveyor James Rennell as 'very little cultivated in the neighbourhood of Goalpara and Jugigopa ... with the woods abound [ing] with several kinds of wild animals ... and so full of trees and jungle as to be scarcely penetrable'.[19] This thick forest cover continued into the middle of the nineteenth century when almost all the zamindari estates had large stretches of forested and uncultivated lands, the estate of Chapar being the only one which consisted of land that was 'populous and cultivated like Bengal' (Mills 1854: Appendix A). Large areas of several estates 'were chiefly hills and mountains covered with forests ... [or] undulating country covered with Sal forests' (ibid.). Several communities continued to live independently on the margins of settled society, while others alternated between settled and migratory lifestyles. Conversely, the forested and hilly areas frequently had large clearings that were sites for shifting cultivation practiced by several communities along with areas that were marked out as common grazing grounds for cattle. A letter from the manager of the zamindari of Bijni had the following observation about the ryots on the estate:

The inhabitants are all Mechis, but they are much less advanced than the people of the same tribe in Koontaghat. The Raimana and the Repoo Mechis have not yet attained the idea of occupying permanently particular spots of land. One family (or two and more families in common) will cultivate a patch of land for one year, and in the following year, will break up new soil. While another family may take up the land thus abandoned ... few of the Raimanee or Repoo ryots took sufficient interest in their homesteads as to plant bamboo trees and none on them planted such trees as the mango, jack, soparee etc., which take a long time to yield fruit. The Mechis of Koontaghat have partly advanced beyond this stage of nomadic cultivation, but yet even then, the patgiri or collector of a village has to keep a sharp look out to see that Mechi ryots do not decamp suddenly without making good the current year's rent.[20]

Evasion of oppressive taxation regimes combined with the demands of the techniques of shifting cultivation and the availability of arable land could explain the mobility of several groups. Whereas villages with settled forms of cultivation would have discouraged much peasant mobility, in areas such as these, where cultivation anyway tended to rotate on account of less population and where other forms of conservation, including manuring and crop rotation, were less practiced, movement, sometimes involving entire villages, was likely to have involved fewer costs and more benefits for the peasant.

Overlapping Territorialities and Shared Sovereignties

Towards the north, there was a similar coexistence of peasant settlements and non-sedentary communities in the Bijni and the Sidli estates and in the Eastern Duar region. A report from an expedition prior to the British occupation of the Eastern Duars described the region as:

[A]narrow strip of land, ranging in breadth from ten to twenty miles, which runs along the base of the lower range of the Bootan Hills from the Darjeeling District to the Frontier of Assam [and] extends from the Dhansiri river to the River Teesta on the west. The land within these limits is by nature singularly rich and fertile; it is formed of the richest black vegetable mould, is washed by many rivers, and has a southern slope from 1,500 feet to the level of the plains of Bengal (Eden 1865: 2).

Rich in ecological resources and suitable for the cultivation of cotton, the eastern part of the Dooar region separated the towns and trading ports of southern Goalpara and eastern Bengal from their markets inland in Bhutan and Tibet. Sal trees, which were an important source of timber for the railways (and hence a significant factor behind the colonial occupation of the Duars in 1866) constituted a large portion of these thick wooded tracts of the Duars.

Colonial economic interests in northern Goalpara, however, had to first contend with the conditions of overlapping territoriality and sovereignty, which characterised the indigenous polity of this region. In the perspective of the colonial state, the Duars, particularly the area included within the zamindari estates of Bijni and Sidli, was 'an anomaly, wherein chieftains who considered themselves independent Rajas paid revenue to the British government for half of their estates, whilst for the other half they continued to acknowledge the authority of the Government of Bhutan'.[21] Officials cautioned 'that previous to arrangements being made for the management of the forests, or for the settlement of the soil, it is incumbent on the government to decide upon the status of the two persons who call themselves Rajas, and who between them, claim the whole land between the Manas and the Godadhar rivers'.[22] What followed, as is elaborated later on in this chapter, was a period of complex negotiations over notions of political space between the state and local powers.

In most other parts of the country under British rule, and on all questions of tributary relationships, rights and territoriality, colonial officials were frequently divided into groups that offered different interpretations and proposed policies accordingly. So it was in the nature of the relationship between the Bhutan monarch and the zamindars of Bijni and Sidli. In their search for documentary evidence to determine the 'legitimate rights' and 'claims' of the local powers and whether a particular tributary was independent or an integral part of the Bhutanese kingdom, colonial officials relied on the sanads of the Deb Raja of Bhutan to these chieftains and were frequently confounded by the 'ambiguous nature' of this tributary relationship.

The sanad of the Deb Raja of Bhutan to Kumud Narayan, the chieftain of Bijni, stated that 'it had been customary during a long time for the Dhurma Raja to send a present of horses to the Bijni Raja and for him to send as presents dried fish, oil, endi silk and salami, all of which were furnished every year.'[23] It then dwelt on the rights of the Bijni chieftain over the Cheerung forests in return for the grant of which the latter had to pay the Bhutan officials three loads of salt and 200 pieces of *endi* (coarse woven cloth) to purchase goods worth Rs 300 from Bhutan, including a fan decorated with peacock feathers. It also warned him to abstain from 'oppressing anyone' in disregard to the orders of the Bhutanese official, the *zimpe*.[24] In short, this was a statement of both superiority and interdependence, of rights and duties expressed by the exchange of 'gifts'.[25] Again, a sanad from the Deb Raja to Indranarayan, the Raja of Sidli, listed the following articles: one pair of ivory tusks, 11 pairs of nine kinds of cloth, one rhinoceros horn, one tiger skin, one jari [water pot], 1 brass batta [betel box] 1 khora [cup] of pewter, one sari [frock], one mosquito net, one punkha [fan], one shade of peacock feathers, one Tangun pony.[26] In return, he received from the Deb Raja a golden *jampe* or an ornament for a head dress, a *jauna* or a robe, a gift of Tangun horses and ponies, mounds of salt, a gong and a drum. The incorporation and submission of the tributary rulers were, therefore, also accompanied by a certain degree of reciprocity, with the rewards from the Deb Raja often being of greater value than the tribute from Bijni and Sidli.

Unfamiliarity with the system of authority that was reflected in these sanads led colonial administrators to offer contradictory interpretations. At the same time, these interpretations reflected a shared inability to recognise the 'complicated set of categorisations and gradations of kinship relations'(Dirks 1986: 312) that the gifts in the sanads entailed, an understanding of indigenous rights that assumed 'opposition and not complementarity' (ibid.). Thus, in his reading of one such sanad, Geddes argued:

> The Booteahs looked upon all men as removable from office and recognized no proprietary right in the soil arising from lengthened tenure. These people [the Bijni and Sidli zamindars] who occupied an intermediate position between the *tehsildar* of the present day and the zamindar of the Mughal empire were usually left to make what arrangements they thought fit, and their conduct was not questioned unless grievous complaint of oppression came up or the revenue fell into arrears.[27]

J. C. Haughton's response to Geddes refuted the latter's arguments but shared his view of property rights, citing evidence of occupancy rights of the zamindars spreading over more than a century under the Mughals and then under the Bhutan and the British administration as sufficient proof of their proprietorship, 'so far as such rights can exist under arbitrary governments'.[28]

The ideology of the colonial state, then, did not allow for a conceptualisation of space and authority that recognised the hierarchised nature of local authority existing within spheres of non-exclusive territorial sovereignties. Within the state's official discourses, therefore, relationships between local powers were frequently reduced to familiar economic transactions and linear hierarchies. For instance, Mackenzie seems to have judged these objects purely in commercial terms, asserting that 'the British government was most tenacious of its rights in matters of bargain ... and it would not consent to be swindled even in such things as yak tails ...' (Mackenzie 1884: 10). In another example of the colonial state's unfamiliarity with the local system of authority as reflected in the sanads, officials dismissed the ritual exchange of gifts between the Bhutanese monarch and the kingdoms of Bijni and Sidli as insignificant for the debate over the status of the chieftains of these areas.[29] The exchange of gifts between the Bhutan king and the chieftains of the Duars, when evaluated in monetary terms, appeared 'ludicrously in favour of the Booteahs', when in return for a *mangon* or demand for money by Bhutanese officials, the chieftains received 'some trifling article, as a piece of silk'.[30] Relationships were invariably represented as 'compulsory exchanges of food and benevolent fines' imposed by a more powerful state, with detailed lists of commodities that construed gifts as utilitarian objects rather than as a means of communicating the reciprocal relationship of these powers.

There were other kinds of confrontations induced by these differing notions of political space. In response to a plea by the Raja of Sidli that he be allowed to retain his title, 'as the Bhutan government used to recognise his status as a Raja by sending him honorary presents every year',[31] Geddes argued that in the absence of any documentary evidence, 'there were no means of determining the exact status accorded to the occupant of Bijni by the Bhootan government'.[32] Colonial officials failed to discover any fixed hierarchy or common system of titles; frequently titles were used without reference to any definite distinctions of status (Cohn 1983: 191) producing arguments such as: 'No importance whatever could be paid to the fact that the petitioner bears the title of the "Raja", or as he calls himself, "Maharajah". In Bhutan, anyone whose collections of revenue were so extensive as those of Sidli and who exercised judicial authority, would be called a Raja'.[33]

There were similar petitions from the Rani of Bijni in support of her minor son, Kumud Narayan. The Rani pleaded that: 'The Raja of Bijni was independent for so long that it was not necessary for him to obtain the title of Raja from any other power. Rajas of recent creation require a sanad but the Raja of Bijnee was a genuine Raja from time immemorial'.[34] In his petition to Bengal government, Kumud Narayan laid claims to the jurisdiction of the territory of Khuntaghat, Habraghat and Bijni on the grounds that, despite having to obtain the protection of the Mughal government, on coming under their jurisdiction, Bijni was distinguished from other landholders by having to pay not a rent but a tribute for these lands.[35] Other petitions included one by the Rani of Bijni, Nageswari Debi. She argued persuasively that the Bhutan monarch concluded periodic settlements with the descendants of Bijni, and more significantly: 'The annexed tract of the Bhutan territory [the Eastern Duars], now under dispute, was neither a conquered one nor a ceded one; it is part of a tributary state and the right and interest possessed by its owner cannot be otherwise but what had been fixed by the conditions of the treaty of peace'.[36] A petition from Gauri Narayan, the Raja of Sidli, claimed to have had judicial and magisterial powers under the Bhutan monarch, including rights to the timber transit duties, while continuing to pay rent to the Bhutia authorities.[37]

Implicit in the petitions of the Bijni and Sidli rulers was not only an awareness of the juridical terms and categories understood by the British, or of the existence of 'a curious form of joint administration' (Rose 1977: 56) but more importantly, suggestions of the existence of multiple sovereignty in the region, which allowed tributary areas to seek protection from a powerful neighbour while continuing to retain their own rights. For the Deb Raja of Bhutan, both Bijni and Sidli were frontier areas bordering his kingdom, the rulers of which could be ordered 'to settle wastelands and manage the taluks' and warned of punishment in the event of 'any injustice, hostility, or an act of disturbance'.[38] These tributaries also continued to receive a robe and scarves of honour from the Deb Raja. The acceptance of these gifts entailed loyalty as well as a recognition of the sovereignty of the smaller powers, including the right to exercise all judicial powers within these territories, by the ruler of Bhutan.[39] A sanad from the Deb Raja to Raja Indranarayan of Sidli, whom Gauri Narayan succeeded, stated, 'No one is to be allowed to go into your jurisdiction and you will exercise all judicial powers. The disposal of murder, dacoity, theft and rape is given to you'.[40] Such practices were rather confusing for officials of the colonial state, who understood property to govern political relations and political space within clearly demarcated boundaries. This was unlike the late eighteenth century, when the early stages of state making ensured that colonialism was still negotiating with local ideas of power, a situation that allowed for not just an acknowledgement but even an acceptance of overlapping sovereignties within official discourses.[41]

The arguments of both Geddes and Haughton drew upon notions of exclusive sovereignty and of fixed territoriality, which negated the possibility that frontiers and sovereignties could overlap. Geddes' understanding of the status of Bijni and Sidli represented the areas as integral parts of the kingdom of Bhutan and located the disputed territories of the Eastern Duars firmly within the sovereignty of the Deb Raja. In one of his several memoranda to the administration on this issue, Geddes argued:

> About 1786, the Booteahs took possession of the Sidli Dooar [and] the place has ever since remained subject to Bhutan. It is true that the Deb Raja did to a certain extent recognise the hereditary succession of zamindars among the Hindus in the Dooars, but this was permitted only as an exceptional arrangement for the sake of revenue, and not by any means as a right, either proprietary or hereditary.[42]

Commenting on the nature of the demands from the Bhutanese government and the manner of payment, Geddes quoted from the last sanad conferred on Sidli which laid down that, 'every year [Sidli] was to give [the Bhutanese monarch] new rice and clothes and likewise ... consignments and contributions and chance fees whatsoever and whosoever we shall ask'.[43] Geddes concluded that this was sufficient proof that the payments were compulsory: it was preposterous to talk of proprietary rights held under such exacting circumstances as these.[44] Bhutan, therefore, was a clearly bound polity, with institutions that could be adapted to colonial rule 'to secure the greatest possible uniformity in the revenue system',[45] and the judicial authority exercised by the rulers of Bijni and Sidli was attributed to administrative necessity, these areas being at the periphery of the Deb Raja's kingdom.

Haughton's spirited defence of the rights of the Bijni and Sidli zamindars, which pleaded for 'the ancient possessors of the soil to be treated with great consideration', was based on the recognition of the sovereignty of these smaller kingdoms. This, he pointed out, was evident in the fact that their rights resembled those of other native rulers, namely to collect taxes and *abwabs*, and to conduct an independent judicial and fiscal system of administration.[46] In his several accounts of the history of the Eastern Duars, Haughton continued to represent the rulers of Bijni and Sidli as independent powers, small kingdoms whose sovereignty was temporarily compromised during invasions by the Bhutan monarch and later by the colonial state. However, he too ignored the existence of a relationship of reciprocity between the Bhutan monarch and the rulers of Bijni and Sidli and, together with Geddes, dismissed rituals of reciprocity — the exchange of gifts between these kingdoms — and attempted instead to identify exclusive sovereignties that would help the colonial state delineate legitimate rights.

Translated into the familiar language of unambiguous sovereignty, whether of the Bhutan king's or of the annexed territories of the Duars, the debates justified the introduction of contractual relationships between the local chiefs and the colonial state in the region and erased any existing ambiguities over rights to the ecological resources of the area. The British recognised the Bhutanese monarch as the sole possessor of sovereign rights over these resources in the pre-colonial period in opposition to the smaller chieftains. They identified a well-defined revenue collecting mechanism under his rule, which had 'the *soubahs* as the highest officer and the tehsildars or the *katams* under him followed by the jotedars, in a clear hierarchy of power'.[47]

Quoting from a sanad from the Deb Raja of Bhutan to the Rani of Sidli, Geddes observed that:

> the terms of the sanad for the Cheerung forests granted by the Deb Raja are so extensive as to enable the Rani to work the forests of Sidli in addition to the ones she has hitherto held ... [T]he people of Bijni and Sidli have found their interest in arranging such things quietly and avoiding interference from their controlling authorities.

Geddes concluded: 'There is no doubt that the forests have always been looked on as state property. They have been expressly treated as such by the Bhutan authorities and even by the Bijni family'.[48]

Other colonial officials agreed: they too needed to establish an ideologically coherent basis for the collection of revenue. Thus, Metcalfe suggested that in dealing with the present Raja of Sidli, 'it seems clear that the only claim that he can put forth is that of his family having collected the rents of the Cheerung Dooar for several generations'.[49] 'The sanads granted to the Sidli family by the Bhutias [were] clearly worded as if the Bhutan government regarded the Dooars as a part of the Kingdom and delegated its authority for a certain purpose'.[50]

Colonial intervention thus reduced complex relations to a law of property. If local rights had been totally contingent on an arrangement with the sovereign of Bhutan, then his successor, the colonial state, would have the forest resources at their disposal. Such readings of local political conditions also gave the colonial state the legitimacy it needed to rule the area.

> In this respect they and ourselves are equal' [observed Haughton], 'the inhabitants here as elsewhere in India have to choose between masters;... [T]hey are willing to choose the English and reject Bhutia rule and hence even though we may be disliked as foreigners, we shall not be so much disliked as the foreigners we have displaced'.[51]

The practical question, therefore, as one colonial official pointed out, was 'how the two objects of preservation of existing Bhutanese institutions and their harmonisation with the British revenue system could best be accomplished'.[52]

The representation of Bhutan as a bounded polity is of significance, particularly since there is evidence of alternative representations of the region and its inhabitants in colonial writings from the period preceding the annexation of the Eastern Duars. Tour reports by officials from the mid-nineteenth century frequently alluded to the rather 'fragmented' and 'patchy' power structure that was the Bhutan polity, the features of which appeared more pronounced in the Duar region, and which remained the chief source for revenue for the officials of the kingdom until the determination of boundaries by the colonial state. William

Griffiths, a medical officer travelling through Bhutan in 1837, as part of a political mission to the state, described the Bhutan government as 'a many headed government, each *deb*, each *pillo*, each *soubah*, each officer ... bent on enriching himself at the expense of his subjects or his inferiors' (Griffiths 1865: 159).

Griffiths' observations suggest that political spheres under Bhutanese rule were determined not by fixed territorial markers but by power relations. While the 'authority regarding the internal economy of the country [was] vested in the Deb Raja ... his power appeared to be extremely limited. The pillo [had] no check on him, his province [was] far from the capital' (Griffiths 1865: 159). Several of these pillos as well as the soubahs below them were on the margins of the power of the Bhutanese monarch, deciding on arbitrary tributes from the inhabitants of the Duars. 'Plunders, fines, reversion of property by death of owners, trading, and the proceeds of lands in the plains' formed the chief sources of their income in the absence of any fixed salaries (Eden 1865: 9). Colonial records observed that 'the amount of the tribute [was] entirely dependent on the generosity of the soubahs who regarded the people of the plains with the same sort of feeling as the task masters of Egypt entertained towards enslaved Hebrews' (ibid.).

Sovereignty and physical boundaries were frequently not conterminous in this region where the powers of these Bhutan officials and those of the rulers of Bijni and Sidli overlapped. Prior to the British occupation of the region, the Kuriapara Duar in the Eastern Duars remained under the occupation of Bhutanese officials for eight months of the year while for the rest of the year other local powers claimed their rights to it (Mackenzie 1884: 10). The collection of tribute from the Duars could also be seasonal: in certain areas the soubah descended from the hills of Bhutan 'only when the cold air of December and January had rendered the region comparatively healthy'.[53] State power was not characterised by plural sovereignties alone; it was apparently a seasonal state as well. The forest resources of the Duars also comprised the chief source of income of the chieftains of Bijni and Sidli. Geddes, referring to the Raja of Sidli, pointed out that 'as chief fiscal officer of the Dooar, he has hitherto levied forest dues of all kinds'.[54] A sanad from the Deb Raja granted the lease of the Cheerung forests to the Raja of Bijni and instructed him to pay the customary fees due to the Cheerung soubah, the official of the Bhutan government.[55]

On the eastern frontiers of the borderland, the Ahom rulers[56] continued to assert rights over the produce of the Duar region and were frequently in conflict with the state of Bhutan. Colonial records from the mid-nineteenth century noted that 'the malarious and deadly character of the tract and their own feebleness in recent years have prevented the Assam Rajas from giving efficient protection to the indigenous cultivators or establishing an undisputed dominion over the soil and its products'.[57] Such ambiguous expressions of political power could result in inhabitants being subjected to exactions from several authorities all of whom could be 'equally obnoxious and equally oppressive in their dealings'.[58] There would also be frequent variations in the rents and tributes demanded. The Bhutanese officials' claims 'changed from one sanad to the next, while the rulers of Bijni and Sidli made whatever demands they thought expedient'.[59]

Several writings from this period suggest that the situation of shared sovereignty was common to other neighbouring kingdoms as well. 'The political relations of the country are as limited as the boundaries', observed William Griffiths in his tour diary of Bhutan. 'With Sikkim they appear to have no intercourse. That they are tributary directly to Lhasa and now indirectly to China, there can be no doubt, although they most strenuously deny it' (Griffiths 1865: 158). Thus, when the Raja of Cooch Behar was carried off during a raid by the Bhutan authorities who claimed a right to replace him in another assertion of multiple sovereignty the colonial government sought the intervention of the Dalai Lama of Tibet who then denounced the Bhutanese as 'a rude and ignorant race' (Eden 1865: 3). That Bhutan formed a part of the sovereign realm of the Dalai Lama was evident in the response of the Bhutanese government, which 'agreed to deliver up the captive Raja of Cooch Behar and his brother and to pay a tribute of five Tangun horses for the district of Chichacottah' (ibid.). In another example of overlapping sovereignties, on the eastern borders of Goalpara, the Ahom king sent an annual peshkash or tribute as an acknowledgement of the sovereignty of the Dalai Lama of Tibet over the region (Hamilton et al. 1854: 109).

And finally, adding to all these existing forms of state–making in the region, were the 'unsettled powers' (Bayly 1983: 29), the bands of various kinds of peripatetic groups whose activities towards the end of the Mughal imperium routinely transformed the Duar areas along with the southern plains below into realms of relative political autonomy through the late eighteenth century into the early decades of colonial rule. Colonial records refer to several such groups of 'robbers and free booters who used the Dooars as their rendezvous from where they could march into Assam villages' and observed that 'in these harassed pergunnahs, the tenantry has mostly given up fixed residence: many of them have retired within the British boundary, while others cross the river to cultivate the fields in Assam and return at night to sleep in safety'.[60] A possible explanation for the flourishing of these groups was to be found in the rather transitional character of the economy of local powers in the region, where despite the immanent sedenterisation, large stretches of land were thickly forested (as discussed earlier in the chapter) and a significant part of the revenue paid to the British continued to be in the form of tribute rather than taxes. Frequently assuming agency for revenue collection and for justice, these groups thrived on their critical connections with local zamindars and the chieftains of the Duars, a factor that enabled them to carry out raids on villages on the Assam border with the latter's resources. Of these, a group led by Ghulam Ali, a former soldier in the Mughal army, wielded considerable power, 'acquiring a kind of sovereignty over 16 villages on the eastern banks of the Manas, from which [it] received a large revenue, readily paid by the inhabitants for protection'.[61] Attempts by the colonial government to check the raids by Ghulam's successor, Manik Ray, were frustrated by Bijni's difficult physical terrain but more significantly, by Manik's negotiations with the ruler of Bijni, whom the British 'strongly suspected of sharing in the burkandezes' depredations'.[62]

Earlier, a letter from the Collector of Rangpur to the Governor General reported with alarm that 'a large body of armed men (had) attacked the house of the Raja of Cooch Behar and forcibly carried off both the Raja and the Rani … with marks of peculiar violence and indignity'.[63] The abduction was carried out by a group of men, comprising of 'Sanyasis, Sikhs and Sepoys, led by Ganesh Ghur Sanyasi who had been given 3,000 rupees in gold and silver for the purpose of raising forces'[64] by loyalists of Khagendra Narain Kumar, a contender for the throne of Cooch Behar. What irked the officials of the colonial state further however, and reiterated its discourse of the turbulent peripheries that were outside of the civilisational order, was the involvement of several tax paying local zamindars in this attack on a British protectorate. The deposition of Hari Ghur Sanyasi, one of the accused, before the Collectorate at Rangpur made this link evident: '… the men began to be collected in the pergunnah Ghurla in the zamindari of Bool Chand Barooah … a very intimate relationship existed between the Ganesh Ghur and Bool Chand Barooah, in whose zamindari the former lives and has a farm of two or three thousand rupees'.[65] Within the official records, the tendency was to view these groups in isolation, as constitutive in their act of mobility and violence in contradiction with those of a settled order and of the state. Officials invariably identified these spheres of 'political anarchy' with the 'peripheries', contrasted with the more familiar settled polities of the plains of eastern Bengal. Thus the estate of Sidli was 'a community no better than an organised band of robbers',[66] while others were 'annual marauders and bandits … sets of vagabonds and dacoits who rally under the standard of anyone who has the influence to collect them and forming themselves into parties in the neighbourhood of Assam towards the close of the rains, take advantage of the fall of the waters to enter the country'.[67] The reality however was more complex, as the above instances indicate, making it difficult to separate the interests of these unsettled powers from those of the local chiefs. Events such as the Cooch Behar abduction, where the zamindar of Karaibari joined forces with the zamindar of Ghurla, sending 'a considerable body of troops to Balrampur to assist Khagendra Narain Kumar, despite warnings about the 'criminality of his conduct',[68] were also important for understanding the negotiated character of colonial state–making in the region, its encounter with local hierarchies of power and the subsequent transformations effected in the institutions and ideology of the state.

Sharing History, Sharing Trade

In the places of memory that came together in later representations of connected histories of the region, there were some that were significant for the collective experiences that constituted them. Marketing practices, everyday forms of exchange and larger

trading networks that wove complex patterns of interdependencies among local polities and communities, were some such sites
in the pre- and early colonial period and this section explores the
history of the connections that they evoked in Goalpara and in the
regions that bordered it. Markets and other trading practices in the
region were important sites, not just as one more material instance
of shared history but also as sites where the shifting, overlapping
notions of power discussed above were produced. By extension,
they were also the most visible spaces of confrontation between
colonial and indigenous notions of space and power. And for
the various communities living on the borderland, commercial
transactions were a constitutive part of the social and political
fabric in the region.

Though often not very substantial in monetary terms, a considerable volume of trade was carried on from the late eighteenth
century onwards in several of the weekly markets and fairs that
were held along the foothills of the Duar area. In particular,
the numerous fairs formed an important element in the trading
network of the region. Some were also held in the plains of
southern Goalpara and were connected to local shrines. Of these
fairs, the ones held at Hajo, Kuriapara and Udalguri were among
the best attended ones. The Kuriapara fair, held in the Duar by the
same name on the borders of the Bhutan kingdom, was under
the shared sovereignty of the states of Bhutan and Tibet, and was
the principal channel for trade between Tibet, China, Bhutan and
Assam. Buchanan offers an interesting description of the fair as:

> An annual event in which traders from all parts of Tibet, from
> Lhasa and places east, west and even north of it were present in
> the crowds, some of them clad in Chinese dresses, using Chinese
> implements and looking to all intents Chinese. Many have their
> families with them and carry their goods on sturdy ponies, of
> which some hundreds were brought down to the fair yearly. The
> annual caravan from Lhasa, carrying silver bullion to the amount
> of about 100,000 rupees and a considerable quantity of rock salt
> halted at Chouna on the confines of the two states of Bhutan and
> Assam and carried back tussar cloth, iron, and lac from Assam and
> otter skins, buffalo horns, pearls, and corals that were imported
> from Bengal.[69]

Colonial expeditions into Bhutan commented on the centrality
of the Duars in the economy of Bhutan and described the

region as forming the most valuable part of Bhutan's territory. 'Through them and from them are procured almost every article of consumption or luxury that the inhabitants of the hills possess. Their principal trade is with them' (Pemberton 1865: 17). Several mountain passes connected Bhutan with the plains of southern Goalpara and Bengal. The expeditions listed 'the numerous passes into Bootan along the frontier, some of which lead direct to the capital' and listed the Bijni, Buxa and Na Duars among the principal Duars or passes (Eden 1865:10). In his notes on his travels in the region, Ashley Eden observed that 'several of these routes connected northern Goalpara to Bhutan, including one which connected Bijni to Wandipur in Bhutan, and others which linked Bijni, Sidli, Bengtoli, Kachubari, Buro Bungloo, Dubleng, Cherrung to the capital of Bhutan' (ibid.). Through these passes flowed a trade in many articles. Woollen cloth, coarse cotton cloth, indigo, sandal, asafoetida, cloves, sugar, ghee and oil were brought up from the plains, while Tangun horses, blankets, walnuts, musk orange and cow tails from Bhutan were sold at the markets of Rangpur in the south (Bose 1865: 198).

In this trade through the markets of northern Goalpara and of the south, timber from the forests of the Eastern Duars was undoubtedly among the most important items. At the turn of the eighteenth century there was already a large timber trade in the region of the Eastern Duars, much of which was not for local use, but largely for export to southern Bengal: 'the traders came with boats from Dacca and Mymensingh during the rainy season to buy up timber in the Duars, on the borders of Garo Hills and up in Kamrup'.[70] Buchanan observed that:

> Merchants of Goalpara usually export to the low country from the forests of Howraghat and Mechpara about 1500 canoes in the year ... [T]he timber was floated down numerous rivers which included the Ai and the Manas, from the Dooar region and also from Nepal and Bhutan, towards the southern ports like Fakirgunj.[71]

The timber was then tied into rafts and then floated down to the port of Narayangunj near Dhaka. The extensive sal forests in the Parbatjoar and Khuntaghat parganas were worked on by several *duffadars* and labourers, several of whom were from the neighbouring districts of Bengal and derived their livelihood solely from felling sal timber.[72] By the last decades of the nineteenth century, trade in timber comprised of the bulk of the trade exports from Goalpara to Bengal. More than 600 boats came up every year from Serajgunj, Dhaka and other places in eastern Bengal for purchasing timber worth about 12,000 pounds (Hunter 1879: 50).

Timber was only one of the several articles that linked this region to the other trading networks of eastern India in the pre-colonial period. A profitable trade in the region was in salt, for which southern Goalpara formed the transit point between Bengal and Assam. Some of the earliest references to the salt trade are in a historical narrative of seventeenth and eighteenth century Ahom rule. Compiled during the eighteenth century, the text reproduces the following response of the Ahom king, Raja Rudra Singha, to a request made by the Mughal faujdar at Rangamati for establishing commercial relations with the Ahoms in June 1793: 'Is it called trade if it is limited to a few maunds of salt from Bengal and the dispatch of a few boats from our place? If the Nawab is intent on the establishment of commercial relations with us, he should send his merchants to Jugigopa and Goalpara, and our leading traders will proceed to Kandahar *chokey* with large quantities of valuable articles. If matters are arranged along this line, they acquire the status of *haat-bat* or trade'.[73]

To return to this section's concern with the significance of markets as transmitters of authority, both in the plains of southern Goalpara and in the hilly areas of the north, the markets and expanding networks of trade were also marked by strong cultural and political underpinnings. Beginning with the late Mughal period, there was an increasing assertion of authority by zamindars and other local powers over trading practices and places of exchange in the region. This was evident in the exaction of several dues for passage at the chowkis set up at several points along the chief waterways. Travelling along the western borders of Assam in the mid-eighteenth century, James Rennell observed several such chowkis along both banks of the Brahmaputra near Goalpara. 'The Assam country begins from the Bonaash [Manas] river on the north side of the Brahmaputra and one of their chowkis is placed directly opposite Gwalpara ... [F]rom the 2nd to the 6th of December we were employed in tracing the Brahmaputra from Gwalpara to the frontier of Assam on the southern side. We were not permitted to land on the northern side or the Assam side, all the way, there being several chokeys placed'.[74]

The rights to the collection of these dues were frequently hereditary and also an assertion of political rights. Colonial authorities noted, however, that:

> Several of the custom houses were also farmed out to the biggest bidder and the whole trade of the country [was] in fact monopolised by these individuals, who in terms of the treaty concluded in February, 1793 ought to leave only 10 per cent on exports and imports but reality extort what they choose (Hamilton et al. 1854: 102).

The chowkis on the Assam border were similarly regulated by the Ahom state with those custom houses 'towards the frontier of Bengal (being) farmed to two Rashi Barhmons, Komol and Parusuram … called Baruas (while) the chief custom house, Kandahar, usually called the Assam Chauki by the English (was) situated at a place called Hadira in Pergunnah Bausi, nearly opposite Goalpara'.[75] The agent of the Assam government at Kandahar was the Dooaria Baruah or the Kandahar Baruah who paid an annual rent of 90,000 rupees and had the right to levy a rather moderate duty of 10 per cent on export and import. In practice, however, the 'custom has long been to leave this entirely to their discretion, and although there is no absolute law to prohibit the merchants from Bengal from carrying their goods to Jorhat or Guwahati … yet the Barua may be said to have complete monopoly and the whole trade passes through his hands'.[76]

> The Dooaria Baruahs realised the duty on all exports and imports. They received advances from the Bengal merchants for the delivery of Assam goods or accepted Bengal goods on credit. Goalpara on the south bank, Jugigopa and Rangamati on the north are the three eastern outposts of Bengal from where the merchants conducted their trade (Martin 1976: 477).

This intervention by traditional political authorities in commercial exchanges persisted into the early decades of the nineteenth century. Buchanan noted with much dismay the various transit duties and the rights exercised by the zamindars and local chieftains during this period. These included the right 'of levying a share of all goods sold at the markets as well as transit duties on all goods carried from one place to another in the markets of southern Goalpara'. 'In some places', he added, 'it was even alleged that they granted small monopolies on several of the most important articles sold, such as cotton, salt and mustard seeds'.[77]

A particularly good example of marketplaces serving as 'an extension of a vision of patrimony' (Sen 1998: 6) in southern Goalpara was the weekly market on the borders of the Garo Hills. The Garo Hills were an important economic resource for the zamindars of Karaibari, Mechpara and Kalumalupara, who sustained themselves through relationships with the Garos, the locally dominant people who lived in the hilly regions surrounding their estates and carried on a flourishing trade in cotton with the inhabitants of these estates. Colonial records noted that large areas of surrounding woodland on the fringes of these estates were eminently suited for the zamindars who 'held all the low country under the Garo Hills on that side ... and as all the cotton, then the staple of the internal eastern trade, came from these hills, the Choudhuris had established at all the principal passes, *haats* or markets guarded by their burkandezes' (Mackenzie 1869: 21).

The taxes levied in these haats on both merchants from the plains and on the Garos formed one of the main sources of income of these choudhuris (ibid.). This conformed to similar practices in the late Mughal period, wherein in frontier areas, where the *mal* or the produce from the land was sparse, the greater proportion of the revenue came from the ability of the zamindars to extract a *sair* or commercial tax on all kinds of goods that passed through their territory. Thus, the zamindars of Goalpara, 'while paying a small tribute to the Mughal faujdar of Rangpur as acknowledgement of their loyalty, were to all intents and purposes independent. They were bound in fact merely to supply a certain number of elephants or a small quantity of *aghur*, a precious wood, to support the maintenance of garrisons and the artillery park at Dacca. Their estates were never subjected to land revenue assessment and they paid what they did pay from their sayer and not from the mal. The faujdar generally made advances on account of cotton to these great choudhuris, as the zamindars were called, and received from them yearly consignments of that article' (Mackenzie 1884: 21). The revenue of several of the permanently settled estates of Goalpara was paid in cotton during the initial period of colonial rule as well, and the zamindars depended not only on taxes collected from the settled peasantry, but also on the resources garnered by raiding the neighbouring Garo hills. The frequent raids by the zamindars of Karaibari and Shusang into the Garo areas, however, were not accompanied by an incorporation of these marginal areas into the territory of the chieftains. Occupation was only temporary, as when the zamindar of Karaibari built forts in the trading passes to assert control over the cotton trade; the aim of these attacks was to compel a weaker polity to submit its allegiance. The sovereignty and independence of the Garos chieftains were allowed to coexist with that of the other local chieftains. The Bemulwa or independent Garos, for instance, formed a significant proportion of the population of the Garo Hills and were responsible for several of the innumerable raids on the Goalpara plains.

What were later described in colonial records as 'stories of violence and murder by a few independent savages'[78] were often a means of asserting the shared rights of communities over the resources of the area as also of correcting the often unequal economic relationship conducted through the market. The Garos could hardly be defined as isolated communities defending themselves against an economically and politically more powerful civilisation of the plains. Rather, through different strategies, of which frequent raids were the most visible, they routinely asserted their control over the resources of the region while continuing to retain their political and economic independence. The passage below illustrates the same:

> In those parts of Kalumalupara which border the hills, it is no uncommon practice with the Garos to enter the villages and make demands of pigs, goats, fowls, or any other articles ... which the ryots are of course glad to comply. Such occurrences, if unaccompanied by homicide, are seldom reported to the police officer ... when such acts become too frequent for endurance, they either desert the village and retire to some more secure spot or purchase the forbearance of the Garos by an additional donation Matha Rakah, a species of black mail, very generally paid by the ryots in remote situations in that pergunnah to the neighbouring Garo chief, for the preservation of their heads as the term denotes.[79]

Periodic looting and plunder of the estates continued through the nineteenth century, establishing the position of the Garo chieftains as tributaries who were autonomous and sovereign in their own right. In the winter of 1816, Garos living on the borders of the Mechpara zamindari estate carried out a violent attack that lasted for more than a month wherein 'they wounded the zamindar, massacred his servants besides several of the ryots and burnt and plundered his zamindari Kutcherry together with several villages situated in the same estate'.[80] The deployment of more troops by the Magistrate of Rangpur appeared to have little effect, for a report from the daroga of the Rangamati outpost stated that a burkandez had also been beheaded by the rebels.[81] Illicit duties imposed by the Mechpara zamindar on the cotton trade had evidently triggered off the immediate violence as the burning of the office records of the zamindar by the Garos was accompanied by the burning of the cotton that had been collected over five years and three or four adjoining villages.[82]

The relationship between trade and authority acquired greater significance in the northern frontiers of the borderland, an area where exchanges in the market place were frequently the most visible articulation of regional political powers. Contrary to what colonial records wrote, the region that later formed the northern part of the colonial district of Goalpara was neither an integrated part of the state of Bhutan, nor was it under the exclusive sovereignty of the chieftains of Bijni and Sidli. This was reflected in the existence of shared rights of these powers over the resources of the area discussed in the previous section. Rather, the Eastern Duars was an area of shared sovereignty, with its rulers tied in relationships of tributary submission with those of the more powerful Bhutan and Ahom polities, which in turn were within the 'power fields' of the Dalai Lama of Tibet.

The role of the market in enforcing indigenous notions of political space in the region was, therefore, of considerable significance. The peshkash paid by the Ahom king was offered at Chouna, a site for a market in the Eastern Duars. It took two months from the market to Lhasa, the Tibetan capital (Mackenzie 1884: 16). There were similar markets established at Gengushur, four miles away from Chouna. Prior to the occupation of the Duars, the Sath Rajas, who were Bhutia chiefs who controlled the Kuriapara Dooar and were considered subordinates of the

Towang Raja, a tributary of Lhasa, paid their tribute through the purchase of cotton and other goods at the Udalguri fair, all of which were then sent to Lhasa and Towang (Mackenzie 1884: 16).

Further, the flow of pilgrims into the Duars and the plains below were a significant accompaniment of the trade between the southern plains of the borderland and Tibet. Several of the fairs in the region of the Eastern Duars formed part of a larger sacred topographical space. Descriptions of the nature of trading in the Dooar area tend to suggest that this region could have been perceived as part of one such religious space, that of the sacred sovereign realm of the Bhutanese monarch. Ethnographers and travellers to the region noted that 'the Bhutias considered the Dhurma Raja as their spiritual, incarnate deity, whose trade with "inferior" chiefs in the Dooar region was more in the nature of some nuzzerana or offering from these chiefs' (Griffiths 1865:189). Religious motifs were also used to define the relationship of submission between the rulers of Bijni and Sidli and the Dhurma Raja of Bhutan. 'You will furnish everything well and in good order', stated a sanad to the Raja of Bijni, Kumud Narayan, 'so the Divine Dhurma Raja and the holy Mahakal will always bless you.'[83] And the town of Hajo was an 'important point in the sacred topography of the region ... boast[ing] of a large establishment of priests [who were] attached to a temple, which [was], by the Bhutiahs and the Kampas, considered very sacred, and to which both these tribes, but specially the latter, resorted annually in large numbers' (Griffiths 1865: 125).[84]

The Reorientation of Trade in a Colonial Borderland

The last section, which brings the trajectory up to the late colonial period, is an exploration into the significant alterations effected in the larger trading networks and local marketing practices by colonialism. As Goalpara transformed into a hinterland for the Bengal market during this period and past historical connections were reoriented when not erased, the market emerged once again as a critical site for the complex forms of contestations that it contained, including contestations between local and colonial concepts of political space. Over the eighteenth century, salt emerged as the most important article in the trade between Assam and Bengal, with a vigorous trade being carried on through a few towns in Goalpara. Several European companies and individuals vied with one another for control over the market during this period and resisted the claims of local powers. Among these companies was the Society for Trade, established by Robert Clive for the sole purpose of trading in salt. The company was closed down in 1768 after the East India Company was briefly deprived monopoly over the trade. Colonial records mention several individuals who participated in the salt trade from Goalpara, of whom Daniel Raush and George Lear appear to have been the most prosperous. The former, according to these records, was a 'respectable Hanoverian and the principal merchant at Goalpara in 1769' (Hamilton et al. 1854: 103). The latter was an English merchant who resided in Rangpur and, like Raush, had established an independent salt factory and salt emporiums in the town of Goalpara besides several warehouses at Dhaka.[85] Ganganarayan Roy, a Bengali salt merchant residing in Dhaka had also stationed his agent Robert Bigger at Jugigopa in the Goalpara district.[86]

The French East India Company also had a branch established in 1755 by Jean Baptiste Chevalier who was deputed from Chanderanagore on this project and had a salt factory at Goalpara. Until 1778, when they were recalled to Calcutta by the government, there were several French merchants at Goalpara trading independently (Bhuyan 1928: 3). The frequent skirmishes between these several trading groups required the intervention of the local powers who now 'negotiated disputes amongst the Europeans who [were] settled at Goalpara ... to more effectually secure the peace of the country and to protect Assam from free booters ... so that commerce may be carried out to the mutual advantage of both kingdoms'.[87]

The period also saw several officials of the East India Company struggling to gain exclusive rights over the sites of production and distribution of salt. Hugh Baillie emerged as a persuasive representative of the Company's interests in the salt trade. In a memorial to the East India Company in 1793, Baillie outlined the significance of this trade and Goalpara's position in it, while arguing persuasively for the appointment of an agent which would make way for a further control of the Company over the market

(Bhuyan 1949: 71). He argued that his experience as an agent of Clive's Society of Trade had allowed him 'the opportunity of acquiring a knowledge of the Company's business at Rungpore, and also of the interior parts of Bhutan and Assam, and the countries adjacent to Gualparah, which had never been explored by any European before'. Baillie offered to be a salaried agent of the Company, supervising the salt trade at Goalpara (ibid.). Baillie's appointment as the superintendent of the Company at Goalpara in 1787 reflected the contradiction within the colonial political economy. An apparent freedom of trade coexisted with the need to control the market. By the end of the eighteenth century the Company was dealing in more than 100,000 maunds of salt in the region, imported from Khulna and Dhaka in eastern Bengal through the towns of Goalpara and Jugigopa.

These trade links continued to be vibrant through the early decades of colonial rule, evident from the lists of commercial centres in Eastern Bengal in Francis Buchanan's writings on Goalpara. Buchanan suggests that the region of southern Goalpara and the Eastern Duar area were integrated into the extensive trading circuits of Narayangunj, Serajgunj, Murshidabad and the Mughal port city of Dhaka. Connections existed through the waterways of the Brahmaputra and other smaller rivers like the Godadhor and the Gangadhar. These also linked Mymensingh in southeastern Bengal to the external trading circuits of Bhutan and Tibet, the rest of Bengal and the internal trade networks of Assam.[88] Buchanan noted:

> By far the greater part of the grain [from Goalpara] goes to Seerajgunj in the Moymonsingh district and to Narayangunj near Dhaka but a part also is sent to Murshidabad, Calcutta and the intermediate towns. The grain that is imported, chiefly mustard seeds, comes from Bhutan and from Bihar and from Assam. These areas were also the centres of the cattle trade ... the greater part of which is exported to Seerajgunj and Narayangunj.[89]

Bhutan also exported horses, musk and paper to Murshidabad and Assam. Trade in several other products, including an illicit one in opium, linked Goalpara with the ports of eastern Bengal, while silk cloth from Murshidabad and cotton from Dhaka were imported into Assam from Rangpur and Goalpara.[90] The chief routes connecting Assam with Bengal passed through Goalpara.

Accounts from the period suggest that there were three overland routes from Bengal to Assam:

> The first by Murshadabad, Mauldah [Malda], Dinagepore [Dinajpur], Rungpore and Goalpara. This is the line of the Calcutta dak but it is almost impassable during the rains. The second route is via Dacca, Dumari, Pucuoloe, Jumalpore, Singimarry and Goalpara, also nearly impassable in the rains. The third passes by Sylhet, Chirra, Nunklow, Ranneygodown, Cannymook and Gohatti [Guwahati], but from its crossing over the Khasya hills, it is impracticable for any land carriage and beast of burden (Pemberton 1865: 9).

Colonial records indicate that the bulk of the trade of Goalpara was now carried on directly with Calcutta. The principal exports were mustard seeds, silk cloth, timber, and cotton and lac obtained from the Garo Hills. The growth of several towns, including that of Dhubri, was also linked to their relative importance as transit points for the trade with Bengal (Gait, Allen and Howard 1905: 519). Dhubri, a vibrant centre of trade from pre-colonial times, had the added advantage of a location that made it a natural harbour for colonial trade (Jenkins 1868: 7–8). A list of articles that passed through the river ports of southern Goalpara, provided in Table 2.1, indicates the significance of the region in the trade between Bengal and Assam in the first half of the nineteenth century.

Anxious to promote a more regulated form of trade and commerce, the colonial state intervened in specific ways in the markets and marketing practices in the region. Significant among the administrative interventions was the prohibition of the exercise of indigenous privileges through local taxes and chowkis. These were seen as obstacles in the growth of free trade. Following the views of classical political economy proclaimed by the Company, Buchanan had perceived these practices as 'prejudicial to the public', since they checked cultivation and commerce.[91] He regarded the duties levied by the zamindar of Bijni on the transit and sale of goods as a 'gross usurpation' of the rights of the ordinary trader and merchant.[92] There was a gradual restriction and prohibition of local taxes and dues levied at markets, on ferries and, most importantly, by zamindars on the boat and timber trade. In March 1835, Hadira chowki, which had been

Table 2.1
List of articles that passed through the river ports of
southern Goalpara

Exports from Bengal in 1809	Rupees	Exports from Assam in 1809	Rupees
Salt, 35,000 maunds	1,92,500	Stick lac 10,000 maunds	35,000
Ghee, 1,000 maunds	1,600	Moonga silk	11,350
Fine pulse	800	Black pepper	500
Sugar	1,000	Long pepper	500
Stone beads	2,000	Cotton (with seed) 7,000 maunds	35,000
Coral	1,000	Ivory	6,000
Jewels and pearls	5,000	Bell metal vessels	1,500
Spices	1,000	Mustard seeds	20,000
Gold and silver cloth	1,000	Iron hoes	600
Copper	4,800	Slaves	2,000
Red lead	1,000		
English woolens	2,000		
Tafetas	2,000		
Satin	1,000		
Benarasi khinkobs	500		
Muslin	10,000		
Shells	100		

Source: Pemberton (1865: 82).

the most important site for the collection of dues by local rulers
during the Mughal imperium, and even earlier, was closed down
(Barpujari 1963: 243). Buchanan had earlier described the complex
layers of authority that governed trading rights in this chowki,
which along with the many other 'subordinate custom houses on
the banks of the rivers ... and several on various routes by which
good might pass',[93] was a site for transactions and negotiations
over trading rights between the European mercantilist companies
and local rulers. Its closure affected a sharp rise in the trade with
Bengal, aided further by the introduction of regular river traffic
on the Brahmaputra, the first steam-boat being put into service in
1847. By the second half of the nineteenth century, more changes in
the trade with Bengal were in place. The growth of the tea
industry in the province of Assam now replaced lac, cotton and
ivory with tea (followed closely by jute and mustard) as the prime
commodity of trade. The extension of tea cultivation in upper
Assam and the operation of coal mines demanded an increase in
the import of iron and steel needed for the laying of the railways,
apart from the large influx of indentured labour from eastern and

central India into the tea estates. By 1900, almost the entire trade of Assam was with Bengal, trade with regions other than Bengal amounting to less than one per cent (Barpujari 1992: 124).

The growth in the Bengal trade was accompanied by a gradual decline in the trade with Bhutan. John M'Cosh observed that 'in former times, an extensive trade was carried out with Bhutan and there was established a well frequented mart at Seepotah but little of that traffic now exists' (M'Cosh 1837: 66). Colonial reports on trade from the 1870s attributed this decline to the absence of a good communication network.[94] There was a similar decline in the trade with Tibet, which had been lucrative ... in the first decades of the nineteenth century [and] amounted to more than 200,000 rupees [but] which has for many years discontinued.[95] By the first decade of the twentieth century, British officials could dismiss this transfrontier trade as 'of very little importance ... the principal imports being rubber and the principal export, silk' (Allen 1906: 103).

On the eastern side, the fairs held at Darrang, Udalguri and Kherkheria continued to have a considerable presence of traders from Bhutan as well as Tibet into the first decades of the twentieth century. Held during the winter months, between January to March, the principal articles of trade from Bhutan included ponies, lac, wax, blankets, musk, and from the British territories, yarn, piece goods, rice, brass and copper utensils, raw silk, iron bars, tobacco and areca nuts and dried fish. Until at least 1923–24, the fairs had a steady presence in colonial reports on trade.[96] Officials commented on the 'difficulty of getting reliable statistics', which they attributed variously to the nature of the trade itself (it comes down in driblets and it is almost impossible to check)[97] to the more obvious attribution of the absence of a certain notion of classification in the indigenous imagination. From 1916 onwards, a system of registration of the trade at Udalguri was effected and there are figures for that year: Rs 65,000 in imports and Rs 40,000 in exports.[98] The registration evidently did not yield satisfactory statistics and officials worked to put in place a system that would help redirect local practices more firmly towards a colonial classificatory order. 'In the past statistics were collected by trade registrars who were stationed at fixed points on the border and any trader not passing their station was missed', reported the deputy commissioner of Darrang in 1924. 'Next year these registrars are to be abolished and details of trade will be collected from the headmen and principal traders'.[99]

The trade with Bhutan continued to record a steady decline in the following year as well. The trade statistics supplied by the *mauzadars* in 1925 showed a great decrease in the value of exports and imports.[100] By 1926, the economic significance of the trade at the fairs, never considerable in the records of the colonial state, had declined sufficiently for the entire system of registration of trade statistics to be discontinued.[101] This was attributed variously to a 'decrease in the number of Bhutias who came down to Udalguri and Kherkheria' or on unreliable trade statistics.[102] These observations recur through the records of the next two decades, until 1935, when the Darrang fair with the Bhutias disappears altogether from the 1934–35 report. There is a simultaneous decline in the fair at Udalguri as is evident in the following comment of the officer on duty at the fair in 1930–31: 'The Udalguri fair is now of no importance. The ponies and sheep brought down were very poor in quality and sales were few. As I have reported previously, this fair has very nearly ceased to exist and I have proposed that the Udalguri outpost should be moved to Bhairabkund where it will be valuable. If this is done then the temporary Bhutia camp may also be sited near Bhairabkund'.[103]

Among the possible explanations for the decline in trade with Bhutan would be the increasing political control of the British state over the Terai region, evident in the profound transformation that it introduced in the local ecology and in the use of natural resources in the region. Considering the richness of the Duars as reliable sources of strong, durable timber such as sal, a critical resource in the fast expanding rail network in eastern India, it was inevitable that 'forestry became a formal, direct endeavour of statemaking' (Sivaramakrishnan 1999: 145) in the region. Besides the belt of Terai forests at the foot of the Bhutan hills, there were several other precious tracts of forests including the one in the Gooma region of the Eastern Duars, stretching to the estate of Parbatjoar. Most of these forests were of sal trees, next only to teak in its durability, though less easier to season. Other forms of access control accompanied the extension of the regime of the state including the search for alternative, more profitable routes of trade with Tibet through Nepal, the objective of the state in regulating the hill traders appearing 'less to make them productive than to ensure that their economic activity was legible, taxable, assessable, confiscatable, or failing that, to replace it with forms of production that were' (Scott 2009: 5). A lot of the trade with the Bhutanese moreover was conducted through everyday, unregulated forms of exchange across the hills. Official correspondence reported that 'the Bhutias, who are regarded as being under political control, gave little trouble but complaints were received of the Bhutias of Bhutan, who wander along this frontier in the cold weather', necessitating 'prompter measures in the British territory wherever reports of offences are received, but unfortunately this is not always possible ... patrols were sent out to Udalguri post up to a distance of about 12 miles as a preventive measure and on one occasion succeeded on arresting some of these people who had been selling liquor'.[104]

Through a regulation of existing trade routes with Bengal and their improvement through a new infrastructure of roads and railways, combined with prohibitive restrictions on tolls levied by local powers and stricter controls at the borders, the colonial state ensured therefore a westward reorientation of the regional trade, ignoring routes and exchanges of pre-colonial times. On the southern borders of the Garo Hills and Goalpara, there were more examples of the market emerging as a site for conflict between the British Government and local rulers. Here the confrontation between notions of political space and trading rights was less masked, resulting in the colonial state using the market to effect changes not just in the trading practices of the region but in indigenous spatial and cultural practices as well. From the time of the commissionership of David Scott, there are several voluminous records relating to the Garo tribes that argued for a legalising of a separate administration for the Garos[105] and other 'hill communities', introducing in the process 'the master oppositional binary' in the colonial discourse in India — the hill–plain dichotomy (Baruah 2008: 16).

As the preceding section elaborated, the weekly haats border-ing the Garo Hills were as much about the demonstration of pre-colonial power hierarchies as they were about the richness of local cultural dynamics and imaginations of political space. Represented in official correspondence now only as places where the Garos were subjected to a constant succession of fraud and falsehood and to the oppression and injustice of the neighbouring zamindars and other inhabitants of the plains,[106] they helped pro-duce a different spatial order altogether in which ethnic groups were fixed to particular physical spaces (Baruah 2008: 15–16) the 'correct' habitat for the Garos here being the hills. 'The relations between the zamindars and the hill tribes had been so undefined and fluctuating in their nature and so much influenced by local and accidental circumstances...there was considerable trouble fixing the principles by which they would be governed. The separation, however, of the hill tribes from the zamindars appeared to us as measures of the first necessity'.[107]

Scott's proposals on the cotton trade between the Garos and the Goalpara zamindars returned the market as the site for effecting this separation. He 'propose(d) to the government that the delivery of cotton should altogether be stopped and in lieu of this and the Kurm collections made in the northern division, that a tax should be imposed upon the Garos of five rupees per house of the first class and of two rupees on those of the lowest, that a deduction should be made from the gross proceeds of 25 per cent to provide for the expense of collecting the revenue. The collection should be conducted by a native officer. Garo sirdars should get a percentage for the trouble they had taken and also to make them more responsible'.[108] Other regulations included limiting the number of haats along the Garo–Goalpara border to 12 and curbing raids by Garos on the villages in the plains.[109] The latter forced the community to diversify and sedenterise while dismantling a pre-existing system of transient alliances and negotiations with the zamindars in which the Garos had been indispensable trading partners of the latter.

These measures were legitimised as being part of the process of 'protecting' the Garos from the zamindars of Goalpara who having been 'released' from the responsibility of defending the country from the raids of the Garos could not be entitled to derive any profit from the lands over which they had exercised the right of property appertaining to the sovereign rather than those of mere land holders.[110] They were also a good example of the 'British institutional reification of their concept of the old regime within the framework of a new "progressive system" governed by the overarching principles of order and revenue ... The old regime as a political process was dismantled and discontinued ... the fixity of the revenue demand was both a metaphor of this change and the fundamental cornerstone of the new regime' (Dirks 1986: 330). Accordingly, arguments for the introduction of a separate customary law, as distinct from the law in effect in the plains, accompanied these measures and Scott's proposal for the 'the introduction of a system of police and criminal judicature among the population of 30,000 people that the Garos comprise of' that was similar to 'the system pursued in Bhagalapur in regard to the people residing in the hills'[111] was adopted in the Resolutions of the Governor General in Council. A narrative of civilisation and morality that located the inhabitants of the hills/forests in the lowest rung of a temporal and spatial hierarchy neatly sealed this hill–plain binary. As the Regulation X of 1822 (which separated the administration of the Garo hills from that of Goalpara) noted in its objectives: 'To promote the desirable object of reclaiming these races to the habits of civilised life, it seems that a special plan for the administration of justice, of a kind adapted to their peculiar customs and prejudices, should be arranged' (Clarke 1854: 659).[112]

In their ability to represent the correspondence between changes in the local property regimes and trading networks, the economic unification of the colonised territory and the colonial spatial ideology, cartographic practices played an important role. Somewhere between the closing decades of the nineteenth century and the early decades of the twentieth, through a series of triangular surveys and mapping,[113] the modern geographical limits of Goalpara and the regions around it were identified and fixed. The colonial state recognised the significance of reliable maps in a frontier area which was peculiarly situated and of great political importance[114] but the resonance of these new maps with the needs of the political economy of the district had long been established. The details of the navigation routes in the writings of James Rennell, for instance, had led to the discovery of routes of commercial investments.

The search for a definitive geography of the colonial district of Goalpara saw processes similar to those initiated by the state when introducing notions of exclusive sovereignty. The multiplicity of layers of pre-colonial local authority meant that large stretches of territories, particularly the hilly areas around the Duar foothills in the north and the Garo Hills in the south, were zones of shared authority of various powers into which inhabitants of the plains and the forested areas made occasional forays for resources.[115] Understanding the spatial boundaries of local authority proved to be a similarly elusive project for colonial officials in the north:

> I was employed a whole forenoon in tracing the boundary of the estate ... there again I found the same uncertainty of boundary. In one part a rivulet presented a very distinct line for a short distance, in some places a ridge of earth such as is raised in all parts of the country to retain water in the fields ... was pointed out as the boundary whilst for the most part my only direction was the memory of my guide assisted as he was by the different colouring of the grass or other marks of the like, the nature of which seemed to me to exist nowhere but in the fertility of the imagination.[116]

Officials demanded of the local chieftains, particularly those of Bijni and Sidli, and the Bhutanese officials in the Duar region, to provide evidence of written documents identifying concrete historical boundaries. Responses to these queries varied: the documents of 'proof of boundaries' were frequently declared lost, either in plundering raids or destroyed in fires.[117] For the ruling groups in these areas, where oral communication had greater precedence over the written word, the colonial emphasis on the legitimacy of written documents in social and political exchanges was not easily appreciated. In response to one such demand for papers to determine the authority of the Bhutanese monarch over some villages in what was earlier a region of ambiguous sovereignty, the Deb Raja explained: 'It is not customary for us Bhutias to be regulated by records, but by the custom of possession. If paper be approved of, I have plenty concerning the giving and taking of areas ... [T]he English and the Bhutias are very different in their modes of transacting'.[118] The issuance of sanads by the same ruler for articulating ideas of a political realm would appear to indicate that this was not so much a case of the orality and the written being dichotomous categories, as of differing conceptions of political space and authority.

These encounters and the construction of more structured zones out of realms of multiple loyalties by colonialism, although fraught with negotiations and contestations between the rulers of Bhutan, the British, the Cooch Behar Raja and the rulers of Bijni and Sidli,[119] saw a subsuming of the local into the colonial spatial order. The late eighteenth century cartography of James Rennell,[120] information from the few scattered maps from the early nineteenth century topographical surveys of the region, and the fresh surveys of southern Goalpara in the 1870s together came to constitute a body of referential knowledge for the colonial state on which its cartographic project was based.[121] Within the next decade or so, 30 miles of the boundary between Goalpara and Cooch Behar had been marked out by boundary pillars,[122] and Mackenzie's 'debatable tract' of the Eastern Duars was incorporated into the district of Goalpara. The northern parts of this region had been terra incognita for early European travellers and had escaped the surveyor's compass, including that of Francis Buchanan's. This geographical ordering introduced a new conceptualisation of political space that legitimised the use of military force in the annexation of the Duar region. The separation of the Garo Hills from Goalpara and its demarcation as a separate district in 1869 similarly initiated processes of surveying in 'hills which had never been crossed by a European ... and which the Garos believed were inaccessible to Europeans'.[123] By 1872, the several undefined boundaries between Garo villages and the Garo Hills and Goalpara had been mapped and marked, and colonial officials were congratulating themselves on the undoubted success of a survey in a rather difficult terrain. The detailed boundaries of the district, however, continued to be demarcated until the first decades of the twentieth century.[124]

The fixing of these boundaries between communities and territories was not necessarily indicative of an irreversible movement from a fluid zone of multiple overlaps into a territory marked by mathematical precision. Rather, as the chapters that follow suggest, in mapping as in other disciplinary acts of enumeration and classification, the colonial project continued to be contested and appropriated by the colonised. And indigenous notions of political and cultural space persisted, and continued to be practised long after the delimitation of colonial boundaries.[125] Having recognised these continuities, it is imperative also to recognise the dramatic change that was colonialism in the region. Goalpara was now a politically and economically demarcated entity, a unit of the colonial state, separated from several areas with which it shared a pre-colonial connected history. As the chapter has argued, the construction of Goalpara was inextricably linked to the practices of the colonial spatial imagination and to the needs of an expanding market. The next chapter extends these arguments into the period of late colonialism, marked by an intensive sedenterisation and the migration of cultivators from the saturated plains of Bengal. It anticipates a necessary connection between this trajectory of economic and spatial change and the emergence of group identities in the region in the early decades of the twentieth century.

✳

Notes

1. For histories and analysis of the Rangpur *dhing,* see Kaviraj (1972); Guha (1983); Wilson (2005).
2. For a detailed analysis of the emergence of the zamindari system in Goalpara, see Guha (2000).
3. The Buchanan Hamilton Papers Book IV, Mss. Eur. D 75, OIOC, London, p. 177.
4. Ibid., p. 762.
5. Ibid.
6. Ibid., p. 16–17.
7. Father Barbier's letter to the Mission, 15 January 1723, in *Bengal: Past and Present,* 6, p. 200 (quoted in Bengal Political Consultations, File no. 21, 1798, West Bengal State Archives, Kolkata).
8. Ibid.
9. The Buchanan Hamilton Papers, Mss. Eur. D 74, Book II, OIOC, London, p. 2.
10. The Buchanan Hamilton Papers, Book IV, p. 99.
11. Ibid.
12. Letter from the manager of the Bijni Estate to the Deputy Commissioner of Goalpara, Goalpara Papers (henceforth GP), File no. 113, 1873, State Archives, Guwahati.
13. The Buchanan Hamilton Papers, Book IV, p. 102.
14. Ibid.
15. Letter from T. B. Lane, Secretary to the Board of Revenue, Lower Provinces, to the Secretary to the Government of Bengal, 18 November 1869, OIOC, London.
16. The Buchanan Hamilton Papers, Book IV, p. 109.
17. The Buchanan Hamilton Papers, Book IV, p. 96.

18. Buchanan observed that the *dewaniya* seldom does any work, and instead 'encircled his head with a turban and on all occasions is helped first to tobacco and betel' (The Buchanan Hamilton Papers, Book IV, p. 97). The social status commanded by the dewaniya was also reflected in the layout pattern of several Rajbanshi villages in Goalpara, in which the house of the *giri* or dewaniya was located in the centre of the village, surrounded by others belonging to his community (Guha 2000: 45).

19. James Rennell, November 1765, from an extract from the *Memoirs of the Asiatic Society of Bengal*, Vol. 3: 3, 1910, pp. 95–248, published as Appendix 1 in Hirst and Smart (1917).

20. Letter from the Manager of the Bijni Estate to the Deputy Commissioner of Goalpara, 12 June 1873, GP, File no. 113, 1873. The letter attributed this mobility to the 'capricious', 'unreasonable' whims of the people: 'None of them think much therefore of removing suddenly from the homesteads which they may occupy and settling anew in the jungle. They remove capriciously and without any reasonable cause. When one of them loses a near relationship by death at his house, he generally thinks it necessary to remove to another home, build a new hut in the distance ... A whole village will remove this way if a few members are cut off by an epidemic. An outbreak of cholera (and this from their filthy habits is not uncommon) is the signal for a general public flitting' (Ibid.).

21. C. T. Metcalfe, Memorandum on the Bijnee Dooar, 20 May 1865, GP.

22. Memorandum submitted by Metcalfe on the newly acquired territory north of the Gowalparah district in Lower Assam, July 1865, GP, File no. 7, 1866–70.

23. Translation of an undated sanad from the Deb Raja of Bhutan to Kumud Narayan of Bijni, GP, File no. 7, 1866–70.

24. Ibid.

25. There is a substantial amount of literature on the meaning of the 'gift' in pre-colonial societies. Gifts of rights to land, titles, emblems, and honors by kings to their subjects became in cultural terms the dynamic medium for the constitution of political relations. These gifts linked individuals, and also corporations, symbolically, morally and politically with the sovereignty of the king and created both a moral unity and a political hierarchy (Dirks 1986: 311).

26. Translation of the sanad from the Deb Raja of Bhutan to the Raja of Sidli, 1817, in GP, File no. 7, 1866–70.

27. Correspondence between J. C. Geddes, Deputy Commissioner of the Eastern Duars and Colonel Agnew, Commissioner of Cooch Behar and the Duars, 4 July 1866, GP, File no. 385.

28. Correspondence between J. C. Haughton, Commissioner of Cooch Behar and the Government of Bengal, 8 April 1867, GP, File no. 7.

Haughton noted that 'to me, it seems that the sanad is a recognition of the hereditary right, where it is conferred in consequence of the descent of the party to whom it is given from the last possessor', stated Haughton, refuting Gedde's arguments on the grounds that they were based on the premise that 'because the Booteahs considered themselves entitled to break their arrangements at pleasure, and they were not bound by them, those engagements were not be allowed to be of any force'.

29. Correspondence between J. C. Haughton and the Government of Bengal, 8 April 1867, GP, File no. 7.
30. J. C. Geddes, Deputy Commissioner of the Eastern Duars to the Deputy Commissioner of the Bhootan Duars, 18 April 1866, GP, File no. 7.
31. Petition from the Sidli Raja quoted in a letter from J. C. Geddes to the Deputy Commissioner of the Bhootan Duars, 18 April 1866, GP, File no. 7.
32. J. C. Geddes, Deputy Commissioner of the Eastern Duars to the Deputy Commissioner of the Bhootan Duars, 18 April 1866, GP, File no. 7.
33. Ibid.
34. Petition of Rani Nageswari Debi on the part of Kumud Naryan Bhoop, minor Raja of Bijni, 1 August 1866, GP.
35. GP, File no. 7, 1866–67.
36. Petition of Rani Nageswari Debi, 24 April 1867 in the correspondence regarding Bijni and Sidli, GP, 1866–70.
37. Petition dated 18 Pose 1272, from the occupant of Sidli to the Deputy Commissioner of the Eastern Duars, GP.
38. Sanad II, dated 1817 in the Correspondence regarding Bijni and Sidli, GP, 1866–67.
39. Writing about similar pre-colonial forms of power in pre-modern Thailand, Thongchai Winichakul comments on the 'hierarchical conglomeration of towns and cities whose supreme overlord acquired sacred power endowed in various places, objects and rituals': 'In the indigenous polity in which the power field of a supreme overlord radiated like a candle's light, these tiny chiefdoms were always located in the overlapping arena of the power fields … the ambiguous sovereignty of these areas was useful and desired by the overlords. Instead of establishing an independent state as a buffer zone, in this indigenous practice the overlords shared sovereignty over the buffer zones as long as the rulers of the frontier tributaries were loyal to all relevant overlords' (Winichakul 1994: 100).
40. Sanad II, dated 1817 in the Correspondence regarding Bijni and Sidli, GP, 1866–67.

41. 'Necessary orders have been sent to the Faujdar at Rangamatty to be regular in the payments of his customary tribute due to the Deb Raja from the districts of Bijni and Bidiagong. The claim which the Deb Raja has sent to these districts in prejudice to the rights of the natural zamindar will undergo a discussion on the arrival of the Bhutan soubah' (Letter from D. H. Mc Dowall, Collector, Rangpur, to Earl Cornwallis, Governor General, 29 May 1787, Rangpur), Bengal District Records 1928, West Bengal State Archives, Kolkata.
42. Correspondence between J. C. Geddes and W. Agnew, Deputy Commissioner of the Bhootan Duars, April 1866, GP.
43. Ibid., p. 10.
44. Ibid.
45. Letter from the Officiating Commissioner of the Bhutan Duars to the Secretary to the Government of Bengal, 25 September 1865, Bengal Government Papers, 1867–69, West Bengal State Archives, Kolkata.
46. Letter from J. C. Haughton to the Secretary to the Government of India, 8 April 1867, GP, File no. 7.
47. Bengal Government Papers, File no. 385, 1867–69, West Bengal State Archives, Kolkata.
48. Letter from J. C. Geddes to the Commissioner of the Bengal Duars, 20 April 1866 GP, File no. 7.
49. Memorandum by Metcalfe on the newly acquired territory north of the Goalpara district in Lower Assam, July 1865, Correspondence regarding Bijni and Sidli, GP, File no. 7.
50. Ibid.
51. Letter from J. C. Haughton to the Secretary to the Government of India, 8 April 1867, GP, File no. 7.
52. Letter from the Officiating Commissioner of the Bhutan Duars to the Secretary to the Government of Bengal, 25 September 1865, Bengal Government Papers, 1867–69.
53. Memorandum from C. T. Metcalfe, July 1865, GP.
54. Letter from J. C. Geddes to the Commissioner of the Bengal Duars, 20 April 1866, GP.
55. Translation of an undated sanad from the Deb Raja of Bhutan to Kumud Narayan of Bijni, GP.
56. The Ahom kings ruled over an area that comprised of a large part of the Brahmaputra Valley, excluding the region of Goalpara, between the thirteenth and the nineteenth centuries.
57. File no. 5, 1853–55, GP.
58. Ibid.
59. Correspondence regarding Bijni and Sidli, GP, 1866–70.
60. Raush to Lumdsen, 7 May 1792, in Bengal Political Consultations, 8 June 1792, File no. 11.
61. Ibid.
62. Ibid.

63. Letter from D. H. McDowall, Collector, Rangpur to Earl Cornwallis, the Governor General, 14 June 1787, Rangpur, Bengal District Records 1928, West Bengal State Archives, Kolkata.
64. 'Deposition of Hari Ghur Sanyasi', quoted in correspondence between D. H. McDowall, Collector, Rangpur to Earl Cornwallis, the Governor General, 14 June 1787, Rangpur, Bengal District Records 1928, West Bengal State Archives, Kolkata.
65. Ibid.
66. Colonel Jenkins in the GP, File no. 7, 1866–67.
67. Reverend J. A. Long, 'A Report Relative to Assam in 1797', in Selections from the Unpublished Records of the Government of Bengal, File no. 14, 1798.
68. Letter from D. H. McDowall, Collector, Rungpore, to Cosby Burrows, Collector of Mymensingh, 13ʼ July 1787, Rungpore, Bengal District Records 1928.
69. Buchanan quoted in Mackenzie (1884: 16).
70. Correspondence between the Deputy Commissioner of the Eastern Duars and the Commissioner of Cooch Behar, 10 May 1866, GP, File no. 7.
71. The Buchanan Hamilton Papers, Book III, Mss. Eur. D 74, OIOC, London, p. 207. Buchanan noted: 'The merchants of Goalpara were the chief dealers in the timber trade and advanced at the rate of 1 rupee for a pair of timbers, to be delivered at a place where they will float' (p. 215).
72. Ibid., p. 6. Buchanan mentions the ' joldhuyas', a group of about 30 families of the Rabha community living in the town of Goalpara, who cut timber and made furniture and were chiefly employed as wood cutters (The Buchanan Hamilton Papers, Book V, Mss. Eur. D 75, OIOC, London, p. 30).
73. 'The Asam Buranji, from the earliest times to the Swargadeo Gadadhar Singha's recovery of Guwahati from the Mughals in 1682. No. 6' (Bhuyan 1949: 50).
74. James Rennell, November 1765, Appendix 1: Extract from the Memoirs of the Asiatic Society of Bengal, Volume III, No. 3, pp. 95–248, 1910 in Hirst and Smart (1917).
75. The Buchanan Hamilton Manuscripts, 'Nations Bordering Assam', Mss. Eur. D 76, OIOC, London, p. 57.
76. Ibid.
77. The Buchanan Hamilton Papers, Book V, p. 92.
78. Letter from C. T. Metcalfe, Officiating Commissioner of the Cooch Behar Division to the Secretary to the Government of Bengal, June 1873, Government of Bengal Papers, 1873, OIOC, London.
79. Copy of a letter from David Scott to W. B. Bailey, the Acting Secretary to the Government in the Judicial Department, Extract Bengal Judicial Consultations, 16 February 1816, OIOC, London.

80. Copy of a letter from David Scott, the Magistrate of Rangpur, to W. B. Bailey, the Acting Secretary to the Government in the Judicial Department, 31 January 1816, Extract Bengal Judicial Consultations, 16 February 1816, OIOC, London.
81. 'Report from Mussiddin, the Daroga of Thanah Rangamati, enclosed in a letter from David Scott to W. B. Bailey, the Acting Secretary to the Government in the Judicial Department, 1 March 1816, Extract Bengal Judicial Consultations, 16 February 1816, OIOC, London.
82. 'The zamindar stated that he was returning from Mechpara after handing out *takavis* (advances) to the ryots, when he was attacked by the Garos. He was stabbed and had to flee for his life, while the 10 persons who were following him were beheaded by the Garos. The Garos carried away the Rs 2,000 that the zamindar had with him after the collection of *nankar* rents, and the selling of cotton ... They also murdered several ryots and burnt the villages of Phoolpur and Gujeria. Since it was too dangerous for him to remain in his house, the zamindar was now living on a boat in the middle of the river' (Extract from a letter from Mahiram Choudhuri, the zamindar of Mechpara to Gurumohan Chacki and Hariprasad Vakeel, Board's Collection, 1818–20).
83. Translation on the sanad from the Deb Raja of Bhutan to Raja Kumud Narayan of Bijni,16 Pos 1269, GP.
84. Griffiths remarked that 'this pilgrimage [was] however connected more with trade than religion, for a fair [was] held in the same time. Coarse woollen cloth and rock salt form[ed] the bulk of the goods which each pilgrim carries, no doubt as much for the sake of penance as for profit' (Griffiths 1865: 125).
85. Letter from George Lear to Warren Hastings, undated, Bengal Revenue Consultations, 23 January 1781, OIOC.
86. Bengal Revenue Consultations, 12 September 1780, OIOC, London.
87. Warren Hastings to the Asam Raja, 14 June 1780, Calendar of Persian Correspondence, Vol. 5: 1911.
88. Buchanan's list of the places with which Goalpara had commercial links included Serajgunj, a mart which seems to have arisen since the time of Major Rennell's survey and which is now a chief place of trade in Bengal, and stands on the Jhinayi river, Narayangunj, the port of Dhaka, Murshidabad and Calcutta (The Buchanan Hamilton Papers, Book V, p. 5).
89. Ibid.
90. Ibid., p. 73.
91. Ibid., p. 92.
92. Ibid.
93. The Buchanan Hamilton Manuscripts, 'Nations Bordering Assam', Mss. Eur. D 76, p. 57. '... (B)ut all duties are paid at Kandahar, the others are merely to prevent an illicit transit of goods' (Ibid.).

94. Annual Report on the Trade between Assam and the Adjoining Foreign Countries: various years beginning 1878.
95. Ibid.
96. See for various years the Annual Report on the Frontier Tribes of Assam: 1911–24 published from Shillong.
97. *Annual Report on the Frontier Tribes of Assam, for the year 1915–16,* Shillong, 1916.
98. Ibid.
99. *Annual Report on the Frontier Tribes of Assam, for the year 1923–24,* Shillong, 1924.
100. *Annual Report on the Frontier Tribes of Assam, for the year 1924–25,* Shillong, 1925.
101. 'No trade statistics are now maintained in the locality': *Annual Report on the Frontier Tribes of Assam, for the year 1925–26,* Shillong, 1926.
102. *Annual Report on the Frontier Tribes of Assam, 1911–12,* Shillong, 1912.
103. *Annual Report on the Frontier Tribes of Assam, for the year 1930–31,* Shillong, 1931. On the Udalguri fair: 'Much of the glory of this fair has departed during the last few years and this year the attendance was smaller owing it is said, to the superior attractions of Darjeeling and Kalimpong for the larger traders' (Annual Report on the Frontier Tribes of Assam, for the year 1928–29, Shillong, 1929).
104. *Annual Report on the Frontier Tribes of Assam for the year 1929–30,* Shillong, 1930.
105. These include several volumes of The Board's Collection in the OIOC, London.
106. Copy of a letter N. B. Edmonstone and G. Dowderwell, to the Court of Directors, 24 October 1817, IOR/F/4/15050, Board's Collection, 1818–20, OIOC, London.
107. Copy of a letter from David Scott, the Magistrate of Rangpur to W. B. Bayly, the Chief Secretary to the Government, enclosing the Report on the Garo hills of 15 August 1818, The Board's Collection, 1825–26, OIOC, London.
108. Ibid.
109. David Scott's Report of the 20 August 1816, Bengal Criminal Judicial Consultations, 27 September 1816, File no. 47, OIOC, London.
110. Ibid.
111. David Scott's Report of the 16 April 1819 in 'Copy of a letter from David Scott, the Magistrate of Rangpur to W. B. Bayly, the Chief Secretary to the Government', enclosing the Report on the Garo Hills of 15 August 1818. In the Resolutions of the Governor General in Council on the following year '(i)t was agreed that the general regulations should not extend to the Garos or other hill tribes ...

and that civil and criminal justice should be administered by the Commissioner under general rules and ... founded on the usages, local prejudices and the habits of the people ... measures of separating the zamindars from the hills tribes appeared necessary in as much as the latter had formed one chief cause of the acts of violence and revenge perpetrated by the Garos' (Resolutions of the of the Governor General in Council, Board's Collection, 1825–26, OIOC, London).

112. The introduction of a separate law was being proposed as an alternative to the use of military force against the Garos. Thus the Secretary of State observed that 'however necessary it may be to teach the inhabitants of these wild districts that they are not inaccessible to the power of Government, it is very clear that we cannot hope to reclaim them from their savage habits, or to induce them to a higher stage of civilisation by the mere display of military strength' (Mackenzie 1884: 24).

113. For details of the triangular and other surveys of Goalpara during this period, see (Hirst and Smart 1917).

114. Government of Bengal Papers, File nos 33–40, 1871–73, OIOC, London.

115. File no. 8, 1860–62, GP.

116. Letter from Mr T. Sisson, dated 17 March 1815, Bengal Secret Consultations, 27 April 1816, Board's Collection 1818–20, OIOC, London.

117. Correspondence between J. C. Geddes and Colonel Agnew, 28 April 1866, Correspondence Regarding Bijni and Sidli, GP, 1866–70.

118. Translation of a letter from the Deb Raja to the collector of Rungpore, 14 Maung 1193, GP, 1866–70.

119. See, for example, the disputes between the rulers of Bijni, Cooch Behar, Bhutan, the zamindar of Baikunthapur and the British over Pholakota and Rangdhamali Ghat (Board's Collection 1818–20, OIOC, London).

120. Letter from Major James Rennell, with one sketch map, dated December 1767, of Rangpur, Cooch Behar and Bhutan, Mss. Eur. F218/103, OIOC.

121. Government of Bengal Papers, File nos 33–40, 1871–73, OIOC, London. In 1834, Captain Brodie made a map of the Bhutan boundary and also surveyed the boundary between the Ghurla and Parbatjoar estates. There was a survey of the parganas of Aurangabad, Jamira, Dhubri, and Chapar in 1851–52 and of the pargana of Khuntaghat in 1852–53 (Hirst and Smart 1917).

122. Bengal Revenue Department, File nos 34–41, 1873–74, OIOC, London.

123. Administration Report on the Garo Hills, 1872, Government of Bengal Papers, File nos 19–22, OIOC, London.

124. The boundary between Bhutan and Goalpara had 56 boundary pillars and 110 guide marks in 1917. On the south Garo Hills and Goalpara were separated by 87 pillars (Hirst and Smart 1917).

125. Writing on the pervasiveness of the colonial spatial order in the post-colonial politics of northeast India, the political scientist Sanjib Baruah observes: 'Yet one still finds traces of local spatial practices that stubbornly resist the ethnic reductionism of colonial knowledge. For instance, only about 40 miles away from Guwahati, the Jonbil mela still takes place every year, where a descendant of the Gobha king presides over a fair in which Tiwas, Khasis and Karbis that straddle across the hill–plains divide, trade edible roots in exchange for fish' (Baruah 2008: 19).

3

❂

Colonial Spaces:
Land, Law and Migration

By the end of the nineteenth century the need of the colonial state to identify a new class that could extend cultivation and ensure the flow of revenue in the now eastern borderland district of Goalpara that was as yet characterised by the existence of vast stretches of wastelands, meant that the system of political authority and power represented by the zamindars was being gradually challenged. The period saw the emergence of the jotedars as powerful rural magnates, occupying stretches of land that at times comprised of around 300 bighas, a factor that placed them in powerful bargaining positions vis-à-vis the zamindar with whom they were engaged in a series of conflicts over land rights in the areas of expanding cultivation.[1] This chapter studies aspects of this 'peasantisation' of Goalpara during the late nineteenth and early twentieth century, so as to explore the process of social production of the colonial state (Washbrook 1988). The first section looks at the ways in which an entrenched state appropriated its acquired territory, and then proceeded to intervene and reconstitute relations between state and society through the privileging of sedenterisation and the 'settlement of wastelands'. This section and the one that follows, emphasise changes in the region's landholding structures and property rights, particularly after the migration of thousands of cultivators from eastern Bengal in the early decades of the twentieth century. The introduction of a system of colonial law that, among other things, created the domain of proprietary law and marked cultural difference and political identity, is the subject of the last section of the chapter.

Appropriable Landscapes

British officials had hoped that the zamindari settlement in Goalpara, with the aid of fertile soil, rising prices and a continually increasing demand for produce, would prove an extraordinarily successful means of clearing the jungles and settling the marshlands.[2] 'Political relations were channelled into this new domain of proprietary law. The drafters of the Permanent Settlement were convinced that a series of favourable consequences would flow from this single transformation. The principal change they thought would be the redirection of the interests and energies of the little kings from local warfare and intrigue to agrarian management and investment. In short, the zamindars would become the rural gentry, sources of both local stability and a steady flow of revenue' (Dirks 1986: 313). It was argued that the raiyatwari system had not promoted the cultivation of the country and although cultivation has extended to some extent in spite of the system, the total cropped area in the five districts of the Brahmaputra Valley, which were under the raiyatwari settlement, was actually less now than it was five years ago.[3] However, much like their counterparts in neighbouring Bengal, Goalpara's zamindars continued to evade the responsibilities of a potential capitalist gentry and did little to extend the boundaries of settled arable land in the district. At the turn of the century, out of a total area of 4,433 square miles, the area under cultivation was only 2,143 square miles, the rest being 'waste lands', the greater part of which was cultivable (Hunter 1879: 64). In the last decades of the 19th century, the problem still appeared intractable for colonial officials who were attempting to explain the reasons behind the availability of such tracts in Goalpara:

> The death rate was higher than the birth rate in Goalpara in 1891 ... there seems to the Government no necessity to look further than this for an explanation of the non-expansion of the cultivated area. That the zamindari system has certain advantages, the government of India is far from denying, but it cannot check the ravages of malaria or epidemic disease.[4]

The 'wasteland scheme' that was introduced in Goalpara to counter this trend was part of a larger concern of the state with the settlement of the uncultivated areas in the rest of the province of

Assam. Officials described the soil of the region as 'of the richest description', with 'no limit to its productiveness' and immigration, 'far below the requirements of the province accounting for millions of acres still lying fallow'.[5] The disappointment with the local rural gentry coincided with the late nineteenth century perception of land as 'a quantifiable, measurable object of knowledge, and a resource to be controlled and improved in the colonial imagination' (Robb 1997: 16). The 'colonisation of wastelands' project was a product of this ideology. Apart from the more obvious classification of land into the distinct categories of 'waste', 'arable' and 'forested', the project envisaged various inducements to local tenants, as well as to cultivators from neighbouring regions to settle in Goalpara.

The colonial state's reliance on the jotedars who were to restructure rural power relations while maintaining the revenue demand in the permanently settled areas of southern Goalpara has to be then seen against this context. The process of identifying jotedars as owners of the land and creating forms of private property to ensure both a steady source of revenue and the extension of cultivation had begun in the early decades of the century. Officials argued that:

> in the jotedaari system, under which cultivation has extended very rapidly in Bengal, the unit of colonisation is a group of tenants headed by the jotedaar who cultivates with them, finances them and represents them in the dealings with the government and with the police.[6] Such a body of men is better able to face the difficulties of colonisation than individual ryots and some encouraging results have already been obtained by inviting colonists of this description to the waste areas of the Goalpara district.[7]

Jotedars continued to be classified as 'reclamation' tenants well into the twentieth century, as colonial officials identified reclamation as 'the main purpose for the creation of jotes ... in a pioneering district like Goalpara' (Laine 1917: 174). In several estates, this class further strengthened its position by initiating the extension of the boundaries of settled agriculture. This was particularly true for the estates of Chapar, Bijni and Parbatjoar, where the jotedar was still the 'enterprising cultivator who paid a prospecting visit to a likely piece of wasteland and if his impressions were favourable, approached the zamindar for permission to settle' (Laine 1917: 114). The land settled with jotedars by the zamindar of

Bijni, for instance, was 'almost entirely wasteland'.[8] He remained, therefore, the primary agent for creating a settled agrarian order in the district.

Vast tracts of land continued to be available. Also, from the last decade of the nineteenth century, the power of the jotedars was beginning to be derived from surplus agriculture, aided further by the non-residency of several of the zamindars in the region. Hunter's account describes the conditions of sub-infeudation reflected in the 'hopeless intricacy' of the cultivator's holding, both as regards area, rate of rent and other terms of tenancy, and the growing power of the jotedar: 'The actual cultivator very rarely holds his fields from the zamindar or superior landlord ... ordinarily he is the sub-tenant of a man called the jotedar and sometimes he is a subtenant of a sub-tenant' (Hunter 1879: 65).

Of course not all jotedars were equally powerful. Colonial records also identify a second category of jotedar, who was 'a mere intermediary put in by the zamindar between himself and the cultivators'.[9] In this respect, however, they shared something with their more independent namesakes: they would 'seek the position of the jotedar so that they may "Lord it over sub-tenants or under raiyats"'.[10] Officials found that 'the jotedars were now of two distinct classes: the jotedar who originally took the land from the zamindar for the purpose of cultivation ... the raiyats of the Bengal Act VIII of 1869 [and those] who are ... clearly more than the under–tenant of that law'.[11] F. C. Monahan, the then Commissioner of Assam, observed that:

> it may be generally said of this part of India that wherever a man holds more land than he can cultivate by his own labour and that of the members of his family, he sublets part of it as soon as he can find a tenant, and if the difference between the rent which he can obtain from sub tenants and the government assessment is enough to maintain himself and his family in tolerable comfort, he sublets the whole. That is his notion of rising in the world.[12]

The big jotedars of estates like Gauripur and Mechpara[13] had at least three layers of sub-tenures beneath them. They cultivated the land with the help of *chukanidars* and *adhiars*.

> The chukanidars are usually the men with ploughs and cattle and a little land, the man holding land under the jotedar, ... a mere

tenant at will, and if the jotedar delivers him a notice to quit, he either must go at the end of the year or accept whatever terms the jotedar may think for to impose. In most of the estates, the chukanidars had absolutely no right of occupancy and could be ejected even after 30 years of cultivation while their rents could also be enhanced indefinitely. The adhiar is of a still lower standing. Indeed in Goalpara, he is treated as a mere farm labourer who is paid by receiving half the crop which he grows on his master's land. In other parts of eastern Bengal, he is still more numerous, but nowhere does law or custom give him any higher status than that of the under raiyat or the tenant-at-will.[14]

The adhiar or the adhi halua was only one of the several classes of landless cultivators during this period. Hunter lists the six other such classes, including the *bandha* or the bondsmen, who tilled land in lieu of the interest from a loan, the *chakars*, who were servants or were hired to cultivate the land of others, the prajas, who had no land of their own but tilled the land with their own oxen and plough (Hunter 1879: 63).

By the end of the nineteenth century, therefore, the colonial state's drive for agrarianisation was showing visible results. Large stretches of forests, woodland, 'wastelands', and cultivable areas had been measured and classified into fairly distinct geographical domains. Between the 1880s and the 1920s, there was a significant extension of the limits of arable land: the area under sedentary cultivation in Goalpara rose from 677 square miles in the zamindari estates in 1857 (Mills 1854: Appendix A) to 1,040 square miles in the late nineteenth century (Hunter 1879: 57). By 1901 this figure had risen to 366,762 acres with nearly 84 per cent of the population in the district being settled cultivators (Allen 1905: 61).

This growing sedenterisation did not of course preclude the continued existence of other lifestyle strategies. Land rights were frequently ambiguous and several communities continued to practice various subsistence strategies simultaneously. The several *palataka* or abandoned land holdings in the zamindari of Parbatjoar, for instance, were left behind by cultivators who continued to subsist on shifting cultivation, 'frequently abandoning their land without the knowledge of the landlords, when the soil was exhausted and finding fresh jungle land in the neighbouring pargana for fresh cultivation'.[15] At the turn of the century, several of the estates had cultivators holding their land directly from the zamindar without the intervention of an intermediary class, sub-infeudation being primarily a phenomenon in these areas that was associated with the immigration of settlers from eastern Bengal and the subsequent pressure on land. The zamindari estate of Chapar, for instance, had an extremely small number of tenants, who cultivated a fractional part of the whole estate, holding lands directly under the zamindar based upon contracts which were mostly verbal.[16] There were still very few jotedars in Bijni,[17] the largest estate in the district and at the turn of the century large areas of the estates were still under non-sedentary forms of cultivation. The number of settled tenants however, even in prosperous zamindari estates like Gauripur, continued to be few in number, with certain estates settled with as few as 515 tenants as late as 1870.[18] These examples, however, do not in any way reduce the profound nature of change in the political economy, and the emergence of new patterns of authority and power in Goalpara's rural countryside. To quote a historian writing in another context, 'a whole juggernaut of social and political change had been set rolling' (Guha 1999: 168) by the colonial state, and it was only a matter of time before even these few geographical spaces with their more flexible practices were forced into more rigid ways of being.

In the Duar region in the north, the anxiety of officials with the stretches of 'wastelands,' paved the way for state–organised schemes for settling uncultivated tracts. These schemes promoted the extension of agriculture into 'wastelands' and marginal areas through a promotion of settlements of migrant cultivators. The policies introduced to settle the uncultivated areas of the Eastern Duars in northern Goalpara were similar to the ones adopted by the colonial state in the neighbouring Bengal district of Jalpaiguri.[19] It was acknowledged that since 'the policy of settling the land on low rent, with grants of three years revenue free term will not attract jotedars for the colonisation of the Goalpara Dooars',[20] the state would rely on individual cultivators in the Eastern Duars.

Since the inhabitants of the plain areas in the south could not be induced sufficiently to clear the forests of the north, the alternative for the state, therefore, was to encourage the migration of cultivators from 'less crowded tracts in other parts of the country' into the Duar region. The land would then be settled with individual cultivators who would hold it directly from the state. The Duars were ruled by the Bhutanese king from the last decades of Mughal rule until 1865. Unlike the rest of the Goalpara district, the ryotwari and *miyadi* system of land revenue was introduced here. After the occupation of the Eastern Duars by the colonial state 'a 10 year settlement was offered, whereby, the Raja and the Rani of Bijni and Sidli respectively [who held the Eastern Duars] received 20 per cent and a 7 per cent of the gross rental of these estates, which were now held *khas* by the government and settled annually with cultivators like the other Dooars' (Ward 1897: 6). 'There [were] no intermediate tenures ... the Rajas of Bijni, Sidli and others who have received leases, merely standing in the position of farmers' (Hunter 1879: 128).[21]

Officials admitted that the introduction of ryotwari areas in the Eastern Duars was designed to secure a fixed population and limit the spirit of migrating. At the turn of the century, Hunter described the 'migratory habits of the Meches', the community which had the largest percentage of cultivators in the Eastern Duars: 'They seldom stay at one place or cultivate the same soil for more than two or three years; but this can hardly be wondered at, when they have so much virgin soil at their disposal' (Hunter 1879: 117). What a section of officials within the government described as an 'impractical, grand scheme' in 1872[22] was being seriously pursued by the state in 1897 and discussed, according to Denzil Ibbetson, in the Imperial Legislative Assembly and in the British press. Ibbetson identified portions of Bengal and Bihar as the areas from which the colonists would be drawn, and observed that:

> every family that is successfully transplanted to a new colony from a congested district in Bengal or Bihar, is removed from a hand to mouth struggle with poverty maintained on the brink of starvation, to a life of independence, with a certainty that hard work will bring ease and a reasonable amount of comfort.[23]

Ibbetson also listed the necessary markers of ideal colonists for the unsettled areas of Goalpara: 'a sturdy independence, self-reliant resourcefulness, the existence of tribal and village organisation, a small amount of capital and the habit of combination and co-operation'.[24] The colonial state's scheme of settling the Eastern Duars, however, also drew upon discourses on agricultural improvement of the late nineteenth century. Officials, including Henry Cotton, argued that it was 'inadvisable to settle Behari and Bengali cultivators on jungle land ... [Instead] the expedient might be tried of having the land cleared partially by pioneer cultivators of aboriginal tribes'.[25] These ideas were representative of strands within the colonial discourse of this period, which portrayed certain communities as yeomen farmers and stressed their role as pioneers in extending agrarian frontiers.

In the hierarchy of the modes of subsistence that Cotton constructed, 'the rude and temporary cultivation of the nomadic and the aboriginal tribes must be a prelude to the migration of real agriculturists ... these aboriginal people were good at jungle clearing, but are bad agriculturists ... they can cut down trees and secure a crop out of virgin soil. When this is once done and the land requires more careful culture, their restless habits assert themselves [and] it is necessary then to import thither a colony of cultivators and to replace woodcutters by agriculturists'.[26] Apart from the Garos, the Kacharis, the Meches and the Rabhas, who were inhabitants of the region, 'imported Santhals' were identified as another community which 'could constantly move forward, leaving behind land fit for cultivation'.[27]

The suggested representation of 'waste' in official writings was a metaphor for socially marginal regions, and for the limited skills of the inhabitants of these areas. The concept of 'waste', it has been argued, was based on an evolutionist idea of nature being arranged like society into tiers of 'superior' and 'inferior', with productivity as the sole ordering criterion. This discourse made it possible to view 'wasteland' as a synonym for 'idle land', that is, land not being tapped, or perhaps more accurately, not being tapped for commercial purposes. Waste was transformed from a classificatory device into a social norm, indicating a particular type of society and kind of social behaviour — indolent, effeminate and ignorant (Gidwani 1992), the assumption being that society and nature were malleable and therefore amenable to being shaped in the desired image, and that colonial intervention was essential to this transformation. When these arguments were extended into the particular context of nineteenth century Bengal, 'the "primitive" appeared indispensable not only for the imagination of history as identity, but also for the material prosperity of the nation. Both the British and the Bengali middle classes believed that the Santhals, unlike the "civilised" Indians, willingly cleared forests, reclaimed wastes, and made large plantations, like that of tea and indigo possible' (Banerjee 2006: 82).[28]

The 'Santhal experiment' in the Eastern Duars was a direct product of such thinking.[29] The settlement, established at the initiative of the Norwegian Mission in 1880 and initially spread over 25 square miles in the Guma Dooar, was encouraged by the several concessions that it received from the colonial state.[30] The colony appears to have been one of other similar settlements that were encouraged by the colonial state in Bengal. For instance, a few years prior to the establishment of this colony, a group of Santhal 'pioneers' were settled in the Chunchal estate in Malda district. The state defrayed the initial travelling expenses of the settlers, arranged for tracts of land to be reserved exclusively for the Santhals, and fixed the rent at a reduced rate of half the usual charge for the first year of cultivation. The 'experiment' was seen as largely a success, with the settlers managing to bring more than 3,200 acres or one-fifth of the area reserved, under cultivation by the early twentieth century (Allen 1905: 93). 'On the whole I think that the colonists have made as much progress as could be fairly expected ... they have been working hard and doing their best to push on cultivation. The houses have all been finished ... I saw a large number of fowls in every village and the people seem happy and contented,' remarked the deputy commissioner in his tour of the area.[31] This area had increased to more than 16,000 acres by 1915.[32] By the end of the nineteenth century, therefore, these several schemes to extend settled cultivation into the Duar areas were beginning to show results. Officials recorded the migration of several thousand cultivators from neighbouring districts of Bengal into the Duar area of Goalpara.[33]

The encouragement of immigrant cultivators into the Duars was accompanied by an increased control of the state over forest resources, another strategy to create a unified economic territory that could meet the state's demands for revenue. Colonial officials touring the region had identified the forested area in the Eastern Duars of Goalpara as one of the main sources of supply for the towns of Eastern Bengal since they formed the bulk of the sal tree area in the region. 'There are other valuable species which only require to be placed on the market in sufficient and regular quantities to find a steady sale. At present, they are too scattered and this indicates the importance of adopting a system of management which will produce more or less pure crops on definite areas' (Hart 1915: 27). By the early decades of the twentieth century, forest management rules were in place, and the colonial reconstitution of the forests had resulted in the demarcation of large parts of these forested areas as 'reserves'.[34]

Migration and the New Economy

From the beginning of the second decade of the twentieth century, Goalpara's society was subjected to a new set of pressures that led to an expansion of public space through the domain of colonial law. This section looks at the phenomenon which appears to have set in motion much of these changes — the unprecedented migration of thousands of cultivators from the plains of northeastern and eastern Bengal. This sudden demographic change challenged existing local imaginations of social space, with substantial implications for the persistence of older pre-colonial formations as well for the forging of new political identities. Of significance in understanding these trans-formations in local culture is the region's location as a borderland between the now two 'core' provinces of Bengal and Assam.

Migration of cultivators between the region of eastern Bengal and the district of Goalpara was a feature of the regional economy from pre-colonial times and had continued into the early colonial period as well. The pattern of migration had however remained primarily a seasonal one, linked to the demand for labour during the jute season.[35] In the early twentieth century, cultivators from Bengal were being 'invited by the offer of special conditions' to settle in the extensive wastelands of Goalpara, and settlement officials had 'no doubt that Bengali colonists would have come forward in very considerable numbers to take up blocks of land on zamindari tenures, with the concession of a revenue free period'.[36] Officials however expressed concern at the reluctance of cultivators from Bengal to migrate to Goalpara, as well as to the rest of Assam, despite the several incentives on offer, including an exemption from payment of taxes for the three years.[37] In the estate of Chapar during this period, for instance, 'there were still very large tracts of khas unoccupied land and there existed no very hard competition for land excepting in some congested areas and permanent old villages. While the occupiers of the soil are of such primitive habits and not accustomed and trained to use it with a permanent interest, the idea of improved legislation is certainly premature.[38] Attempting to explain this reluctance, colonial records suggested that:

> in the neighbouring districts of Bengal from which the valley is the most accessible, and where the people are accustomed to a climate and surroundings resembling in some degree those of Assam, and are well qualified, physically and otherwise to undertake the task of colonisation, there is at present no great pressure of population to induce them to migrate.[39]

While there was a migration of cultivators from Mymensingh and other districts of eastern Bengal between 1905 and 1907, this does not appear to have affected the ratio of population to land, and a steady annual immigration of about 2,000 was estimated as required to maintain the 50,000 immigrants of 1901 into Goalpara at their existing strength.[40] 'It might be thought that the amount of cultivable land, the fertility of the soil and the low rents prevailing would have induced some portion at least of the over crowded cultivators of Bengal to find their way ... and take up land', remarked E. A. Gait, the Census Commissioner for 1891, 'but this does not appear to be the case'.[41] This was clearly a trend that had persisted from earlier, for at the turn of the century, Hunter had commented on the almost total absence of:

> either emigration from or immigration into Goalpara, except for cultivators fleeing their lands to escape payment of arrears of rent and a few immigrants from Bengal and Hindustan, as well as from Assam [who came] to Goalpara seeking employment or for trading purposes, but their numbers [were] so few that this [could] hardly be called immigration (Hunter 1879: 46).

As late as 1917, colonial officials continued to despair at the land–man ratio in the district, ruing that 'in the zamindari areas over great part of the district there is much more land than population, and plenty of wasteland within short distances'.[42] The situation changed dramatically in the first decade of the twentieth century, which saw an exceptional rise in rural densities in several of the Bengal districts bordering Goalpara, particularly in Dacca, Mymensingh and Faridpur. This was the result of a pushing forward of the margins of agriculture into the rich alluvial tract of the Ganges and the Brahmaputra. In settlement reports from the period, the margins of cultivation had been reached in most parts of Eastern Bengal by the end of that first decade. Demographic pressure, the subservience of a jute-producing cultivating class to market forces, and the near constancy in the yield from cultivable areas, created conditions of impoverishment for the peasant.[43]

Thus, the increasing density of the population in Dacca, as an example, resulted in a situation where it became 'a matter of consideration as to what extent the land could be induced to provide the rapidly increasing members of the cultivating classes with employment' (Ascoli 1917: 50). With a density of 1,118 people per square mile, this was nearly double the average density of population for the whole of Bengal. The population in rural Bengal rose by 6.5 per cent in the 1920s, and the increase in Eastern Bengal was high enough for the colonial officials to suggest that the region 'be marked out as a separate natural division' (Census of India 1921, Assam: Chapter 1). The colonisation of the Madhupur jungles, 'an infertile jungle tract of stiff clay' in Dacca, indicated that the 'superior agricultural land of the region could no longer support its teeming population' (Census of India 1921, Assam: 50).

With a mean density of 823 per square mile, Mymensingh recorded a similarly high demographic growth and a situation of indebtedness with high interest rates 'such that payment constituted a severe drain in the resources of the agricultural population' (Sachse 1919: 27),[44] 'pushing cultivators from the region of Tangail and Jamalpur to settle in the Goalpara char areas of the Brahmaputra' (ibid.: 34). There were several cultivators' tracts published from Mymensingh during this period with descriptions of the conditions that led to the phenomenal migration into Goalpara. Of these, Abdul Hamid's *Krishak Bilap* is particularly poignant and detailed. Although the text primarily focuses on the exploitation of the cultivators by moneylenders, its author also offers images of sorrowful farewells to these cultivators at the Amritganj station in Mymensingh, wondering 'whether the malaria and the *kala azar* of Assam would prove to be even more life threatening than the mahajans' (Shah 1921: 5).

The migration in question involved over a million people in the first three decades of the twentieth century, as cultivators moved up the river Jamuna and northeastwards into the Assam valley up to Guwahati. As Table 3.1 shows below this had a great impact on the population of Goalpara. By 1911, more than 118,000 migrants had moved into the district of Goalpara alone, clearing vast tracts of dense jungles along the south bank of the Brahmaputra and occupying flooded lowlands all along the river, leading to a 30 per cent growth in the population of the district (Census of India 1911, Assam: 8). Officials pointed out that the impact of the immigration could be assessed from the fact that the growth in the natural population of Goalpara was only 15.6 per cent during this period (Census of India 1911, Assam: 10). The effects of 'this extraordinary inrush of settlers' produced almost immediate changes in the district's figures of population density, the mean density per square mile rising from 89 in 1891 to 115 in 1911, and then to 193 in 1921 (Census of India 1911, Assam: 10).[45]

Table 3.1
Variation in the population of Goalpara between 1872 and 1921

1872	1881	1891	1901	1911	1921
387,376	446,741	452,812	462,089	600,685	762,523

Source: Imperial Table II, Census of India, 1921, Volume III, Assam, Shillong, 1923.

What colonial officials had described as the 'commencement of [a] voluntary stream of settlers' in 1911 had, by the end of the second decade of the century, 'extended far up the valley and the colonists were now part of the population of all the four lower and central districts of Assam' (Census of India 1921, Assam: 41). According to the Census of 1921, nearly 300,000 cultivators had migrated to the province of Assam, of which 141,000 had settled in Goalpara alone. Of this 141,000, the highest figure of 78,000 was that of cultivators from Mymensingh (Census of India 1921, Assam: 41). The areas of Golakganj (density of 392) and Dhubri (density of 390) in the western part of the district, adjoining the province of Bengal, continued to be the most affected in 1921 as well, with Lakhipur thana recording a population increase of nearly 90 per cent within a decade (Census of India 1921, Assam: 87). At the end of just a decade of migration, cultivators from eastern Bengal formed 20 per cent of the population of Goalpara district (Census of India 1921, Assam: 41).[46] The level of migration from Mymensingh was high enough for literary tracts to express fears of a depopulation of the district. In the *Adarsha Krishak,* a text from Mymensingh, the author attempts to stem this migration by linking it to the project of national self-discovery in Bengal: 'Aren't you the same people who cleared the jungles and settled this part of Bengal? Our land, our civilisation is superior to that of Assam's and we need more people to cultivate our lands. We will not leave this country ...' (Hai 1922: 32).

The Census Report of 1921[47] had ended on the hopeful note that 'the migration of 1911 was only the advance guard', and that 'the main body was only just beginning to arrive ... as the news of the promised land has spread to other districts beside Mymensingh ...' (Census of India 1921, Assam: 20). The period between 1921–31 obviously did not disappoint for the Census Commissioner offered the following rather dramatic description of the continuing migration in 1931:

> Probably the most important event in the province [of Assam] during the last twenty-five years — an event, moreover, which seems likely to alter permanently the whole future of Assam and to destroy more surely than did the Burmese invaders of 1820, the whole structure of Assamese culture and civilisation — has been the invasion of a vast horde of land–hungry Bengali immigrants, mostly Muslims.[48]

The availability of cultivable land and the migration of cultivators from eastern Bengal in such large numbers emerged as significant determinants of the nature of tenurial relationships in Goalpara in the early twentieth century. It has been earlier suggested in this chapter that the jotedar–chukanidar pattern had gradually emerged as the dominant feature of the agrarian structure of Goalpara. Unlike East Bengal, where there was a predominance of small peasant raiyati holdings (Bose 1986: 15), the pattern of dominance in the several estates of southern Goalpara by the end of the nineteenth century was similar to that of northern Bengal, where the land was parcelled out between big and small jotedars who also advanced credit to the cultivators. There were clear parallels between the consolidation of the jotedars as the dominant class within the village in Goalpara, and a similar consolidation of this class in the neighbouring province of Bengal, particularly in north Bengal, where the availability of large tracts of wastelands placed the jotedars in a powerful bargaining position vis-à-vis the landlords.

In the pattern of sub-infeudation that emerged in the region in the post-migration period, the zamindars frequently contracted with these prosperous jotedars to initiate the task of clearing the land by the East Bengal immigrants. In several zamindari estates, local jotedars granted perpetual leases to these cultivators in order to reclaim wastelands, thereby creating intermediate tenures.[49] The *payal pattas*, as these leases were known, were given for uncultivated tracts, which were made revenue and *khazana* free for three years (Guha 2000: 60). In Chapar, the settling of considerable stretches of wasteland with the migrants and the subsequent 'constriction of privileges' were the causes of severe discontent among the older tenants.[50]

The process of forest clearing and land reclamation initiated by the colonial state produced therefore, complex tenure chains extending from the zamindar at the upper end to the actual culti-vator at the lower end, with numerous jotedars and other tenants in between. A distinct tenurial system emerged, as most often the immigrant peasant also acquired jotes and then went out into the forest or marsh lands to clear or settle land. Colonial officials observed that cultivable land was often being sold at highly profitable rates to the immigrants by the local cultivators: 'In several cases, the migrants took up land cleared by others and only if they could not find such land did they take up wastelands. Many Assamese had sold their lands ... at a good price ... sometimes for as much as Rs 200 per bigha of wasteland.'[51] As Table 3.2 below shows this increased the land holdings of the migrants.

Table 3.2
Figures of area settled (in acres) by immigrants from eastern Bengal in Goalpara

1914–15	1917–18	1922–23	1933–34	1934–35
22,580	41,496	10,256	42,992	43,495

Source: Collated from the Resolution on the Land Revenue Administration of Assam, 1914–35, Assam, State Archives, Guwahati.

In several estates, the migrant cultivators had gradually established themselves as 'de facto' jotedars over whole regions, eventually coalescing into settled communities. In Bijni, for instance, where the cultivators had previously sometimes held the land directly under the zamindar, jotes were now being increasingly settled with immigrant peasants.[52] There was also a sudden rise in the number of 'speculative jotes' being taken up by both the prosperous local tenants and the headmen of immigrant families in the estate of Mechpara.[53] A.J. Laine's survey of the district similarly traced the origin of several jotes in Goalpara during this period to 'reclamation settlements cultivated by the bhatias or the Eastern Bengal Muhammadan immigrants (Laine 1917b:19).

The immigration marked the beginning of a second great period of economic and social expansion in the forests, marshes and the char areas of Goalpara, after the early phase of 'wasteland colonisation'. With nearly 90 per cent of the migrants being drawn from the class of ordinary cultivators, left landless by the pressure of land in their homeland, it was now the cultivator from eastern Bengal who assumed the leading role in the extension of the frontiers of cultivation in the district (Census of India 1921, Assam: Provincial Table IV). There were almost immediate increases in the figures of cultivated acreage in colonial records. The area brought under cultivation by the immigrant cultivators in Goalpara rose from a negligible 2,165 acres in the pre-influx period, between 1904–5, to nearly 23,000 acres in 1915.[54] This was better than anything the state had hoped for in the region and C. S. Mullan, who was the Census Commissioner in 1931, captured the bewilderment of the officials at this sudden change:

> Without fuss, without tumult, without undue trouble to the district revenue staffs, a population ... of over half a million has transplanted itself from Bengal to Assam Valley. It looks like a marvel of administrative organisation on the part of the government but it is nothing of the sort: the only thing I can compare it to is a large body of ants (Census of India 1931, Assam: 51).[55]

Jute Growers, Traders and the Land Market

The acquisition of tenancies of various kinds by the immigrant cultivator was frequently predicated on his knowledge of what were apparently 'superior and more intensive techniques of agriculture'. Officials pointed out that 'in industry and skill, the migrants [were] an object lesson to the local cultivator ... they [had] reclaimed and brought under cultivation thousands of acres of land ... weeded and neatly sown and shown examples of new crops and improved methods',[56] all of which 'was beneficial since the local people seem to be shaking off their old lethargy and responding to the new spirit of competition'.[57] There was frequent praise for the 'migrant cultivators from Mymensingh who were setting examples of good husbandry to the people of Darrang and Goalpara',[58] although countered at times by descriptions of the east Bengal cultivator as 'unruly' and 'refractory'. These were representations that were echoed in various committee findings and surveys of the early twentieth century. 'Unlike the local cultivator, who was conservative in his methods and range of cultivation, the Mymensinghia settlers produced a variety of crops'.[59]

The singular contribution of the cultivators from East Bengal to the regional economy, however, was in the production of jute. Official reports from the nineteenth century indicate that jute was being cultivated by several communities of the region in the pre-migration period as well, particularly by the Hajongs, the Rabhas and the Kacharis, who had 'perfected the technique of cultivating the plant ... and produced a superior quality of jute, though in very small quantities and primarily for domestic consumption' (Kerr 1874: xlviii).[60] According to one such report, one in ten out of the 444, 761 people in Goalpara were engaged in jute cultivation during this period,[61] growing the crop in both the *char* areas as well in the foothills of the Duars: 'the hill tribes towards Majparah ... grow really superfine jute, very clean, though not long. These men do not cut the plant at the root but near the centre, so that only the finest portion of the fibre is kept' (ibid.: 65). The production of the crop, however, expanded considerably only at the turn of the century as Goalpara then begins to be listed among the chief areas of jute cultivation, along with districts of eastern Bengal: 'The Uttariya or the northern jute grown in Goalpara, Rangpur, Bogra and the districts of Sirajganj was rated as among the most superior of jute fibres, along with Sirajganj jute and desi jute from Dacca and was described as "unequalled for length, colour and fineness"' (Carter 1909: 3).[62]

The growth of a market in jute in the late nineteenth century, however, was limited, among other things, by a poor transport network. The descriptions of the Hajong and Rabha communities bringing in small quantities of this jute on their backs for sale to the haats of Gossaiganj, Salamara and Lakhipur in colonial records of the late nineteenth century, indicate that this fine jute had found its way into the hands of local traders, though not into the larger market at Serajgunj (Kerr 1874: xlviii).[63] 'We sell this jute to itinerant traders and rarely send it to Serajgunj. The quantity of jute exported from Gossaigaon is 5,000 maunds of very fine quality, which we bring in ponies or bangies ... from a radius of six miles. There are no pucca roads and only one dak road. We sent our jute to Serajgunj for sale this year at a cost of 3–6 rupees laid down there and sold it at 2–4 rupees to 2–8. [Therefore] we prefer selling this jute locally' (ibid.: xlviii).

All of this changed from the early part of the twentieth century with the integration of Goalpara into the regional trading circuits of Bengal. Several trading firms and jute mills were set up in Goalpara during this period. The Gouripore Jute Mills used jute from Serajgunj and Narayangunj along with locally produced fibre (ibid.: xv).[64] Several itinerant traders, locally called the *bhasania beparis*,[65] made annual trips to Goalpara from Serajgunj in the months of Aughran, Pous and Magha, and purchased jute with ready money (Kerr 1874: xliv). The pattern of jute cultivation and trade continued substantially unchanged into the early part of the twentieth century, with an expansion of the area under cultivation in the district to 35,022 acres, and an annual yield of more than 348,332 maunds.[66] F. C. Monahan, the then Director of Land Records and Agriculture, observed that the jute was grown primarily between the Lakhipur and the Mankachar area of Goalpara:

> on both the south and the north banks of the Brahmaputra, in the tract of the country to the north of Dhubri, lying west of a straight line drawn from that station to the eastern boundary of the Guma forest reserve. The western part of Goalpara district where jute cultivation has spread very rapidly within the last 16 years, resembles more the adjacent districts of northern Bengal than the rest of Assam.[67]

With the influx of immigrants from Eastern Bengal in the succeeding decades of the century, the production of jute was provided with a new impetus. Growing a 'superior quality of jute'[68] in the wastelands that they brought under cultivation, the immigrant cultivators brought about a steady increase in the figures of cultivated acreage under this crop, which now rose to nearly 43,000 acres.[69] Most of the land that was sold to the East Bengal cultivators by the local population was *chapori* land, considered ideal for jute cultivation,[70] and by 1921, jute had emerged as the second most important cash crop in Goalpara, with its cultivation occupying more than nine per cent of the net cultivated area of the district.[71] Developments in the transport network during this period, particularly the extension of the Eastern Bengal railway along the north bank of the Brahmaputra, would have contributed to the growth of the market in cash crops in the region.[72]

This increasing diversification in Goalpara's economy would not have been possible without certain facilities like a fairly well-developed credit network. Jute production, for instance, was dependent on the presence of local moneylenders who advanced money in return for payment in kind. In the nineteenth century, such persons are unlikely to have formed a separate class of professional moneylenders or usurers. Rather, the chief source of credit for the ordinary cultivator was more likely to have been the rich jotedar, who thus exercised effective control over the labour of the ordinary cultivators (Guha 2000: 72). Francis Buchanan describes this class in the district of Rangpur (in which Goalpara was included) as grain dealers or *beparis*, who were large farmers with more than five ploughs and kept cattle for transporting the grain collected from the village to the nearest market.[73] In the early twentieth century, there was also the gradual emergence of a new class of moneylenders who offered advances for growing jute and mustard and were repaid in kind.[74] Thus, in his evidence given to an official report, a local moneylender observed that, 'In Goalpara, the conditions under which advances are made and received are various. In some places, the advancing party ... the mahajan ... advances on the understanding that he is to be repaid in jute' (Kerr 1874: 59).[75] 'We sell jute not to the *paikars* [itinerant merchants] but to traders and mahajans,' reported Shoar Nysho, a cultivator from Teamari in Goalpara (ibid.: xlv).

The existence of this credit network could also explain the ability of the migrants to accept far higher rates of rent than those paid by the indigenous cultivators. Agents of zamindars observed that 'these newly settled tenants, mostly from Bengal, openly declare that they do not mind the increased rents at all, so long as they get good arable lands. Most of them who are industrious and not migratory in their habits have improved their positions ... these new tenants know perfectly well what they are about'.[75] In several of the estate reports from the period, the rates contracted by jotedars with the 'foreign tenants from Bengal' were almost always far higher than the rates paid by the local tenants, who continued to pay rates fixed by the survey and settlement operations of 1869.[76]

By the end of the third decade of the twentieth century, after over 20 years of migration of cultivators from eastern Bengal and a resultant boost to commercial crops such as jute and the expansion of cultivated acreage, conditions had been created for sharp increases in rent and an expansion of the land market in the district. The extensive margins of cultivation in Goalpara appear to have been reached by the early 1930s. The Census Commissioner for 1931 reported that 'there had been a diversion ... of the tide of migration from Goalpara into the districts of Kamrup and Nowgong during this period, most of the cultivable wastelands in the district having by this time been already taken over ... [and] although there was still room for expansion in the district, the great days of mass immigration by the Mymensinghias are over'.[78]

The area brought under cultivation had risen from 10,256 acres between 1922–23 to 45,000 acres between 1933 and 1934.[79] 'In the past, the land was of comparatively little or no value, but with the steady influx of immigrants from Bengal in recent years, and the consequent spread of cultivation, such land has steadily increased and is still rapidly increasing in value', observed A. J. Laine in the Legislative Assembly:

> With its appreciation in value, it has acquired an increased importance in the eyes not only of its owners but also of potential tenants ... land lords claim the right to settle all unoccupied land belonging to them with such tenants, and at such rates, as they may think proper, and in as much as the right to property includes the right to exclude others from possessing it, they likewise claim the right to eject persons who have taken possession of their lands without their consent.[80]

Zamindari records denied any unreasonable increase in rent in the post-immigration period, and instead suggested that 'only a very small number of tenants have been affected by this and the amount at stake is very small'.[81] The numerous petitions from different classes of tenants and their movements suggest otherwise, demonstrating forcefully that the second and the third decades of the twentieth century were marked by a sharp increase in land rents in the district. It is evident that all of the 19 permanently settled estates of Goalpara imposed a sharp increase in the land rents demanded from tenants, the highest being an increase of more than 25 per cent in the estates of Gauripur and Karaibari from 1911–14 (Friel 1914: 5). Assessing the changes effected on local agrarian conditions by migration, officials noted that the competition over land resulting from the rapid extension of cultivation 'have had the inevitable result of enhancing the rent, and this has been facilitated much by the fact that these immigrants have been accustomed to pay very much higher rents elsewhere and readily agree to rates in advance of the old prevailing pergunnah rates'.[82]

To this acceptance of a higher rent was added 'an increase in the cost of living and the introduction of cultivation requiring certain technical skill' [the production of jute], all of which 'benefited the immigrant ... at the expense of his predecessors who are being gradually outbid, bought up and ousted from the better portions of the district with the assistance and the connivance of the zamindars who benefit from this change'.[83] In the estate of Mechpara, suggested the report of H. Savage, an official assessing the need for tenancy legislation in the district:

> the zamindar had adopted the insidious system known in Rangpur as *hajat jamma* wherein the rent is fixed at a high rate but 'as a favour' only a part of it is demanded at present. Even however, the present 'favoured' rate means a considerable enhancement over present rates and this has undoubtedly given rise to general ill-feeling on the part of the jotedars. An enhancement of 100 per cent is extremely heavy in comparison with most current rates in the vicinity. In the Gauripur estate also there is considerable discontent and for the same reason.[84]

The petitions from the older tenants of the zamindari estates protesting against rent enhancements and subsequent ejectments during this period indicate that these conditions affected both the chukanidars and the jotedars. The estate of Bijni was particularly representative. A series of memorials were submitted by Basuram Patgiri and Madharam Das on behalf of the tenants of Bijni in 1912 complained, among other things, of increase in rent without the knowledge of tenants and 'notices of ejectment being served to coerce payment of rent at enhanced rates'.[85] A petition from the jotedars of the Dihi Dolgoma village of Habraghat pargana in the estate of Bijni attributed the several rent suits in the region to the migration, and questioned the right of the Rani of Bijni to eject them from holdings held by them in perpetuity over 100 years.[86] The petitioners accused the zamindar of having 'repeatedly brought suits against the raiyats for arrears of rent as well as ejectment', and pleaded for a sanad, which would 'secure their rights from any future invasion of migrants'.[87] The situation was not very different in the other zamindari estates. A petition from Thanda Ram Das and other jotedars of the Khuntaghat pargana objected to the new surveys being carried out after the settlement of wastelands in the region, as he feared a further increase in rents after having already suffered at the hands of the tehsildar for refusing to meet his exorbitant demands.[88] In Gauripur, more than five petitions were submitted by the chukanidars between 1915–16 in a movement that had as its leaders, Gajendra Rai Sarkar, Jamir Sheikh and Pahali Maha, who demanded that they be given occupancy rights over land cultivated for more than 12 years (Laine 1917b: 23).

The condition of insecurity in the land holdings of the jotedars was reproduced in their tenurial relations with the chukanidars or the under-tenants. Colonial surveys commented on the several cases of ejectment of these under-tenants by the jotedars, 'mostly on account of an inability to accept the terms of resettlement at considerably enhanced rates of rent, the motive [of the jotedar] being the desire of gain which a resettlement with a new immigrant tenant at an enhanced rate of rent would bring' (ibid.: 150). Petitions submitted to the colonial government by groups of chukanidars protested against the growing insecurity in land tenure, and demanded 'a permanent status for tenants who, despite being the actual tillers have no protection ... and were at the mercy of the unscrupulous jotedars'.[89] With most of the available land in the riparian tracts suitable for settlers being already taken up (Census of India 1931, Assam: 52)[90] by the early 1930s, there was not much room for agrarian expansion. Indebtedness had risen by the late 1930s, and officials reported that more than 80 per cent of the population of the district was in debt to local mahajans and Marwari traders.[91] Migrants, who appear to have formed a large percentage of this section of Goalpara's population, were frequently described as 'reckless borrowers, improvident and thriftless', who spent a considerable amount of their money on litigation.[92]

The absence of sufficient statistical evidence in the form of figures of per capita income, indebtedness and land transfers among various communities in the district makes it difficult to offer definitive conclusions about the economic conditions of social groups during this period. From the preceding discussion of the process of settlement of land by the immigrants, however, one could suggest that despite this indebtedness, the 'Mymensinghias' would have also benefitted from the reclamation of swamps and uncultivated tracts. In the reclaimed areas, the high fertility of the soil, the low rents, the favourable land–man ratio, and the cultivation of a variety of crops, including jute, would together have created conditions for their prosperity and placed them in a position which would enable them to bargain for the security of their holdings.[93]

By the end of the 1920s, colonial officials were describing 'the difficulties of regulating and guiding the legitimate land–hunger of a needy but industrious people without encroaching on the rights and aims of the old established tenants' as 'one of the most difficult problems' that they had to deal with.[94] Officials warned that 'unless some remedial measures were adopted, the influx of cultivators from other parts of Bengal would lead to the eviction of the chukanidars or to the enhancement, almost to starvation point, of the rents payable by those men who were the actual cultivators of most of the land in the district'.[95] Some such 'remedial measures' already seemed to have come into force during this period, as government reports stated that 'of late years, the government has adopted the policy of controlling the settlement of the immigrants. Certain areas are set apart where they are allowed to settle and areas reserved for expansion of cultivation among the Assamese are barred to them under penalty of ejectment'.[96] Along with some evidence of an increasing sale of land to non-agriculturists,[97] there were now also suggestions to confine transfers of land holdings to local cultivators, amidst fears that the 'Assamese were losing their land, and would ultimately have no land for themselves'.[98] Instances of conflict over wasteland resources and common grazing areas in villages would have added to these fears.[99]

Law, Custom and Emerging Subjectivities

The last section of the chapter analyses the ways in which these conflicts came to be gradually subsumed within the structures of colonial law. If only partially, this was underscored in the processes which led to the introduction of a new tenancy law for the district in the 1920s. What is also highlighted in these processes is the unstable character of colonial law, its construction in the interstices of endless negotiations with the colonised that includes not just the propertied zamindars and jotedars but also various communities resenting their reduction to the status of agrarian dependents.

To the increasing scarcity of land and its increasing value, the pressure of population and the consolidation of rural power, and to its need for a steady source of revenue, the colonial state responded by identifying the occupancy tenant as the actual producer and reinstating his 'original privileges' (Robb 1997: 2).[100] This was part of a broader process 'whereby state intervention over landed property sought to reach every lower social or tenurial strata ... [it was] part of an ever extending categorisation, the attribution of "properties" defining a wider range of people and institutions' (ibid.: xvi). As with the Bengal Tenancy Act, tenancy legislation in Goalpara, too, appeared to have been informed by such imperatives, by the need of the state to create 'definite categories with rights located within them, as species of property' (ibid.: xxv). The issues being voiced were often an extension of the debates within the official discourse in the preceding years, which had retained the interests and rights of the jotedars and the chukanidars as their common concern. Thus, a report submitted by F. C. Monahan in 1907 had argued against the introduction of the Bengal Tenancy Act in Goalpara on the grounds that the Act was not suited for the protection of the jotedars.[101] Other officials also opposed the Act on the grounds that 'it had failed to protect the cultivator from exactions, legitimate or illegal ... it had led to a great deal of litigation and the poorer was generally at a disadvantage against the richer litigant in the court'.[102] Even among those who supported the introduction of the Bengal Tenancy Act in Goalpara, the justification for colonial intervention continued to be the protection of tenants' rights. In his detailed notes on the issue of tenancy legislation in Goalpara, H. Savage argued:

How would the jotedar stand under the Tenant Act? It has been said above that they are all at present regarded as raiyats with right to occupancy ... To all these and particularly to the occupancy raiyats, the Tenancy Act would afford protection against undue enhancement in future. The case of the chukanidar is different. It is their hope that the Tenancy Act would at least give them the status of raiyats without the right of occupancy.[103]

The presence of migrant cultivators who had a greater degree of familiarity with institutions of the colonial state, offered another reason for the extension of the legal system into new areas of the rural social order. In several estates, estate officials observed that 'it had now become necessary to enumerate the principal conditions of tenancy ... on account of the influx of new raiyats from Bengal who were usually well conversant with the provisions of the Bengal Tenancy Act'.[104] This familiarity of the immigrant community with the workings of colonial law was evident also in the several references in offi-cial records to the 'innate litigousness in the character of the immigrant'. Thus A. J. Laine's summing up of agrarian relations in early twentieth century Goalpara listed 'the less reputable surplus population of the litigious districts of Eastern Bengal' along with 'the several powerful families ... and a mixed peasantry, mostly illiterate, composed partly of obstinate aboriginals' (Laine 1917: 3). Survey officials noted that this increasing precision in the definition of tenancy rights, accompanied by a restriction of traditional privileges of the tenants was more pronounced in the more settled estates of Gauripur, Mechpara and Karaibari.[105] In the estate, reports from the second decade of the twentieth century, the creation and formalisation of boundaries of various kinds within local society, were attributed to the changing social context, with migrants working as a catalyst.

The petitions from jotedars and chukanidars during this period, which gradually exhibited an evident ease in their ability to work the institutions of the state, particularly the law courts, signified such processes of formalisation within the local tenurial strata. From the first decade of the twentieth century, the demand for tenancy legislation begins to be articulated in these petitions, signalling a further expansion of the domain of colonial law that merged neatly with the pro-tenant discourses of the colonial state. The new tenancy legislation was to perform the task of maintaining social order, which in this context meant a preservation of the proprietorial rights of the original ryots without conceding the rights of the zamindars, as well as of meeting the demands of revenue, the assumption being that the legal protection of the tenurial holdings of the ryot would necessarily generate investment in agriculture. Reflecting on the question of change in the tenancy law in the district, P. R. T. Gourdon, the Commissioner of the Assam Valley districts, noted that:

> The demand for the revision of the tenancy law in Goalpara is not a new one. Tenancy legislation was under contemplation as far back as the year 1883. My own experience for this demand dates back from the year 1895, when I was the deputy commissioner of Goalpara. My attention was drawn to the unsatisfactory relations between the tenant and the zamindar which existed, specially in the pargana of Mechpara. The grievances alleged then were very much the same as they were till quite recently, e.g. the grave disabilities under which the tenants laboured owing to their being four separate collecting agencies which harassed the raiyats. The complaints from tenants of this pargana have been constant.[106]

Added to these was resistance from tenants in several estates to several privileges that were continued to be seen by the zamindars as part of their proprietorial rights, including high rates of *salami* and other forms of 'customary dues', which, along with abwabs, remained the largest source of variation in what the zamindar demanded from the tenants. In the more settled estates of Gauripur, Mechpara and Chapar, these dues included the *punya nazar* (paid at the beginning of payment of rent every year), the *bijaya dasami nazar* (paid on the occasion of Durga Puja), and the *pattan nazar* or the settlement bonus.[107]

In the changed context of the post-migration period, the scattered discontent of the late nineteenth century took the shape of more coherent demands for effective occupancy rights. The second decade of the twentieth century saw the emergence of several formally constituted associations of tenants and under-tenants. Zamindari records of the Bijni estate mention the activities of one such association, the Habraghat Hitsadhini Sabha, which organised a collective resistance of the jotedars against increased rent in the estate.[108] The Jotedar's Association was another organisation which occupied considerable public space, and put forward consistent demands for a steady extension of tenants' rights and a curtailing of the rights of the zamindars. The Association resisted the passing of the Assam Landlord and Tenant Procedure Bill, which was the state's response to the rise of competition rents that threatened the already uncertain domain of the tenant–landlord relationship. The Act, which proposed to make arrears of rent recoverable as arrears of land revenue,[109] favoured the landlords by providing them with the means to improve rent collection. The protests against this Act from other organisations, including the Goalpara Krishak Sanmilani[110] and the Goalpara District Association, were sufficient indication of the strengthening of the jotedars as a new class of interests. The intense debates over this bill, and later over the introduction of the Goalpara Tenancy Act during the 1920s, in the Assam Legislative Council, provided an early instance of the emergence of revenue law, as the most important arena of political dispute

Law courts, therefore, were emerging as the 'new battlefields', 'an arena for political dispute that was as all-consuming for some of its litigants, as it was non-threatening to the state' (Dirks 1986: 332). The marked rise in the incidents of litigation and cases about landed property in the district was illustrative of this. Between 1907–12, which was also the peak period of migration from eastern Bengal, the number of rent suits in the Dhubri Courts rose from 169 in 1907 to 662 in 1912. There was a similar rise in cases in the Goalpara Courts, from 53 in 1907 to 677 in 1912 (Laine 1917: 5). Nearly 70 to 80 per cent of the rent suits and pure ejectment suits, respectively, were successful (ibid.: 152). In one such series of rent suits brought by jotedars of Gauripur estate between 1905–15 at the Dhubri Court against some chukanidars, the *munsif* argued that the findings of a local enquiry had stressed that 'regular traffic [was] going on in ejecting old tenants and settling new ones from the immigrant community on heavy salami. Many sub-tenants had been ejected without reason by the occupancy tenants, when the former had originally cleared the land and held it for many generations'.[111]

Formal associations, representing new classes of interests, and their institutionalised protests couched in the new legal language were but one form of response of the local society to the widening arena of colonial law. Tenancy legislation in Goalpara, and its accompanying project of social categorisation, had to frequently negotiate with local notions of shared tradition and custom particularly when the latter was evoked to validate rights in land. This was particularly evident in the Eastern Duars in northern Goalpara, where the reinvention of custom emerged as a powerful political weapon for communities resisting their reduction to the status of agrarian dependents, as the forest no longer remained a strategic resource for them. The several petitions and memorials submitted from the late nineteenth century onwards indicate that the subsistence patterns of several communities, particularly the Garos and the Meches, had been irrevocably transformed by the settlement and forest policies of the state. The most visible impact was that the mobility of these communities was severely circumscribed by a ban on all residence or cultivation within the forest reserves.

> Those who remained committed to the mobile and independent lifestyle — now forager, now cultivator, now warrior — found the agricultural frontier closing around them and were left to the tender mercies of the Forest Department that came into being from the mid-century. Their fate has been sketched (Guha 1999: 163).

The official perception of *jhum* as a method of cultivation that caused 'significant injury to valuable timber by the firing and clearing' was followed by steps to prohibit it altogether. The enlisting of the services of the Garos in the felling of forests within the reserves by offering them 'favourable terms', in the hope that such terms would induce the Garos to 'abandon their destructive hill jhuming were products of such policy framing' (Hart 1915: 29). These were accompanied by measures to establish forest villages in the Duar region. Those in Kachugaon were set up in 1902 to provide an uninterrupted supply of labour for the neighbouring reserve of Ripu (Allen 1905: 79). Forced evacuation of the residents of surrounding villages was frequently required in order to settle them in the protected areas (Hart 1915: 2). The impact of the changes on the political economy of the region was evident from the fact that the 'forest reserves' were already being marked out at the turn of the century to 'provide a refuge for these tribes who were being pushed out by more astute and energetic races'.[112]

The restrictions introduced by the colonial state, however, were not easily implemented, and resistance to these policies saw local groups drawing upon shared memories of customary rights and tradition to articulate their protest. They demonstrated yet again the complex ways through which colonial law came to be enforced in the region. Here, it is necessary to direct attention to the 'number of agrarian movements caused by the encroachment or fancied encroachment by each estate on the lands of the neighbouring estates or on government land, peopled mainly by aboriginals' (Laine 1917: 4). Through the late nineteenth century and the early decades of the twentieth century, Garo, Bodo and Mech cultivators on several zamindari estates continued to confront the authorities with allegations of zamindari oppression, including the practice of *begar*[113] and the encroachment of lands. A memorial from the Garo cultivators on the estate of Bijni complained that the 'Hindu zamindar of Bijni had for many years been encroaching on lands which properly belonged to the Garos'[114] In a memorial submitted to the colonial authorities in 1904, Mech cultivators recorded their protest against the formation of forest reserves and the subsequent loss of 'valuable privileges which they had previously enjoyed'.[115]A redrawing of boundaries between Garo villages and zamindari estates and the exclusion of certain tracts from the permanently settled areas (including the entire pargana of Habraghat) were among the demands set forth in the memorial of Sonaram Sangma, who led a sustained defiance of state regulations by Garo cultivators.

Several other instances of resistance from indigenous communities to loss of customary rights continued to be reported. The petitions that followed invariably contended that these communities had 'the right to collect fuel and straw, to fell sal trees required for the construction of their houses or their ploughs, to graze cattle and to cultivate in the sal forests, and fell trees standing on their homestead land'.[116] Not surprisingly, cutting sal trees from reserved forests was among the primary charges against the Meches and the Garos in the several criminal cases that were instituted during this period. 'In most of these cases,' colonial officials observed, 'the Garos or the Meches do believe that they have the right to cut from the reserved forests timber which they require ... for certain purposes.'[117] In the *King Emperor v Guman Singh Garo case*, the court noted that 'the accused pleads not guilty to the charges and alleges that he cut four posts himself ... believing he had the right to cut sal trees ... since this is their custom from time immemorial'.[118] In the judgements of all these cases and in the debates within official circles, customs were significant for legitimating practice, and colonial officials set about fixing their meanings in the act of encoding them:

> As regards the complaints of the Garos, the formation of the forest reserves deprived them of valuable privileges, the wasteland was being treated as being at the disposal of the Government, and no compensation was given for such lands. It is now proposed that ... any area which is found not worthwhile to retain, be surrendered to the villagers. Compensation representing roughly the approximate value of the land should be paid as an act of grace.[119]

Several other judgements reflected similar concerns. In a case where six Garo cultivators were convicted by the magistrate for cutting trees without permission in the reserved forests of the Bijni Raj, the conviction was later overturned by the Sessions judge who ruled that, 'the gradual regulation of these privileges has of course been objected to by the tenants as infringement of immemorial rights. It may be that some people have actually come to believe that they possess the right. The mere fact that the Raja has forbidden them to cut the trees is sufficient to put them in the wrong, but ancient customs and privileges cannot be set aside in this summary manner. In my opinion, the conviction is wrong'.[120]

The customs of local communities and the terms of their validity were therefore to be decided by courts and imperial officials, as colonial law sought to reorder the rather 'untidy' world of indigenous practices in the region. This need to seek or protect 'new rights' by generating and generalising 'old claims' was visible in the permanently settled southern areas of the district as well. Official reports of the conditions of tenancy legislation pointed out that almost all the rights of the jotedars that were 'denied in theory' in the zamindari estates, continued to prevail through customary usage.[121] These included the right to a resettlement on the expiry of the term of the lease and the right to inherit, sell, transfer or mortgage the land. For instance, in the estates of Parbatjoar and Bijni, which had vast stretches of uncultivated land and a less complex tenurial system, the heritability of the jotedar's holdings was 'passively recognised, although their position remained uncertain'.[122] On the other hand, despite the recognition of the occupancy right of the tenant by the Act VIII of 1869 if he had been in occupation of the land for 12 years, it was pointed out by colonial officials that this right of the tenant 'remained very vague indeed, as its precise incidents were not determined under the existing law'.[123] The estate reports of Gauripur, Mechpara and Karaibari clearly denied all such rights to the jotedars.[124] The 'exact nature' of the occupancy rights of jotedars remained a central concern of civil litigation in the early twentieth century. In an ejectment suit brought to the Calcutta High Court, for instance, the judge pointed out that 'the Act VIII of 1869 also failed to distinguish between raiyats and under–raiyats'.[125]

Illustrating the regional variations that accompanied the implementation of the Permanent Settlement, the rights claimed by the jotedars in this part of eastern India, including the right to sublet, inherit and transfer the jote, had to be validated through custom and collective memory long after they had been identified and legitimated by colonial law in other parts of the country. In the absence of any protective legislation, petitions from jotedars appealing against increasing rent and ejectment described their rights in the land, as timeless and immemorial, 'held in perpetuity over hundreds of years'.[126] Memory was summoned to provide the necessary validity to their assertion of the 'liberty to settle or cultivate any part of the land that they pleased without the permission of the landlord', the relationship with whom was based on long prevailing customary rules.[127] Shared customs and traditions of the local agrarian community, also institutionalised in relationships like the dewaniya–chengra system, played as significant a role in determining the relationships of various groups to the land, as did the recognition of rights by colonial law in Goalpara during this period.

The rights of the chukanidars were similarly represented as characterised by ambiguity in colonial land records, their conditions of tenancy described as being frequently based on 'mere verbal settlements of the vaguest nature'.[128] The state often found the origin of the tenancies of this class of tenants, who were drawn predominantly from the indigenous communities of Goalpara, difficult to define. In 'many cases their ancestors were probably cultivating the land long before the zamindars spread their authority and considerable numbers probably came from time to time as the original squatters'.[129] This ambiguity, not unsurprisingly, was the central concern of the several petitions submitted by this class of tenants through the late nineteenth and early twentieth century. Between 1910–13, for example, the chukanidars of several zamindari estates claimed ancient occupancy rights in the land, but failed to establish them (Laine 1917: 9).

When the Goalpara Tenancy Act was finally passed in 1929, it enhanced the security and certainty for a majority of the 'settled' ryots, who had until then enjoyed continuity of residence and land holding de facto. The Act recognised the rights of occupancy of the tenant, hitherto held by custom, as well as the rights of a settled under–raiyat to land held continuously for 12 years (Laine 1917: 171). The new rent law sought to restore the proprietary rights of the cultivator and to protect groups that were already entrenched in the agrarian sector as owners or tenants. It also provided for 'a new classification of tenures and tenancies, based on local conditions', which divided Goalpara's society into categories of proprietor, tenant and under tenant (ibid.).

The discussions around the tenancy law were equally significant for highlighting the ways in which history, culture, economy and the state came to be closely forged together in this region during the late nineteenth and early decades of the twentieth century. In the noisy legislative council debates from the period, Goalpara's economy and culture emerge as closely interwoven sites of tension. As a member from Sylhet put it: 'The Tenancy Legislation which is to adjudicate the rights between the tenants, the jotedars and the landlords, will be made the occasion for a fight for the spread of Assamese and Bengali culture. (This Bill will) be made the occasion for the bigger issue — what should be the boundaries of the province of Assam'.[130] Although opposition from Goalpara's zamindars to the introduction of the tenancy legislation was couched in the familiar language of modernity and development (such as the absence of cadastral surveys and the still peripatetic lives of cultivators)[131] the discourse at once overlapped with that of cultural nationalism as the following quote from the speech of a fervent proponent of the bill would make evident: 'Is it prejudice to think of our own people? We are not against Bengali culture. We do not care if Bengali culture comes to Assam or not. We are concerned with the conditions of the tenants. Is it to be believed for a moment that if the condition of the tenants improve, they will discard Bengali culture? If the tenants are really in favour of Bengali culture, then certainly they will improve Bengali culture when their own living conditions improve. Is it supposed that Bengali culture can be forced on the tenants only if their condition remains poor and is as miserable as it is at the moment?'[132] Goalpara's emergence as a circumscribed unit of the colonial economy of eastern India, the changes in the region's agrarian structure and its inclusion into an expanding market of global capitalism, therefore, were all inseparably tied to the production of regional cultural imaginings, to questions of linguistic, territorial and political autonomy. The chapter that follows understands these critical linkages through an exploration of the links between the constitution of a colonial borderland, and the articulation of cultural difference in the realm of speech practices.

✳

Notes

1. For a discussion of some of these conflicts, see Guha (2000: 38–41).
2. Note by the Chief Commissioner of Assam on the extension of cultivation in Assam and the colonisation of wastelands in the Province,
   24 Sept. 1898, Assam Secretariat Proceedings (henceforth ASP),
   Revenue A, Nov. 1898, File nos 128–38, State Archives, Guwahati.
3. Ibid.
4. Colonisation of Wastelands in Assam, Revenue A, Nov. 1898, File nos
   128–38, State Archives, Guwahati.
5. Colonisation of Wastelands in Assam, Revenue A, Nov. 1898, File nos
   128–38, State Archives, Guwahati.
6. 'The jotedaars of Rangpur, the talukdars of Chittagong, the kunkatidars
   of Chota Nagpur ... are but different names for the reclaimers of the
   jungle, who exercise a sub-proprietary right in the land that they have
   brought under cultivation (Colonisation of Wastelands in Assam,
   Revenue A, Nov. 1898, File nos 128–38, State Archives, Guwahati).
7. Correspondence between the Chief Secretary to the Government of
   East Bengal and Assam and the Secretary to the Government of India,
   31 May 1906, Revenue A, Oct. 1906, File nos. 106–16; 'The system of
   jotes as at present known in Goalpara was originally introduced from
   the Bengal districts of Rangpur and Jalpaiguri where this system has
   been in existence from time immemorial. Whatever their economic
   utility now, there is no doubt that in the past jotes have served a very
   valuable colonising purpose. By this means, the zamindar is enabled,
   with a minimum of risk and expense to himself, to gradually open out
   and colonise the wastelands of this estate' (Laine 1917: 113).

8. In Mechpara, the jotedar was 'the man who applied for waste land and expected to make a middleman's profit by subletting to kolijans or under tenants at a far higher rate than he would pay to the landlord' ('Mechpara Estate Report', in Laine 1917: 66).

9. Copy of notes recorded by H. Savage, 22 Apr. 1909, Commissioner's Conference, 1909, in Revenue A, Feb. 1913, File nos 6–9, File no. IIT/R, 1913, OIOC, London.

10. Ibid.

11. Ibid.

12. General Department, Revenue A, June 1905, File nos. 176–78, ASP.

13. F. C. Monahan estimated the size of the jotes in Goalpara to be between 1,000 and 5,000 bighas (Report No. 1503 R & F, 30 May 1907, Commissioner's Conference, 1909, Revenue A).

14. Copy of notes recorded by H. Savage, 22 Apr. 1909, Commissioner's Conference, 1909, in Revenue A, Feb. 1913, No. 6–9, File no. IIT/R, 1913, OIOC, London.

15. 'Parbatjoar Estate Report' (Laine 1917: 80).

16. 'Report from the Estate of Chapar' (Laine 1917: 100).

17. According to B. C. Allen, Bijni had an area of 943 square miles while Gauripur, the second largest estate, had an area of 423 square miles (Allen 1905: 111).

18. 'Report from the Estate of Parbatjoar, in (Raine 1917: 78).

19. Ray, 'Jalpaiguri Under Colonial Rule', Chapter 3.

20. Colonisation in the Goalpara Duars, Revenue A, July 1905, File nos 38–41, OIOC, London.

21. 'In the temporarily-settled Eastern Duars, pattas or leases were granted to the cultivators in Bijni, Sidli, and the Ripu Duars, and to the jotedars in Guma Duar, determining the rates at which they were bound to pay for the land in their possession. The rates of assessment in Bijni, Sidli, Chirang and Ripu Dwar were fixed as follows: homestead and winter rice land, Rs. 1.8.0 or 3s an acre; pharingati or dry land growing miscellaneous crops, 12 annas or 1s. 6d per acre; patit or jungle land included in the holding 1½ annas per acre. In the case of Guma, rents were fixed at the reduced rates of R. 1 (2s), 8 annas and 1½ annas respectively'(Hunter 1879: 69).

22. Correspondence between Henry Hopkinson, the Commissioner of Assam and the Secretary to the Government of Bengal, 6 Apr. 1872, Board of Revenue Papers, 1859–72, File no. 145, OIOC, London.

23. Correspondence between Denzil Ibbetson, the Secretary to the Government of India and the Chief Commissioner of Assam, 2 June 1897, Revenue and Agriculture, File nos 1–28, OIOC, London.

24. Ibid.

25. Note by the Chief Commissioner of Assam on the 'extension of cultivation in Assam and the colonisation of waste lands in the province', p. 10, 24 Sep. 1898, Revenue A, Nov. 1898, State Archives, Guwahati.

26. Ibid., p. 11.
27. Ibid.
28. 'Only people like the Santhals, who had proved their "primordial" worth by reclaiming post-famine Bengal, seemed capable of clearing Assam of this aggressive wildness' (Banerjee 2006: 95).
29. For a discussion of texts such as Dhirendranath Baske's, 'Saonthal Ganasangramer Itihaas' (Calcutta 1996) that tells the story of the Santhal migration to Assam, see Prathama Banerjee's 'Travel, migration, and the conduct of time' (Banerjee 2006: 82). Baske's text has the account of Chotrae Deshmanjhi, who was persuaded by the missionaries to go and settle in the new lands of Assam. 'Yet the narrative rang with live memories of disease and pain and of not entirely voluntary dislocation to an unfamiliar land. There seemed no 'indication' that the Santhals moved "naturally" to Assam in the course of their habitual migration, as Skrefsrud (the missionary) had claimed. According to Chotrae, Skrefsrud had told officials: "Do not worry, I shall get as many subjects as you want, to clear as large a tract as you can grant". The point clearly was to make Santhals migrate — Chotrae realised — so that the "wilderness" of Assam could be reclaimed' (quoted in Banerjee 2006: 106).
30. Letter from the Assistant Secretary to the Commissioner of the Assam Valley, 12 Nov. 1880, Home Proceedings 1881, OIOC, London.
31. Extract from the diary of T. J. Murray, Officiating Deputy Commissioner of Goalpara, 23 July 1881, in File no. 132G, Goalpara Papers, ASP, 1881.
32. Resolution on the Land Revenue Administration of Assam for the year 1914–15, p. 3, State Archives, Guwahati.
33. Letter from the Officiating Deputy Commissioner of Goalpara to the Commissioner of the Assam Valley, 11 Oct. 1880, Home Proceedings 1881, OIOC, London.
34. By 1905, there were 787 square miles of reserved forests in the district, divided into seven reserves. There was also an area of 558 square miles of 'unclassed forests', which was classified as 'simply waste land at the disposal of the Government'. The earliest reserves in the Dooars were formed in 1875' (Allen 1905: 78).
35. Administration of Land Revenue in East Bengal and Assam, p. 3, State Archives, Guwahati. In the rest of the Assam valley, however, migration was a significant factor in the increase of population. The first significant wave of migration into Assam began shortly before the middle of the nineteenth century, and was connected to the tea plantations. This was followed by a wave of migration of educated Bengali Hindus into the administrative and professional positions in Assam when Bengali was introduced as the language of instruction in the province. In the Census of 1891, it was estimated that one-fourth of the population of the Brahmaputra Valley was of migrant origin.

36. Letter from L. J. Kershaw, Secretary to the Chief Commissioner of Assam, to the Secretary to the Government of India, 5 June 1905, Shillong, Revenue A, June 1905, File nos 176–78, ASP.
37. Letter from the Secretary to the Chief Commissioner of Assam to the Commissioner of Assam, 27 Feb. 1905, Revenue A, Mar. 1905, File nos 6–8, ASP.
38. 'Chapar Estate Report' (Laine 1917: 102).
39. Letter to the Chief Commissioner of Assam from F. J. Monahan, General Department, Revenue A, June 1905, File nos 176–78, ASP.
40. Copy of notes recorded by P. G. Melitus, 25 May 1909, Commissioner's Conference, 1909, Revenue A, Feb. 1913, File nos 6–9, File no. IIT/R, 1913, OIOC, London.
41. Quoted in the Census of India 1921; (Assam: 40).
42. Commissioner's Conference, 1909, Revenue A, Feb. 1913, File nos 6–9, File no. IIT/R, 1913, OIOC, London.
43. For a detailed analysis of the material conditions in Eastern Bengal which led to the immigration of cultivators to Goalpara and the rest of Assam, see Bose (1986).
44. The settlement officer also reported that 'cultivation had almost reached its full limits' in the district of Mymensingh (Sachse 1919: 29).
45. The most spectacular rise was recorded in the western parts of the district, where the thanas of South Salamara, Lakhipur and Bilasipur showed an increase of 70.15 per cent, 61.81 per cent and 38.65 per cent in the population, respectively.
46. The net variation in population in the district between 1872 and 1921 was +96.8 per cent (Census of India 1921; Assam, Subsidiary Table IV).
47. For variation of population in Goalpara between 1872 and 1921, see Table 3.1 in this chapter.
48. Mullan in (Census of India 1931, Assam: 49).
49. 'The jotedari system has spread in this district,' remarked R. Friel (1914: 5). 'These jotedars are practically middlemen and the zamindars are thus saved the trouble of dealing directly with the innumerable cultivators, who can only get their land from the jotedaars'.
50. Note from the Chief Commissioner of Assam, Revenue A, June 1927, File nos 24–28, ASP.
51. (Evidence of the Assam Provincial Banking Enquiry Committee 1930: 478).
52. 'Bijni Estate Report' (Laine 1917: 36).
53. 'Mechpara Estate Report', in Laine 1917: 75. The figures of those who drew their income from rent of agricultural land rose from 52,571 in 1901 to 106,781 in 1921.
54. Resolution on the Land Revenue Administration of Assam for the year 1914–15, p. 3, State Archives, Guwahati. Colonial officials writing in the late 1920s calculated an increase of 700 per cent in the

settled years during the previous 20 years in the neighbouring district of Kamrup (*Report of the Assam Provincial Banking Enquiry Committee 1930*: 23).

55. For the statistics of the area settled by immigrants between 1914 and 1935, see Table 3.2 in this chapter.
56. 'Report of the Deputy Commissioner of Kamrup' in the (Census of India 1921, Assam: 40).
57. 'Report of the Deputy Commissioner of Nowgong', in the (Census of India 1921, Assam: 40).
58. Report on the Land Revenue Administration of Eastern Bengal and Assam, 1908–9, p. 3, State Archives, Guwahati.
59. (*Evidence of the Assam Banking Enquiry Committee 1930*: 446).
60. Locally, jute was called 'Pat', 'Pata', 'Koshta'and 'Kankhura' (Kerr 1874: 5)
61. In 1874, Goalpara had an area of 15,000 acres of a total arable area of 2,769,280 acres under jute cultivation. This area yielded more than 225,000 maunds of jute in 1872 as against the high yield of 1,260,000 maunds from Mymensingh. It was, however, far higher than the production figures of jute from the neighbouring Assam districts of Kamrup and Darrang: 4,650 and 2,790 maunds of jute respectively (ibid.: 65).
62. Kerr's report quotes the following observation of Shoar Nysho of Teamari in Goalpara: 'Within the last seven or eight years, the people in our part of the district have taken to the cultivation of jute on a large scale. Before that, small quantities were raised by us for local consumption' (ibid.: xliv).
63. There was a trade in local products including mustard seeds, which were being bought by traders from lower Assam trading centres like Sualkuchi and Barpeta.
64. By 1873, the firm of Jyth Mull Dhunraj had already been trading in jute and other items in Gauripur for over two decades. All these firms exported jute to the markets of Serajgunj, where it was sold as 'Gouripore paat' (Kerr 1874: xliii).
65. A term used in Goalpara for traders from Eastern Bengal.
66. F. C. Monahan, Director of Land Records and Agriculture, to the Secretary to the Chief Commissioner of Assam, 7 Feb. 1898, File no. 814, Revenue A, ASP.
67. Ibid.
68. Report on the Administration of Land Revenue in Assam, 1907–1908, State Archives, Guwahati. p. 1.
69. Ibid.
70. (*Evidence of the Assam Banking Enquiry Committee 1930*: 478).
71. Census of India, 1921; Assam: Subsidiary Table 1. The figures of 1921 for the cultivation of jute were an increase from 1911, when it was

grown on 6 per cent of the total cultivated area (Census of India 1911; Assam: 4).

72. Previously jute from Goalpara 'was taken in steamers ... to Calcutta at a charge of 9 annas to 12 annas a maund' (Kerr 1874: xliii). Jute was also sent to Serajgunge in 'Bengali boats' (ibid.: xliv).

73. The Buchanan Hamilton Papers, Book II, Mss. Eur. D 75, OIOC, London.

74. *(Report of the Assam Provincial Banking Enquiry Committee 1930: 2).*

75. 'We deal in jute. Either we buy it for cash or make advances to ryots to cultivate it for us. When making the advances, we sometimes fix the price at which the jute is to be delivered' (Kerr 1874: xlvii). 'About one-eighth of last season's produce still remains unsold with the mahajuns and the paikars, but none of it is in the hands of the actual growers' (ibid.: xliii).

76. Report of the Diwan of Bijni on the allegations made by certain tenants at pargana Habraghat and Dihi Botiamari, Revenue A, Sep. 1913, ASP.

77. Ibid., p. 36.

78. Mullan in (Census of India 1931, Assam: 15).

79. Resolution on the Land Revenue Administration of Assam for the year 1933–34, p. 2, State Archives, Guwahati.

80. Assam Legislative Council Debates, 7–9 Mar. 1929, V/9/1367, OIOC.

81. Report of the Diwan of Bijni on the allegations made by certain tenants at pargana Habraghat and Dihi Botiamari, Revenue A, Sep. 1913, ASP.

82. Note from the Chief Commissioner of Assam, Revenue A, Sep. 1915, ASP.

83. Ibid.

84. Copy of notes recorded by H. Savage, 22 Apr. 1909, Commissioner's Conference, 1909, in Revenue A, Feb. 1913, File nos 6–9, File no. IIT/R, 1913, OIOC, London.

85. Petition from certain raiyats of the Bijni estate, 1912 (Laine 1917b: 23).

86. Petition from certain raiyats of the Bijni estate complaining of certain matters in connection with the management of the estate, Revenue A, Sep. 1913, ASP.

87. Ibid. Several similar petitions were given to the Diwan of Bijni during his tour of the estate in the preceding year, including one signed by 500 tenants, dated 3 Nov. 1912, Revenue A, Sep. 1913, ASP.

88. Petition dated 20 Jan 1913 from Thanda Ram Das, Kali Ram Das, and others of Bajitpara and Batiamari, pargana Khuntaghat, Goalpara, in Revenue A, Sep. 1913, ASP.

89. 'Petition from tenants of Parbatjoar, headed by Kali Charan Brahmo' (Laine 1917: 25). There were at least five more such memorials

submitted from the estate of Gauripur alone stating similar demands. between 1913 and 1914.

90. There was a decline in the productive capacity of the soil in areas other than the chars settlements, with a bigha of land producing three maunds of paddy during this period, instead of the previous five maunds (Evidence of D. C. Chakravarty, Dewan of Gauripur Estate, in the Evidence of the Assam Provincial Banking Enquiry Committee 1930: 431). The continuing burden of abwabs along with the increased rent, however, would have left the peasantry with little means to initiate improvements in agriculture.

91. (Evidence of the Assam Provincial Banking Enquiry Committee 1930: 444).

92. Evidence of Maulavi Osman Ali Sarkar, an immigrant from eastern Bengal who settled in the district of Nowgong in Assam, in Evidence of the Assam Provincial Banking Enquiry Committee 1930: 360. In their evidence to the committee, several moneylenders stated that their business was more with the 'Mymensinghia people than with the local people' (Evidence of the Assam Provincial Banking Enquiry Committee 1930: 438).

93. The Report of the Assam Provincial Banking Enquiry Committee, 1929–30, stated that 'many of the Mymensinghia settlers are more prosperous than in other districts higher up the valley as they have been settled here for a longer time' (p. 25). The evidence in this report also frequently suggested that the immigrant cultivators from eastern Bengal were 'materially better off' than the local tenants. 'The Mymensinghias spend much on food and live well … unlike the Assamese, who are idle'. (Evidence of D.C. Chakravarty, Dewan of Gauripur Estate, in the Evidence of the Assam Provincial Banking Enquiry Committee 1930: 434).

94. Resolution on the Land Revenue Administration of Assam for the year 1927–28, State Archives, Guwahati, p. 3.

95. Copy of notes recorded by H. Savage, 22 Apr. 1909, Commissioner's Conference, 1909, in Revenue A, Feb. 1913, File nos 6–9, File no. IIT/R, 1913, OIOC, London. There was a sharp increase in the number of ejectment suits instituted against the under–tenant by the jotedars and the zamindars: 42 in 1911, 64 in 1912 and 80 in 1913 (Laine 1917: 27).

96. (Report of the Assam Provincial Banking Enquiry Committee 1930: 6).

97. 'There are touts and speculators whose business it is to buy land and sell them again at a profit. We did our best to introduce provisions in the Rent Law by which non-agricultural speculators may be kept out.' (Evidence of D. C. Chakravarty, Dewan of Gauripur Estate, in the Evidence of the Assam Provincial Banking Enquiry Committee 1930: 430).

98. Evidence of Jagannath Bujar Baruah, in the (Evidence of the Assam Provincial Banking Enquiry Committee 1930: 478).

99. In the legislative assembly debates of 24 Mar. 1924, for instance, a member pointed out that 'more than 150 houses of the Mymensingh settlers at Leptamari grazing reserve in mauza Bishwanath were set on fire to by the orders of the Deputy Commissioner, Darrang' (Assam Legislative Council Debates, 24 Mar. 1924, V/9/1358, OIOC).

100. Partha Chatterjee terms this 'a rationalisation of [the colonial state's] policies into a faith in the capacity of small peasants ... to evolve the most efficient organization of production', in his essay 'Agrarian Structure in pre-partition Bengal' in Sen, Chatterjee and Mukherjee (1982: 115). For more on the intellectual roots of the concept of the 'original raiyat', see Robb (1997: 195–200).

101. Copy of notes recorded by P. G. Melitus, 25 May 1909, Commissioner's Conference, 1909, in Revenue A, Feb. 1913, File nos 6–9, File no. IIT/R, 1913, OIOC, London.

102. F. C. Monahan's report, No. 1503, R & F, May 1907, in the Commissioner's Conference 1909, Proceedings and Connected Papers, Eastern Bengal and Assam, Revenue A, Feb. 1913, OIOC, London.

103. Copy of notes recorded by H. Savage, 22 Apr. 1909, Commissioner's Conference, 1909, in Revenue A, Feb. 1913, File nos 6–9, File no. IIT/R, 1913, OIOC, London.

104. 'Report of the Gauripur Estate', in Laine (1917: 49).

105. Revenue A, June 1927, File nos 24–28, ASP.

106. Revenue A, Nov. 1917, File nos 42–44, ASP.

107. 'Chapar Estate Report', in Laine (1917).

108. Report of the Diwan of Bijni on the allegations made by certain tenants at pargana Habraghat and Dihi Botiamari, Revenue A, Sep. 1913, ASP.

109. W. J. Reid, in the Proceedings of the Assam Legislative Council, 29 Mar. 1922, V/9/1357, OIOC.

110. In a letter to the Chief Secretary of the Government of Assam, the President of the Sanmilani warned that 'such an Act would surely cause grave discontent among the tenants' (Revenue A, Nov. 1922, ASP).

111. Suit Dh Muns 229, Oct. 1915, Dhubri Munsif's records. There was also an increased registration of the transfer of land holdings during this period, indicative of the ability of landlords to couch their control in the new legal language. The number of sales registered in Dhubri, for instance, rose from 347 in 1907 to 957 in 1916 (Laine 1917: 25).

112. This was the Garo and Mech reserve with an area of 30.7 square miles and set up in the Alipur subdivision in 1895 (Monahan 1910: 24).

113. A movement of Bodo–Kachari villagers against begar in the forested areas under the leadership of Pratap Chandra Brahmo in 1921 elicited some support from the local workers of the Indian National Congress as well (Guha 2000: 68).
114. Memorial dated 8 Feb. 1905, reprinted in a letter from the Chief Secretary of the Government of India to the Chief Secretary of Eastern Bengal and Assam, 20 Mar. 1908, Revenue A, OIOC, London.
115. Memorial of Sonaram Sangma and others to the Chief Commissioner of Assam, 13 Dec. 1904. Reprinted as Appendix IV (Barman 1994).
116. These were the common concerns of most petitions from Garo and Mech cultivators from the forested Duar area of Goalpara during this period. The above quote is from the Petition of Mangal Singh and other Garo Raiyats of the Bijni Raj, submitted to the Chief Commissioner of Assam on 12 May, 1916, Revenue A, 1929, OIOC, London.
117. Judgement in the Court of Sessions Judge of the Assam Valley Districts, 13 May 1920, Order sheet for Magistrate's Records, Dhubri Collectorate.
118. King Emperor v Guman Singh Garo, Case no. 77, Section 411, I.P.C., Order sheet for Magistrate's Records, Dhubri Collectorate, Dhubri.
119. Correspondence between the Chief Secretary of the Government of India and the Chief Secretary of Eastern Bengal and Assam, 20 Mar. 1908, Revenue A, OIOC, London.
120. Judgement in the Court of Sessions Judge of the Assam Valley Districts, 13 May 1920, Order sheet for Magistrate's Records, Dhubri Collectorate.
121. (Report of the Assam Provincial Banking Enquiry Committee 1930: 27).
122. 'The Gauripur Estate Report', in (Laine 1917: 55).
123. (Report of the Assam Provincial Banking Enquiry Committee 1930: 27).
124. The Gauripur Estate Report defined a jotedar as a tenant who was 'bound by contract, with no occupancy rights, and liable to enhancement of rent after the expiry of his temporary lease' ('The Gauripur Estate Report' in (Laine 1917: 48).
125. Appeal No. 316 of 1918, in The All India Reporter, Calcutta, 1918, p. 76.
126. 'Petitions from certain raiyats of the Bijni estate', Revenue A, Sep. 1913, ASP.
127. 'Memorial of the tenants of Goalpara', submitted to the Chief Commissioner of Assam, 16 Sep. 1919, Revenue A, Dec. 1919, ASP.
128. Letter to the Chief Commissioner of Assam from F. J. Monahan, General Department, Revenue A, June 1905, File nos 176–78, ASP.
129. Ibid.

130. Brajendra Narayan Chaudhuri in the Debate on the Goalpara Tenancy Bill 1927, 20 July 1927, Assam Legislative Council Debates, V/9/1364, OIOC.

131. 'It is not that I am opposed to the principle of the settled raiyat but to me it appears that the present undeveloped condition of the district is most unsuitable for the immediate application of this principle, specially in those areas under the Bijni Raj, under the Court of Wards, where a system of cultivation known as uthit patit, or karari ashu mahals prevails ... under this system a tenant cultivates a parcel of land one year, then abandons and takes up another plot the second year ... The concept of a settled raiyat introduced by Laine and his committee in the hope that the principle will not come into immediate operation but it will take some time to define a village, to survey and prepare a record of rights under the authority of the Government after which the principle will have its application.' (Promothesh Chandra Barua in the debate on the Consideration of the Goalpara Tenancy Bill, 1927 as amended by the Select Committee, 4 March 1929, Assam Legislative Council Debates, V/9/1367, OIOC).

132. Rohini Kumar Chaudhuri in the Debate on the Goalpara Tenancy Bill 1927, 20 July 1927, Assam Legislative Council Debates, V/9/1364, OIOC.

4

❂

Framing a Region: Politics of Speech in a Borderland

This chapter looks at some of the connections between speech, political culture and economy in Goalpara. It focuses on the tensions involved in the relocation of boundaries of language and the construction of linguistic autonomy in a region that was by the second decades of the twentieth century, emerging as a significant locale for the cultural production of a borderland identity. This was marked by a hyphenated existence between proto-Bengal and proto-Assam. Because this production was frequently in contestation with the standardisation of language that was promoted by Assamese nationalist imaginations, the chapter discusses the debates between the proponents of the more 'fixed' narratives of Assamese, and those struggling to ascribe fixity to the more fluid speech practices of the borderland. This is the subject of the first section of the chapter. It anticipates the agenda of the next section which examines the instability of this narrative, through an analysis of other stories of speech practices and histories of language and literature from Goalpara, as also from parts of eastern and northern Bengal that bordered it, and the district of Kamrup. The last section focuses on two sites around which the politics of speech came to be centred in Goalpara and Assam: the census, and the practice of 'local option' during the 1920s and the 1930s. The former was an exposition of the new links between the politics of community and the colonial project of classification in Goalpara and the rest of Assam during this period. The latter, exercised through a stream of letters and petitions to local authorities, with frequently the village headman as their signatory, was an illustration of the exceptionalism that often tended to characterise colonial governmentality in perceived 'transitional' zones such as these.

Producing the Assamese Language

The politics of Assamese linguistic nationalism of the late nineteenth and early twentieth century relied on the ability of the local intelligentsia to negotiate sufficiently with the project of colonial cultural production and to coalesce its interests into a social class. The determining of the boundaries of the Assamese language saw the emergence of vernacular textual production as the primary site of conflict in a contest that was marked for the exclusion of other counter discourses from the region by this intelligentsia. An expanding vernacular sphere, though rather circumscribed by the rule of colonial difference, had come to exist with the introduction of education through the vernacular and the spread of print capitalism.

Printing presses were initially set up as an adjunct of Christian proselytisation in the Sibsagar district of Upper Assam[1] but the publication of the first Bibles and other religious tracts in Assamese were soon followed by several elementary texts, a dictionary and a grammar (Misra 1987: 67).[2] The philological enterprise of the state helped 'discover' the roots and standard structures of the Assamese language. A resolution passed in 1873 introduced Assamese as the official vernacular and stated that 'the facts and memorials of the past few years have shown that the Assamese language is still the vernacular of the people. No amount of argument about derivative affinity can get over the fact clearly testified to, and nowhere really contradicted, that the people of Assam do not understand Bengali'.[3] This was preceded by a period of agitation which saw the formation of the Assamese Literary Society in 1872 and the Asomiya Bhasa Unnati Sadhini Sabha in 1888. These organisations, both of which were in Calcutta, helped institutionalise the language. The project of a colonial education in Assamese gave a new territorial fixation to the imagined vernacular linguistic community. The spread of printing was accompanied by a growth in vernacular prose, indicating that the emerging intelligentsia consciously emulated and appropriated the standardised Assamese and chose it as their primary media for imaginative expression.[4] Located between the language of 'high' culture and the several dialects spoken in the Brahmaputra Valley, vernacular Assamese print emerged as the most potent symbol for forging regional identities in the region.[5]

Early twentieth century linguistic nationalism in the region required that for the boundaries of the vernacular of the province of Assam to be fixed, its relationship with local history should be constructed as a continuous process. The new vernacular had to be given a 'suitable ancestry' and the new Assamese nation, an unruptured continuity. Some of the earliest references to the language were claimed to have been found in the travel writings of Hieun Tsang who visited the region in the seventh century AD and had described Assamese as 'a separate and distinct language, similar to the those of Madhya Bharat' (Bezbaroa 1910c: 172). Lakshminath Bezbaroa[6] dated the earliest books in the language to 1000 AD, cautioning the reading public that 'out there were still many old *puthis*, heirlooms in families treasured with care but decaying and rapidly becoming illegible awaiting deciphering and publication' (Bezbaroa 1910a: 286).

Like several other writers in Assamese, Bezbaroa too found the roots of the Assamese literature and language in the religio–cultural traditions of the region, with the legacy extending at least to the sixteenth and seventeenth centuries and hence inextricably linked to the growth of the Vaishanava religious tradition under Sankardev. Bezbaroa saw this period of literary activity in Assam as one which was 'synchronous with a similar period in Bengal ... [for] in both countries the religious effects were identical. Sankardev however had of necessity to compromise with the instincts of his followers and so arose the Mahapurushis sect whose sacred seat is Barpeta [bordering Goalpara]' (ibid.). 'In both Vaishnavite sects', he pointed out, 'we find that the literature takes the same form — the translation of sacred books and the writing of hymns' (ibid.: 285). The representation of Assamese as a language of popular communication as against Sanskrit, indicating parallels with the teachings of the reformed Vaishnava religion as against classical Hinduism, allowed for its historical continuity as well as a certain dignity. The claim that Sankardev had used Assamese instead of Sanskrit for spreading his message among the people [leading to] the composition of texts, songs, recitation of the *Bhagavad* and the *Mahabharat* appeared frequently in several writings from the period (Bordoloi 1925: 21).[7]

The redrawing of historical frontiers then was a necessary requisite for the production of a political community around the notion of language and linguistic pride. Several of what had been claimed as ancient Assamese texts, including some of Sankardev's early compositions, were traced to the court of the Naranarayan, the Koch ruler who ruled over a kingdom that in the sixteenth century straddled the colonial districts of Jalpaiguri, Rangpur and the kingdom of Cooch Behar. The boundaries of this kingdom were believed to have roughly coincided with those of the ancient kingdom of Kamarupa. This region was now identified as the repository of ancient Assamese language and literature. 'The Assamese will always hold Cooch Behar in high regard. It is, after all, the place of origin of our language. Our earliest texts were composed there', stated Benudhar Rajkhowa in his address to the Assam Sahitya Sabha in 1913 (Hazarika and Goswami 1955, 1957: 211). Several of the editorials in the Assamese newspapers and periodicals of the period expressed similar views. Others credited Naranarayan with the patronage of Sankardev and of the Assamese language and with having 'arranged for the translation of several Sanskrit texts to the *desiya bhasa*'.[8]

The shifting of historical boundaries meant that most of northern Bengal and parts of eastern Bengal could now be appropriated within the new historical past of the Assamese language. Resisting similar appropriations of this border area by the narrative of Bengali nationalism, Assam's nationalists emphasised on its historically shared elements with Assamese (Bezbaroa 1910c: 174). Reflecting a strand within Assamese nationalist thought during this period, which argued for an extension of Assam's contemporary political boundaries to create a 'Greater Assam', by including the Bengal districts of Jalpaiguri, Rangpur, Dinajpur and Cooch Behar, Gyananath Bora suggested that:

> as a part of the ancient kingdom of Kamrup, Jalpaiguri is of Kamrup and its language is Kamrupia, that is Assamese. Rajbanshi, the language of this area, has transformed over time into Assamese ... although our Kamrup does not exist anymore, its culture and language live on in these districts of north Bengal (Bora 1932: 258).

The idea of a 'Greater Assam' captured the imagination of nationalist historians and Assamese scholars alike, extending into an argument in the early decades of the century of an administrative appropriation of parts of Bengal.[9]

The appropriation of the history and language of Goalpara within the expanding grand narrative of Assamese nationalism was thus a logical extension of the process of subsuming the old past of the region into the new past of the Assamese nation. In the imagined language map of the Assamese intelligentsia, the 'centre' or Upper Assam spoke chaste Assamese while the speech of Goalpara, at the peripheral frontiers, was represented as a pale imitation of the language of 'Assam proper'. The movement from the centre to the periphery appeared to suggest, therefore, a different value along with a difference in form. Along with this was an acceptance of the idea that national identity at the borderlands tended to be diluted. Thus it was acknowledged that 'Goalpara's Assamese language is mixed with Bengali to a certain extent, a phenomenon common to languages in frontier and marginal areas ... where certain sections of the population do not even know whether their mother tongue is Assamese or Bengali' (Bezbaroa 1910a: 350). Like Goalpara, Cooch Behar was another *bhati* area,[10] the language of which had been similarly influenced and appropriated by the neighbouring Bengali language (ibid.: 367). The linguistic situation in these areas was explained by the historical occupation of the region by Bengalis.[11] As Bezbaroa argued, 'in reality it is difficult to deny that the language of Goalpara is Assamese, although a little corrupt and twisted' (ibid.: 350).

Inherent to the standardisation of a vernacular was the idea of an authentic and pure language and the recognition of a hierarchical relationship between a 'standard language' and a set of dialects. Ideally, such a language had to be 'geographically centred and socially hierarchical',[12] a condition well brought out by Bezbaroa: 'Under the availability of suitable conditions, the local dialect of a particular place might become strong enough to establish its dominance over other contemporary dialects ... transforming a dialect into a language' (Bezbaroa 1910d: 44).[13] Accordingly, the privileging of the dialect of Sibsagar, which was closer to the print language was defended as 'the adoption of the language of the historic capital city of the Ahom kings ... it was an established fact that the language of the capital becomes the language of the entire kingdom' (ibid.: 45). Implicit in the process of standardisation was also the concept of an infinite refinement of literary styles and a suggestion of increasing social difference:

'the Assamese language [was] not the language of either Upper or Bhati Assam. [It was the language] in which Sankar and Madhav had composed their texts, the language in which the upper classes speak' (Bezbaroa 1910d: 43).

Lodged in the democratising aspects of print were therefore inequalities of a different kind, for standardisation clearly differentiated dialects from a 'high' language. In Goalpara, these inequalities were more pronounced also on account of the geographical proximity of Namani (Bhati) to the northern districts of Bengal which allowed its residents a greater degree of mutual accommodation in speech than the people staying in Ujani. This became increasingly suspect in the new discourse of language activism in Assam as several Bengali nationalist scholars made concerted efforts to define a 'Greater Bengali' identity inclusive of the administrative divisions of Orissa, Assam and eastern Bihar' (Kar 2008: 55). As Bezbaroa put it, 'The people of bhati are welcome to speak their dialects at home. It is an expression of their love for their birthplace. But Assamese is the public property of the entire Assamese community and its best to keep differences aside' (Bezbaroa 1910d: 43).

There were protests through the late nineteenth and early twentieth century against what was clearly perceived as a deliberate choice of the language of Upper Assam as the criterion of modern Assamese identity. A petition signed by the 'people of Lower Assam' in May 1872 questioned 'the designation of the language of Upper Assam as the Assamese language ... a dialect spoken only by a small portion of the population of Assam, [and] altogether unimportant and meagre and its capabilities and chances to make itself the language of the entire district ... extremely limited'.[14] Equating the levels of comprehension of the 'Upper Assam patois' with that of Bengali, for the people of Lower Assam, the petitioners focused on the richness of the language and literature of the region. They argued that 'though presumptuously stigmatised by the Upper Assam people as provincial *dhekeri* the language of Lower Assam, on the contrary, does manifest a remarkable and marked superiority in this respect over its rival, as the large majority of written works, and all the most approved publications, together with the sacred and religious writings of the people of Assam, are found to have been composed in it'.[15] The petition dismissed the publications from the Baptist Missionary press at Sibsagar as 'a highly objectionable dictionary and one or two flimsy grammatical primers'.[16]

In the beginning of the twentieth century, resistance to standardisation was primarily articulated within the pages of the several periodicals and newspapers that reflected the growing print culture in the province. Of these, the journal edited by Taranath Chakravarty and Pratap Chandra Goswami, *Assam Bandhav*, was particularly significant for its propounding of the cause of the Kamrupia language.[17] In his memoirs, Goswami traced the idea of publishing the *Assam Bandhav* to increasing disapproval among sections of scholars from Lower Assam of the standardised form and style of Assamese prose which was marked by an absence of Kamrupia words.[18] Founded 'to create an understanding between the language of Upper Assam and that of Kamrup', the periodical engaged in a series of debates with the contributors of *Banhi* on issues of standardisation (Goswami 1971: 119).[19] The tenth volume of the *Assam Bandhav* carried a critique of contemporary Assamese grammar (Saikia 2000: 171) *Banhi* itself published several essays which questioned the emergence of this new language of power. In its emphasis on the need for an increased publication of books in the Kamrupia language, Bholanath Kakati's essay, for instance, was a conscious effort at encouraging the literature of Lower Assam (Kakati 1910).

Contesting Narratives and the Idea of the 'Goalparia'

At the turn of the nineteenth century, the pre-eminence of Goalpara's traditional elite, which consisted of the zamindars and other landed classes, and sustained by institutions of the colonial state, such as the Court of Wards, was being gradually replaced by a new middle class with better potential for political investment for the colonial state. The intelligentsia that emerged in towns such as Dhubri and Goalpara was a part of this class. Despite the steady erasure of the pre-colonial moral economy and their subordination to colonial institutional structures, the landed elite however demonstrated a remarkable ability to not just preserve what remained of their earlier sovereign powers but to also learn how to negotiate with these structures and ideologies. Of the several strategic choices that they made during this period, their involvement in the shaping of the new vernacular for Goalpara was of significance, for it allowed the local traditional elite to reinsert themselves as a social group into the political imagination of the early twentieth century. That their interests and upper caste social origins were shared by the new intelligentsia ensured that the debates over the boundaries of the vernacular in the borderland, while countering discourses of the state and of Assamese nationalism, remained an exclusionary one.

Reconstructing the linguistic unity of the borderland that was Goalpara, these writings almost invariably began with the story of a historical unity of the region. Goalpara was represented as part of a kingdom and ruled by dynasties with a political history that was independent of both the provinces of Assam and Bengal.[20] Based on this historical narrative of a politically unified entity, the local elite identified 'Rajbanshi bhasa' as the language of the region between the Sonkos and the Manas, the two rivers that were believed to have been the historical borders of a kingdom that included the districts of Rangpur, Cooch Behar and Goalpara (Shastri 1930: 8). The territorial location of Rajbanshi is continuously reiterated in several writings and was obviously central to the imagining of some form of lingual autonomy of the region. 'We speak Rajbanshi, which is a distinct language of this region and we need to work for its greater spread and usage', asserted Prabhat Chandra Barua, the zamindar of Gauripur estate, in his address to a meeting of the Goalpara District Association (Barua 1928: 10). In an essay on indigenous music traditions in a collection believed to have been written in the early 1930s, Nihar Barua, the daughter of the then zamindar of Gauripur, began by firmly locating Rajbanshi as the language of this region:[21] 'This area has its own geographical and historical distinctiveness and despite being administratively amalgamated into Assam these hundred years, it still retains its links with the Rajbanshi language and culture. For generations, the spoken language of both Hindus and Muslims in this region has been Rajbanshi' (Barua 2000: 57). 'The people of Cooch Behar, where it continues to be the spoken language of the majority of its population, have given this language respectability', wrote Barua, while also identifying certain genres of music composed in Rajbanshi and citing these as evidence of it being a living language of Goalpara and northern Bengal (ibid.).

That these speech practices of the frontier were represented as the vestiges of the now more modern forms of vernacular being imagined for Assam and Bengal, was a matter of great resentment in Goalpara. In his response to the assertion of Dineshchandra Sen, the author of *Bangabhasha O Sahitya*, 'a historical account of Bengali language and literature that fuelled much of the nationalist–expansionist fantasy of a "Greater Bengali" identity in the first decades of the twentieth century,' (Kar 2008: 64) that the language of a recently recovered local text was from Chattagram in Bengal, Gaurinath Shastri, the Dewan of the Gauripur Raj asserted, 'We live in a place that is at a long distance away from Chattagram. Unlike Dinesh Babu, therefore, we do not find the language complex. This is because the language of the text is Rajbansi, the language spoken in Rangpur, Cooch Behar and Goalpara' (Shastri 1930: 8). Shastri continued: 'Dinesh Babu discovered three Pargali Mahabharatas, one written 204 years ago, another 200 years ago and the third written 250 years ago. We have not had the chance to read these texts, but from the sections of the texts that have been reproduced in his *Bangabhasha O Sahitya*, we have seen and understood that these are all texts of this region, written in Rajbanshi, although certain regional variations may have crept in' (ibid.: 9).

The debate was centered on the possible date of composition of the recovered text, the *Kabindra Mahabharat*, and had import-ant implications for Rajbanshi's claims to antiquity. Predictably, the proponents of this vernacular claimed that the earliest texts in Rajbanshi could be dated to the eighth century AD unlike those written in the dialect of Chattagram (Shastri 1930:13). Such claims were strengthened by the strategic appropriation of Ananta Kandali's *Ramayan*, a seventeenth century text identified by the Assamese nationalists as an essential part of their historical past, and of its author as a poet in the court of Naranarayan.[22] The most significant appropriation, however, for the incredulity that it evoked among Assamese linguistic nationalists, was the claiming of the vast literature produced by the Vaishnava reformers, Sankardev and Madhavdev as 'Goalparia'. 'These great thinkers have written all their great works in the language of Goalpara' asserted Prabhat Chandra Barua, whose role in the recovery and preservation of these 'jewels' of local literature was frequently appreciated (Barua 1928: 9).

In this situating of Rajbanshi, and thereby, a questioning of the validity of the linguistic boundaries drawn by the colonial state and by Assamese nationalist ideology, Goalpara's traditional elite could draw upon George Grierson's idea of languages, not just as contained entities within demarcated geographically areas, but also as speech practices that tended to change slowly and imperceptibly over distances. The detailed defence of the distinctiveness of the language of the *Kabindra Mahabharat*, for instance, ends with a citing of Grierson's *Linguistic Survey of India* as the authority (Shastri 1930: 16). Grierson's survey had defined Rajbanshi as a 'well marked dialect ... spoken in the country to the northeast of that in which Northern Bengali is spoken', and extending 'into the Goalpara district of Assam, in which it gradually merges into Assamese' (Grierson 1903: 166). As with other languages in his survey, Grierson's method also located, counted and represented the speakers of Rajbanshi on statistical charts.[23] He then identified with considerable precision the exact geographical boundaries of its territory:

> The dialect is not confined to the Bengal Province ... [i]t is the language of the west and the southwest of the [Goalpara] district. To the south it is stopped by the Tibeto Burman language of the Garo Hills. In Bengal, it is bounded on the east by the Brahmaputra, with the Garo Hills on the opposite side. In its extreme southeast corner, it just touches the Eastern Bengali of Maimansingh, also across the river. On the south and the west, it is bounded by the northern Bengali and on the north by the Tibeto Burman languages of the Lower Himalayas. It is spoken in the following districts: Rangpur, Jalpaiguri, the Tarai of the Darjeeling district, the Native State of Cooch Behar, together with the portion of Goalpara already mentioned (Grierson 1903: 163).

In the 1920s and the 1930s, Grierson's findings were extended to defend the objectives and location of several of the literary meetings and conventions that were held in Goalpara, primarily through the initiative of the zamindar of Gauripur, Raja Prabhat Chandra Barua. These included several sessions of the Uttar Banga Sahitya Sanmilan, held at Gauripur, and at Kamakshyadham in the Kamrup district (Goswami 1971: 121). Severely criticised in Assamese newspapers for what was seen as a courting of Bengali, around which nationalists had constructed an elaborate theory of 'otherness',[24] these literary meets were significant for their expressions of linguistic pride and ideas of shared, connected histories, in this context across Goalpara and northern Bengal. 'Our objective is to revive the language of this region and restore its lost pride' stated the President of the fifth session of the Uttar

Banga Sahitya Sanmilan. He then went on to evoke a collective historical consciousness, institutionalised in the Kamrup Anusandhan Samiti which had been formed with the explicit purpose of 'recovering the lost history' of the region (Uttar Banga Sahitya Sanmilan 1917: 50).

The territorial fixation of Rajbanshi was accompanied by a few scattered arguments about the distinctive structure of the language and the evolutionary nature of its grammar. Gaurinath Shastri, for example, attempted to demonstrate the distinctiveness of Goalpara's language through an exercise that involved comparing some representative specimens of sentences in Rajbanshi with Assamese and Bengali (Shastri 1928: 18). The preface to the *Kabindra Mahabharat* also traced a few grammatical differences between Rajbanshi and Bengali (Shastri 1930: 18). These attempts however remained rather unconvincing and despite the writings from Goalpara attempting to follow the standardised conventions of constructing speech into language, it was clear that the autonomy of Rajbanshi was to be found not so much in its formal linguistic structure, but in its territorial identification as the language of a region.

The production of a sense of political community around the Assamese language was therefore accompanied by a redrawing of the frontiers of speech by Goalpara's traditional elite and sections of its emerging middle class. That Rajbanshi itself was spoken over an area that transcended colonial and later, nationalist cultural and political borders, added to the history of cultural liminality in the region while rendering language ineffective as a crucial marker of Assamese identity. Table 4.1 below indicates the numbers of Rajbanshi speakers in the early twentieth century, in Assam and Bengal. Indicative also was a reinvention of the roles by the traditional elite, visible in their abandoning of the old language of protection, loyalty and kinship and their adoption instead of the new vernacular public space for expressions of a new collective self. These expressions of a separate linguistic identity also raised uncomfortable questions about the production of vernaculars through social practices as against the essentialisation of linguistic categories within the discourse of Assamese nationalism. In the second decade of the twentieth century these arguments also extended into demands for a politically autonomous area consisting of parts of northern Bengal and Goalpara and marked

Table 4.1
Figures of Rajbanshi speakers in the early twentieth century

Jalpaiguri	568,976
Rangpur	2,037,460
Cooch Behar (native state)	562,500
Darjeeling (Bahe sub-dialect)	47,435
Total for Bengal	3,216,371
Goalpara	292,800
Total for Assam	292,800
Grand Total	3,509,171

Source: Grierson (1903: 163).

by its fluidity and heterogeneity: 'We have never been either Assamese or Bengali. They are both our neighbours. Who are we? We are neither of the two. We are we. We are the people of this area. We are Goalparia … we are distinct and so is our culture, customs and traditions' (Shastri 1928: 33). Shastri also argued that several cultural elements, including the cuisine, attire and social norms, were illustrative of this distinctive borderland identity and could be used to evoke a new people (ibid.: 32–38). 'Our district has become the victim of "political football"', mourned Prabhat Chandra Barua. 'We have been forced to accept as our mother tongue the languages of those communities which have scored a goal' (Barua 1926: 7).

Both Shastri and Baruah were influential members of the landed gentry, the social class which dominated the debates in Goalpara over the construction of a vernacular for Assam and the reshaping of political imaginations. Through much of the early decades of the century, Goalpara's zamindars continued to be the best organised and effective of collectivities in the district, with several organisations continuing to favour their interests until the end of colonial rule. That this class could also claim to be representative of local society implied that 'the colonial public sphere could yield a relatively homogenous discourse with potentially hegemonic dimensions, not necessarily through processes of discussion and accommodation, but more on account of the virtual exclusion of subaltern counter-discourses from the domain of cultural production'(Naregal 2001: 45). This discourse of exclusion was underscored in the ways in which the tension over language came to be used to validate claims for land rights and legislative representation of the landed elite. In a letter to the government in 1912, Prabhat Chandra Barua used the history of shared speech practices of the region Goalpara and the contiguous Bengal districts of Jalpaiguri, Rangpur, Cooch Behar and Dinajpur, as a justification for the demands of local zamindars for a common tenancy law for the region.[25] These arguments were also used to support claims for separation of the permanently settled estates from Assam and their eventual assimilation into Bengal,[26] drawing upon an older discussion in official documents over the transfer of Goalpara to Bengal: 'The prayer [of a transfer to Bengal was] based on a community of feeling arising out of past history, traditions, ties, language, religion and land tenure — all of these being substantially similar to those governing the zamindars and people of the adjoining districts [of Bengal]'.[27] Another memorial expressed fears of 'being completely swamped by the Khas Mahal holders of the Assam Valley — a body with which they had nothing in common'.[28]

The debates in the legislative council resonated these concerns of the zamindars, including the formation of the permanently settled estates into a separate territorial unit transferable to Bengal. Their arguments were also illustrative of the ways in which claims about a necessary spatial overlap between the local culture and economy came to be framed in this region. Thus representatives from the region protested against 'the antipathy in the Assam Valley against the Goalpara landlords and those in that district who side with Bengali culture'.[29] In the several meetings of zamindars during this period, earlier anxieties with the lack of sufficient zamindari representation in the legislature were now linked to fears of 'a movement to foist the Assamese language on Goalpara'.[30] In a letter to the colonial government, the president of one such meeting asked: 'If it is absolutely necessary to keep us in Assam, can we not reasonably expect that the Rent Law in Goalpara should be the same as in Bengal and our language should not be in any way interfered with ...?'[31] The idea of Goalpara as the 'favourite hunting ground of the Assamese'[32] too found considerable support among members of local associations. Despite opposition from certain members, the Goalpara Association in 1918 passed a resolution which recommended in turn, that the Assam Association pass a resolution stating that 'Goalpara being mainly identical in race, language, social customs and system of land laws with Rangpur, Jalpaiguri and Cooch Behar, ... it [should] be placed under the same laws and administration with the [above] districts'.[33] Several petitions, one of which was signed by 6,863 signatories, cited 'close resemblance with the people of North Bengal' and 'a growing discontent with the introduction of Assamese' to explain the need 'to reunite the district with Bengal.'[34] Prabhat Chandra Barua, an important spokesperson of the movement, addressed himself to village headmen and tenants of Chapar and Bijni[35] and organised several public meetings in Goalpara's villages through the late 1920s and the 1930s against both the proposed Goalpara Tenancy Act and the introduction of Assamese.[36] In its edition of 28 October 1929, the *Amrit Bazar Patrika* reported that one such meeting of the All Goalpara District Conference had an estimated gathering of 'about 10,000 people, including 400 ladies, representing all classes of people and of all shades of opinion'.[37]

That the zamindars of Goalpara continued to exercise much hegemonic influence in the public space despite their declining political power was a matter of considerable concern for sections of the Assamese intelligentsia. This explains the tensions over the use of the tenancy debate as a site for the representation of the zamindar as the primordial provider and protector and hence as a powerful instrument of solidarity. Listing the several memorials that he had received from tenants in support of a new tenancy law, Nabin Chandra Bordoloi described Goalpara's landlords as 'those born with silver spoons in their mouths ... thriving at the expense of tenants and who live in Calcutta in the grandest style possible'.[38] The objectives of the *Prantobashi*, a weekly Bengali newspaper published from Dhubri with several zamindars as its patrons,[39] similarly, were 'not to fulfill the interests of the poor praja but to emphasise instead on the understanding between the king and his ministers'.[40] 'From the "kumar" title prefixed to the name of the editor, we know that he belongs to a zamindari family. The zamindars, who are mere puppets in the hands of the Bengali *amlas* and the Brahmans, Jotedars and Talukdars who are their loyalists, claim to be speakers of Bengali. The *Prantobashi* is a foreign Assamese newspaper ... a conspiracy of these rich sections'.[41]

Arguments about the distinctiveness of Goalpara's speech practices, including those shared with northern and eastern Bengal were reconstructed in the nationalist discourse from Assam as but another example of the inevitable zamindari genuflection towards the Bengali language. The zamindar of Gauripur, it was reminded, had been 'the President of the Assam Association ... [and] an Assamese [although] Bengali influence may in the meantime, have caused a change in his mentality and he wants to go to Bengal now'.[42] As the nationalist rhetoric from Assam moved to appropriate Goalpara within 'the immemoriably ancient community of the Assamese' revealing the extent to which the 'policing of the frontier speeches in extensive areas of Goalpara, Kamrup, Darrang and even Nagaon (had become) strategically crucial for the Assamese language activists' (Kar 2008: 55), it exhorted the people of these frontiers to recognise the zamindars as the Bengali 'other', responsible for the fraught linguistic situation in the region: 'I ask my Goalparia brothers! How long will it be before you are stopped being swayed by people with a foreign language ... and recognise instead the greatness of your civilisation and ancient pride? A few zamindars may wish to be Bengali. Why let their propaganda affect you?' appealed Lakshminath Bezbaroa in his address to the Dhubri session of the Assam Sahitya Sabha.[43]

Practices of Exception

The linguistic boundaries of Goalpara continued to be debated upon long after its political boundaries as a colonial district were firmly drawn. Late nineteenth century exchanges between officials described Goalpara as 'a debatable land', 'with respect to its language as well as its administration and physical aspect'. Apart from the several distinct communities with their separate languages, there were also 'a considerable number of pure Bengalis ... and the so-called Assamese, whose ethnological and philological relation with the Bengalis [was] so warmly disputed'.[44] Thus, the Resolution which had introduced Assamese as the official vernacular in 1874, advocated 'a policy of dichotomy for Goalpara' on the grounds that 'the people of the district had expressed their choice for both Bengali and Assamese'.[45] This policy was extended into the early twentieth century when J. B. Fuller decided in 1903 to discontinue Bengali as the language for teaching Assamese but accepted that Goalpara had to continue to be exempted from the order.[46] Several petitions favouring Bengali and counter petitions in support of Assamese had been submitted in the last decade of the nineteenth century and it is likely that Fuller's response was shaped by these inputs.[47]

Around this time, there are discussions in official correspondence about the impossibility of locating boundaries of intelligibility in an area, where one language shaded into another more starkly than it did elsewhere in the province of Assam, a situation that would have been rendered more complex by Goalpara's proximity to Bengal. For a more 'precise' definition of Goalpara's language, the state relied on Grierson's survey. However, his findings, while offering a definition of Rajbanshi as the dialect of western Goalpara and elaborating the colonial analysis of languages, also appreciated the existence of broad frontiers in languages, where one regionally dominant pattern of speech merged into another.[48] Grierson's analysis and findings informed the Census of 1901, which, like the preceding census, used language as a key indicator for determining identity. The emphasis on inscribing culture into legible spaces and categories meant however that the frontiers of speech had to be made to correspond to the recently fixed administrative boundaries of colonial units. The Census of 1901 had columns for the categories of Assamese, Bengali and other recognised languages. Rajbanshi was not returned, although Koch, also classified by Grierson as a dialect, was given a column in this and in later censuses as well.

Of significance is the extent to which the institutions and ideologies of the colonial state were produced in negotiation with local contexts. In his reply to a query in the legislative council in 1914, regarding the introduction of Assamese in the district, A. W. Botham described the issue to be as 'under consideration'.[49] In the same year, in an apparent acknowledgement of the impossibility of disciplining the speech practices of the district, the government order created a provision for the principle of 'local option'. The 'local option' allowed the villages of Goalpara to petition for or against the introduction of either Assamese or Bengali in the local schools.[50] Official records note that 'in 1914 ... an enquiry was made to ascertain what really was the vernacular of the district. It appeared that neither pure Assamese, as spoken in Central and Upper Assam, nor Bengali as spoken in Nadia, was the vernacular of the district ... in the eastern part, most of the people spoke a form of Assamese similar to that spoken in the adjoining district of Kamrup, while in the western portions, the dialect was closely akin to the Rajbanshi dialect of northern Bengal.'[51] Responding to the enquiry, the Chief Commissioner's order laid down that 'both languages should be taught, the choice in each case being in the hands of the majority of the inhabitants of each village … and the change from one language to another could only be brought about by an application from the majority of the villagers concerned'.[52] Later official correspondence noted that 'the deciding authority, although this was not expressly stated, was to be the Deputy Commissioner'.[53]

Over the next few decades, the principle of 'local option' emerged as a defining element in the colonial state's language policy in Goalpara. There is evidence of several petitions being filed by village headmen for changes in the local medium of instruction and records of the resultant changes. On 3 February 1914, a petition filed by the headman of the village of Hakma, near Bilasipara, asked for a substitution of Bengali by Assamese in the lower primary school. This was followed by a counter–petition which opposed the change and was signed by a greater number of signatories. Numerical majority being the deciding condition of the principle, the language of the school remained unaltered.[54] In response to a petition for the introduction of Assamese in another school in Bilasipara, however, the Deputy Inspector of Schools for Dhubri agreed to effect the necessary changes.[55] The language used in the petitions was a crucial element for reinforcing the arguments of its signatories. A petition from the village of Adalguri in Bijni in Assamese demanded the removal of Bengali on the grounds that 'although [Bengali] was prevalent for quite sometime in the region, our spoken language remains Assamese.'[56]

Several similar letters and petitions from different villages of Goalpara during this period reflected some of the ways in which the colonised found ways of not just circumventing, but also working with the projects of the state. Petitions for change were filed from Tipkai, Kamalsing, Binnakhata, Fakiragram, Lakhigang and Barkanda through the second decade of the century.[57] In Lakhigang and Barkanda, Bengali was reintroduced and teaching resumed with the help of teachers who had Bengali as the medium of instruction, 'although they also imparted instructions with the assistance of their own local terms'.[58] In Fakiragram, on the other hand, orders for the introduction of Assamese had to be revoked after 21 villagers signed a petition in favour of Bengali.[59] Colonial officials noted that the extract from the petition in the records was in Assamese, 'which indicated the home language in that locality'.[60]

Some of the petitions interrogated the political and intellectual leadership of the local elite and intelligentsia. As an example, the school at Tipkai, with a Middle Vernacular status, was started in 1914 for the Brahma and non-Brahma sects in the Bodo community. Through a series of petitions that resisted attempts by the traditional elite to appropriate them, the community pleaded for the introduction of Assamese in their school. The petition of 7 March 1914, for instance, was signed by '49 leading Brahmas and non-Brahma Meches of different Bodo villages for introduction of Assamese in all schools attended by the children of their tribe'.[61] Official correspondence noted that by 1917, several localities in the district had successfully effected changes on the medium of instruction in their area. Evidently then, an engagement with the colonised affected the social production of the colonial state, a factor that was underscored powerfully in the debates over the censuses of 1921 and 1931. In both these years, the census emerged as the site of diverse and apparently irreconcilable claims of different groups from Goalpara and Assam, primarily over the issue of how speech was to be socially constituted.

The Census of 1921 was a defining moment in the debates over linguistic representation in the region. Goalpara's language continued to defy any easy generalisations and posed, according to the Census Commissioner, the same conflict that had arisen between Bengalis and Assamese in the previous census (Census of India 1921, Assam 1923: 116). The Census Commissioner attempted to resolve the problem 'by ordering that the language (of Goalpara) should be entered as returned by each person for himself, thereby ensuring that the language question was taken out of the hands of the subordinate staff as far as possible and instructions given for the language taught in the village school to be entered for the corresponding area. (However) even this was found to be unsatisfactory in several instances' (ibid.). The final return showed the proportion of Assamese to Bengali speakers somewhat less than the corrected estimate made in 1911 and much greater than the tabulated figures of 1911 (ibid.). Table 4.2 indicates the wide variations in the schedules of Bengali and Assamese speakers in the census figures of the first three decades of the century.

Table 4.2
Figures of Bengali and Assamese speakers in the
Census of 1901, 1911 and 1921

	1901	1911	1921
Assamese	11,397	115,436	138,810
Bengali	320,050	317,365	405,710

Source: Figures compiled from the Imperial Table X, *Census of India, 1901, Assam,*
Shillong, 1902, *Census of India, 1911, Assam,* Shillong, 1912, *Census of India,*
1921, Assam, Shillong, 1923.

That the categorisation of language in this liminal area appeared to demand a softening of boundaries was evident also in this statement from the Census Commissioner:

> To illustrate this difficulty in this district, I quote the opinion of a former Chief Commissioner who had the knowledge of the rural life of the province. He said, 'We may take it as settled fact that as long as we attempt to work upon a basis of "Bengali" and "Assamese", the language statistics of Goalpara will be worthless. The plain fact is that the people of Goalpara all speak "Goalparia". At the Bengal end, they speak it with a tinge of Bengali; at the Assam end with a tinge of Assamese and in between with a tinge of both' (Census of India 1921, Assam 1923: 117).

However, the preoccupation of the state with the reliability and validity of the census ensured that neither Goalparia nor Rajbanshi was returned as a column in census reports. Official policy either did not recognise the existence of this language or refused to record it on the grounds that it would upset the projections of previous censuses.

The anxiety of the Assamese intelligentsia and of the landed groups of Goalpara over the results of the census indicated yet again the control of the elite over the means of generating a discourse on the fixing of the vernacular in these regions. There were allegations of a 'vitiation of census schedules' from the vernacular Assamese press (Das 1940: 225) and in an analysis published in the periodical *Awahan*, the writer argued that the variations in the census figures had led to 'an inexplicable rise of the Assamese speaking community in Goalpara by 11 per cent between 1911 and 1921' (Phukan 1935: 600). There had been similar expressions of discontent in the legislative assembly after the 1911 census when members from Assam had commented on the 'absurdity of the

Goalpara language schedules' and quoted from the report of the Census Superintendent. The report had noted that 'where parents born in Kamrup were shown as speaking Assamese, those of their children living in the same house who were born in Goalpara were returned as speaking Bengali, while their brothers born in Kamrup apparently followed their parents'.[62]

Responding to the allegation that the 'returns were vitiated, mostly in the direction of showing fewer Assamese and more Bengali speakers than actually existed', the colonial official present in the council acknowledged 'the difficulty of discriminating absolutely between Assamese and Bengali as spoken in the district of Goalpara'.[63] Eventual changes in the returns after an official inquiry resulted in an increase in the speakers of Assamese and a decrease in the speakers of Bengali respectively.[64] The figures for Assamese speakers rose from 85,329 to 115,436 and those of Bengali speakers decreased from 347,772 to 317,365 (Census of India 1911, Assam 1912: 97). As in 1911, the demands for an inquiry into the census returns of 1921 were followed by an inquiry that colonial officials claimed 'required the visiting of every house by the Deputy Commissioner' and a subsequent revision of the language figures for Goalpara.[65]

Through the remaining decades of British rule, too, the categorisation of language and linguistic identities continued to reflect the ways in which rulers were sometimes forced to re-examine their own hegemony and effect alterations in their policies when challenged by their subjects. On the one hand, despite a representation of Goalpara as a region that 'historically and ethnologically differed considerably from the rest of Assam',[66] the centrality of the notion of unambiguous political boundaries and the accompanying idea of exhaustive citizenship continued to determine the state's response to claims of separation and autonomy. This also allowed officials to argue against the idea of a shared history of tenancy legislation between Goalpara and Bengal.[67] On the other hand, however, a closer reading of the colonial sources indicates an attribution of more coherence to the state's enterprises than they actually warrant. While dismissing the possibility of contemplating the transfer of the district by any 'process of consent',[68] the state continued to reveal competing agendas for using power as well as doubts about the legitimacy of the venture in its language policy during the last two decades of its rule. Throughout this period, local communities in rural Goalpara continued to petition and initiate changes in the medium

of instruction. Among others, the people of Bagribari petitioned successfully against the introduction of Assamese in the
local lower primary school.[69] Again, in response to a letter from
the Goalpara District Association, which alleged an imposition
of Assamese on the students of the Dhubri subdivision,[70] E.
Soames, who was the Second Secretary to the Government of
Assam pointed out that 'the language had been introduced in six
schools, eight years ago, after a local verification of the wishes
of the people of the locality and the Government did not think it
advisable or expedient to revert to Bengali'.[71]

In the changed context of the 1930s earlier mechanisms of
assessing the 'local option' were critiqued and replaced by efforts
that reflected a continuous refashioning of the relationship of
difference between the coloniser and the colonised.[72] In 1929, the
'mere opinion of the schools committee' or of the 'parents or
guardians of the pupils' was ruled out as a factor for determining
change in the medium of instruction. Application for change,
instead, was to come from the villagers.[73] Writing about the 'vexed
question of languages in the schools of the district', the Inspector
of Schools noted that 'the propaganda by zamindars to introduce
Bengali had been so active that in a number of schools which
took advantage of the orders of 1914 and adopted Assamese, Bengali
had been re-introduced'.[74] Counter petitions from Assamese
nationalists expressed 'great alarm' at the manner in which
'Assamese was being driven out of the local boards of Goalpara
district'.[75]

Reflecting on these petitions, officials acknowledged the
difficulties of working with the 'local option'. 'Originally it was
assumed that once a majority of villagers voted for a particular
language, there may be no demand … from the public for a change
again', pointed out M. Saadulla, the then Minister of Education.
However, in a situation 'where a petition for change was invariably followed by a counter–petition',[76] modifications clearly had
to be made in colonial policies. Instructions needed to be laid
down, asserted officials, regarding 'whether a school should be
allowed to change the language as often as there is a petition from
a number of people'.[77] The introduction of bilingual schools[78]
was seen as a possible solution to the controversy but these were
abandoned on grounds of potential government expenditure,
including the production of textbooks in two languages and an

increase in the school staff.[79] Offering a temporary resolution to the colonial state's predicament, R. Friel suggested greater powers for the local boards in ascertaining that the majority of the villagers who may be concerned with the school were con-sulted. Friel also suggested a provision that allowed the minority community in the village to demand an extra teacher in their language on the condition that they contributed towards his salary,[80] thereby keeping the option of bilingual teaching open. That the borderland continued to defy any unambiguous categorisation of its language was evident yet again in the report of the Census Commissioner of 1931, C. S. Mullan, who observed that 'as might be expected in a district which is the meeting place of two languages, [it] has developed a dialect of its own ... the true boundary of Assam from a linguistic point of view would be the line drawn from the north to south almost exactly half way through the middle of the Goalpara district' (Census of India 1931, Assam 1932: 177). Mullan observed that the new category of bilingualism that was introduced in the Census of 1931 applied to the people of Goalpara alone. Exceptionalism continued to define the colonial linguistic policy in the region in the 1940s as well, although Assamese was by then the medium of instruction in the rest of the valley (Kar 1975: 33).

The post-colonial state in Assam relied on the institutional continuity of the census but also enforced the idea of a 'majority' language in its attempt to accord legitimacy to the Assamese regional linguistic identity:

> The question of protecting the Bengali speaking minority of Goalpara district does not arise ... the geographical territory of Assam can no longer be disturbed on any grounds of linguistic basis ... Assamese must be the state language of the province. So the question of language must be solved once and for all. The Assamese people as a whole will not tolerate any other language or culture imposed on them. All the languages of different communities and their culture will be absorbed in Assamese culture.[81]

The new nation's preoccupation with homogenisation, its deep suspicion of cultural fluidity, as also the reluctance of the Assamese intelligentsia to produce inclusive cultural practices, would produce many quotes such as these. The next chapter looks at another such practice of significance, that of writing narratives of the past, to reiterate yet again the persistence of the sometimes incipient, powerful alternative narratives that retold the story of the contested and contingent nature of such nationalisms.

✳

Notes

1. 'Upper Assam' was one of the administrative divisions created by the colonial government after the occupation of the region in 1826. The division was restored to the Ahom ruler, Purandar Singha, but was brought back under colonial rule in 1838. 'Lower Assam' was another administrative division and had its headquarters at Guwahati. For more details, see Bhuyan (1949: 553–70).
2. The Baptist missionaries of Sibsagar continued to be among the early pioneers of printing in the language and published the first Assamese periodical, the *Orunodoi*, from the Sibsagar Mission Press in 1846. The first Assamese Bible was printed at the Serampur Missionary Press in Bengal.
3. Resolution by the Government of Bengal, 19 April 1873, File no. 171 G 1874, Assam Secretariat Files (henceforth ASF), State Archives, Guwahati. 'The only real difficulty in the way of recognising Assamese as the vernacular of the province', continued the Resolution, 'was the paucity of high school books in the language'.
4. In an essay published in the journal *Banhi*, that he edited, Lakshminath Bezbaroa lists some of the Assamese texts from the nineteenth century. The list included Jaduram Barua's *Assamese Dictionary* (1831), Mrs Wood's *Vocabulary in English and Assamese* (1894), Nathan Brown's *The Assamese English Dictionary* (1867), Hemchandra Barua's *Hemkosh* (1900), *Kaniyar Kirtan* (1861) and Gunabhiram Barua's *Asam Buranji* (1875) (Bezbaroa 1910a: 314).
5. For an excellent study of the creating of a vernacular for Assam from 'the mutable, heterogeneous and fluctuating speech practices', see Kar (2008). For a detailed analysis of the movement to promote the use of the language in public life and the debates in the public arena over the status of Assamese, see Misra (1987: 144–76).
6. Lakshminath Bezbaroa was one of the most prominent writers in Assamese in the late nineteenth and early twentieth century.
7. These were recurrent themes in several of the addresses to the Assam Sahitya Sabha in the early decades of the twentieth century.

8. S. K. Bhuyan, 'Address to the History Session of the Assam Sahitya Sabha', Dhubri, 1926, in Hazarika and Goswami (1961: 38).
9. See Rabha (1931).
10. The term here broadly refers to the colonial districts of Goalpara, Darrang and Kamrup.
11. Bezbaroa defended his analysis of Goalpara's language by arguing that 'Goalpara had been under the rule of the Nawabs ... and Bengalis from professional classes have settled here as well. All of this has contributed to the strong influence of Bengali on Goalpara's language' Bezbaroa (1910a: 367).
12. 'They (named languages) form the presence of those who dominate a country. For the rest, they have a working language that sets up the possibility of mutual intelligibility as 'it' goes, and they go, from here to centres of dominance' (Burghart 1993: 771).
13. In his review of *Beula*, a book by Taranath Chakravarty, a scholar from Lower Assam, Bezbaroa observed that 'it was difficult to recognise the language of certain sections of the book as Assamese' (*Banhi*, Vol. 8, No. 8, 1912).
14. Letter from the people of Lower Assam, signed by 1,226 persons, to the Lieutenant Governor of Bengal, Fort William (enclosed in the letter from the Officiating Inspector of Schools, Assam Circle, to Colonel Hopkinson, Agent, North East Frontier and Commissioner of Assam, 30 January 1873), Assam Commissioner's File no. 471, ASF, State Archives, Guwahati.
15. Ibid.
16. Ibid.
17. The *Assam Bandhav* was published from Calcutta and later from Dibrugarh, from 1908 onwards.
18. Apart from Taranath Chakravarty and Pratap Chandra Goswami, protagonists of Kamrupia language and literature during this period included Lakhikanta Misra and Sarat Chandra Goswami (Goswami 1971: 119).
19. The closing down of the periodical was similarly attributed to the fact that 'literature now had an equal number of words from Lower Assam and Upper Assam and there was an end of differences between the two' (Goswami 1971: 120).
20. As the next chapter will discuss, in the late nineteenth and early twentieth century, there emerged in Goalpara a tradition of writing alternative histories of the region that resisted appropriations by nationalist historical narratives from Assam.
21. 'The objective of my essay is to rejuvenate the language of North Bengal and Goalpara — Rajbanshi or Bahebhasi, as it is commonly called' (Barua 2000: 56).
22. 'Dinesh Babu has mentioned Ananta Kandali's *Ramayan*. This text belongs to our region. It has been kept with care in the homes of

many people of Goalpara ... Another text composed in the language of our region is Ramsaraswati's *Mahabharat'* (Shastri 1930: 13–14).

23. See Table 4.1 in this chapter.

24. See Bora (1928) and Lakshminath Bezbaroa's series on the 'Asamor Gauripurot Bangla Sahitya Sabha' in the issues of *Banhi*, July–October 1910.

25. Note from Prabhat Chandra Barua to Sir Charles Bailey, Lieutenant Governor of East Bengal and Assam, through the Raja of Dighapatia, 12 January 1912, in Some Memorials (1925: 14).

26. Some of the earliest articulations of this demand were in the last decades of the nineteenth century, when several zamindars petitioned for the region to be placed under the jurisdiction of the laws of Bengal. See also the 'Petition from the inhabitants of the Dhubri Subdivision praying for a transfer of that subdivision from Goalpara to Rungpore' Home Judicial B May 1874, File nos. 27–29, National Archives of India, New Delhi.

27. Memorial from the zamindars of Goalpara to John Napier and Baron Chelmsford, Viceroy and Governor General of India, 12 March 1919, Ninth Despatch on Indian Constitutional Reforms, Q/IDC/46, Appendix IV, OIOC, London.

28. 'Memorial of the Zemindars of Goalpara to Mr Beatson Bell, Chief Commissioner of Assam, 18 September 1918', in Some Memorials (1925: 33).

29. Brajendra Narayan Chaudhuri in the Debate on the Goalpara Tenancy Bill 1927, Assam Legislative Council Proceedings (henceforth ALCP) 20 July 1927, V/9/1364, OIOC, British Library, London.

30. Proceedings of the Goalpara Zamindar's Conference relating to the Goalpara Tenancy Bill, September 1927, Revenue A, ASF nos. 42–53. This was echoed in various memorandums submitted by zamindars, including the Memorandum by the Goalpara Zamindar's Association to the Indian Statutory Commission, May 1928, Confidential B, ASF nos 212–23, State Archives, Guwahati.

31. Ibid.

32. Brajendra Narayan Chaudhuri , ALCP, 20 July 1927, V/9/1364, OIOC.

33. Resolution passed on 15 December 1918 in the Proceedings of the meeting of the Goalpara Association, Gauripur, APAI 4-1-19 to 6-12-19, PHA, File no. 97/292, State Archives, Guwahati.

34. Memorial by the people of Goalpara to the Viceroy, sent by the President, Goalpara People's Memorial Committee, Dhubri, April 1920 in Some Memorials (1925: 67–70).

35. APAI, 4–1–19 to 6–12–19, PHA, File no. 97/292, State Archives, Guwahati.

36. 'Agitation against the Assamese Language and the Tenancy Bill', APAI, September 1927–October 1927, PHA, State Archives, Guwahati.

37. 'Goalpara Conference', *Amrit Bazar Patrika*, 28 October 1929, Calcutta.

38. Nabin Chandra Bordoloi, ALCP, 20 July 1927, V/9/1364, OIOC, London.

39. Proceedings of the meeting of the Goalpara Zamindar's Association, 25 October 1927, Education, 1928, ASF nos. 662–64, State Archives, Guwahati.

40. T. Chakravarty in 'Extracts from the Political History of Assam', File No. 5, 1927, Assam State Archives, Guwahati.

41. Nabin Chandra Bordoloi in the Debate on the Goalpara Tenancy Bill 1927, ALCP, 20 July 1927, V/9/1364, OIOC. Speaking in the same debate, Bepin Chandra Ghosh, a representative from the district, saw such representations as 'the idea of an insignificant minority, i.e., of the zamindars, led by the Raja of Gauripur, who is by birth an Assamese [but] 'instigated by his foreign amlas to join the agitation'.

42. L. Bezbaroa, 'Address to the Dhubri Session of the Assam Sahitya Sabha, 1926', in Hazarika and Goswami (1955, 1957: 1880).

43. Ibid.

44. R. Cornish, Assistant Commissioner, in a letter dated 16 November 1872, 'Assamese language 1862–73', File no. 471, Assam Commissioner's Files, State Archives, Guwahati.

45. Resolution by the Government of Bengal, 19 April 1873, File no. 171 G 1874, ASF, State Archives, Guwahati.

46. File nos 52–57, August 1903, Home A, ASF, State Archives, Guwahati.

47. A protest memorial signed by 3,366 people, favouring the introduction of Bengali in Goalpara, and some counter–petitions were submitted to the Deputy Commissioner in 1896, Home A, nos 50–54, December 1897, ASF, State Archives, Guwahati.

48. Thus while Grierson explained that the language spoken in western and southwestern Goalpara was pure Rajbanshi, he suggested a more fluid category for the eastern part of the district, which he claimed, spoke 'western Assamese, which is Assamese influenced by the Rajbanshi dialect' (Grierson 1903: 394).

49. A. W. Botham's reply to Padmanath Barua, 5 January 1914, ALCP, V/9/1350, OIOC, London.

50. Chief Commissioner's order No. 177E, dated 16 January 1914, quoted in a letter from the Deputy Inspector of Schools, Dhubri, 7 August 1923, Education B, September 1924, nos 273–89, ASF, State Archives, Guwahati.

51. Letter from J. E. Webster, Chief Secretary to the Chief Commissioner of Assam, to the Secretary to the Government of India, 12 March 1919, Shillong, Ninth Despatch on Indian Constitutional Reforms, Q/IDC/46, OIOC, London.

52. Note from J. H. Cunningham, Education B, September 1924, ASF nos. 273–89, State Archives, Guwahati.

53. Ibid.

54. Letter from the Deputy Inspector of Schools, Dhubri, 7 August 1923, Education B, September 1924, ASF nos 273–89, State Archives, Guwahati.
55. Ibid.
56. Letter from Deputy Inspector of Schools, Dhubri, 5 April 1924, Education B, October 1924, ASF nos 300–1, State Archives, Guwahati.
57. Ibid.
58. Ibid.
59. Ibid.
60. Ibid.
61. Ibid. Other petitions included one by Kalicharan Brahma, the founder of the Brahma sect among the Bodo community, dated June 1912.
62. Quoted by Tarun Ram Phukan in the ALCP, April 1913, V/9/1350, OIOC, London.
63. W. M. Kennedy in the ALCP, April 1913, V/9/1350, OIOC, London.
64. 'The revised figures showed an increase of 30607 for Assamese and a decrease of 30907 for Bengali' (L. Bezbaroa, 'Address to the Dhubri Session' in Hazarika and Goswami 1955, 1957: 1878).
65. Letter from the Deputy Inspector of Schools, Dhubri to the Inspector of Schools, Assam Valley Circle, 7 August, 1923, Education Department B, September 1924, nos 273–89, ASF, State Archives, Guwahati.
66. Letter from J. E. Webster, Chief Secretary to the Chief Commissioner of Assam, to the Secretary to the Government of India, Appendix IV, Ninth Despatch on Indian Constitutional Reforms, Q/IDC/46, Appendix IV, OIOC, London.
67. ALCP, Debate on the Goalpara Tenancy Bill 1927, ALCP, 20 July 1927, V/9/1364, OIOC, London.
68. Letter from J. E. Webster, Q/IDC/46, Appendix IV, OIOC, London.
69 Note from E. Soames, 20 May 1924, Education B, September 1924, nos 273–89, ASF, State Archives, Guwahati.
70. Letter from Nabin Chandra Pal, Secretary of the Goalpara District Association, Dhubri, to the Chief Secretary to the Government of Assam, 19 December 1923, Education A, 21 December 1923, ASF, State Archives, Guwahati.
71. Note from E. Soames 26 May 1924; in a report to the government dated 20 October 1923; J. Cunningham encouraged 'petitions which complained of infringement, to provide materials for enquiry', Education B, September 1924, nos 273–89, ASF, State Archives, Guwahati.
72. Colonel Gourdon, the Commissioner of the Assam Valley Division had suggested that either the 'Deputy Commissioner, Mr. Laine, or a European Officer of the Education Department, or Shri Durgadas Barkataki, should go around the villages ... assemble the parents of the children and ask them one by one whether they wish their

children to be taught in Assamese or Bengali' (Education A, January 1914, nos 92–98), ASF: State Archives, Guwahati.

73. Note from the Director of Public Instruction in schools in Goalpara, Education A March 1929, nos 28–33, ASF, State Archives, Guwahati.

74. Correspondence between the Inspector of Schools, Assam Valley Circle, and the Director of Public Instruction in schools in Goalpara, Education A March 1929, no. 29, ASF, State Archives, Guwahati.

75. Letter from Chandradhar Barooah, Secretary of the Jorhat Sarbajanik Sabha, to the Government of Assam, 8 February 1929, Education A March 1929, no. 30, ASF, State Archives, Guwahati.

76. Correspondence between the Inspector of Schools and the Director of Public Instruction, March 1929, 19 December 1928, Education A March 1929, nos 28–33, ASF, State Archives, Guwahati.

77. Letter from G. A. Small, Acting Director of Public Instruction, Assam, to the Secretary to the Government of Assam, 8 January 1929, Education A, March 1929, Assam Secretariat Proceedings, State Archives, Guwahati.

78. In a letter dated 20 October 1923, E. Soames stated: 'Where is there is a strong volume of opinion in favour of either of the two languages, I do not think it would be advisable to disregard the opinion altogether ... Where the opinion is substantiated strongly, provisions should be made for teaching in both the languages (Education B, September 1924, ASF nos 273–89, State Archives, Guwahati. There is a similar argument being made in the correspondence between the Inspector of Schools, Assam Valley Circle and the Director of Public Instruction, where it was noted that 'it appears that there are already a number of schools in the district where both the languages are taught' (Correspondence between the Inspector of Schools and the Director of Public Instruction, 19 December 1928, Education A, March 1929, nos 28–33, ASF, State Archives, Guwahati).

79. J. Cunningham's report to the Government, 20 October 1923 (Education B, September 1924, nos 273–89, ASF, State Archives, Guwahati).

80. Letter from R. Friel, Secretary to the Government of Assam, to the Director of Public Instruction, Assam, 19 February 1929 (Education A, March 1929, no. 31, ASF, State Archives, Guwahati).

81. Nilmoni Phukan in the Assam Gazette (1948: 581–82).

5

❂

Histories, Memories and Identities

If the formation of a region is about the production of different prerequisites at different moments of time and place, then, for the newly created colonial province of Assam in 1874, a critical prerequisite was the production of a narrative of history that could assure a contested and contingent nation the anachronistic comfort of an unbroken past. Over half a decade, beginning with the colonial annexation of the Ahom kingdom in 1826, a series of military conquests in the easternmost frontiers of the colonial territories in India had identified and fixed the limits of this province. The incorporation of the region of Goalpara which colonial officials recognised was 'ethnically disparate and historically unconnected to the rest of Assam'[1] into this province, the demarcation of boundaries between the region of the Garo Hills and Goalpara and annexation of the Eastern Duars from Bhutan, were all processes that created conditions for the writing of a new history from Assam. This history was intended to be able to accommodate and satisfactorily explain the dramatic political changes of the late nineteenth and early twentieth centuries within a narrative of continuity, in a manner very similar to other nationalist narratives such as those of nineteenth century Siam that the historian Thongchai Winichakul writes about: 'the demand for a new account at a time when there is a tension in the moments of continuity and discontinuity is not uncommon … the turbulent times were never suppressed or erased from memory. Rather they were fully recognized but only to be shaped and explained in such a way that the ruptures were accommodated to an enduring past' (Winichakul 1994: 142).

This last chapter explores the generation of this narrative of history and its production of the Assamese national subject.[2] Its first section argues that this story of a glorious and continuous past of modern Assam could only be written by presenting it as uniquely able to accommodate and absorb variety, a practice that hinged on the inevitable appropriation and repression of other competing narratives, such as histories from the borderlands. The second section of the chapter considers these other histories, with their other meanings of peoples and events, which often falsified Assamese nationalist historiography and resisted its appropriations. It studies these contestations through the category of 'historical memory'[3] which makes it possible to see 'a complex interaction between scholarly and popular commemorations ... (even) as it points to the need to retain the distinctiveness ... of scholarly historiography' (Deshpande 2007: 6). Oral literature and songs and the representations they produced were therefore a constitutive part of historical memory and as the concluding section discusses, powerful ideological resources for framing local practices of cultural identity, space and authority.

The Assamese Nation and Its Histories

While not always constituting a tightly coherent historiography, there was little ambiguity within nationalist histories from Assam from the late nineteenth century onwards about the trend of re-producing the linear modes of Enlightenment history that identified the nation (or the region, as the case may be) as the primary historical subject. Equally evident in these histories was the process of transfer of difference from geography to history (Morris–Suzuki 1996: 63) which identified cultures of administrative frontiers as survivals and repositories of an ancient past and hence as a ready resource for consumption by the project of cultural nationalism. Demonstrating these trends and negotiating with the colonial re-ordering of spaces and the fixing of previously differently accented practices, were several general histories from the region. Of these, the *Asam Buranji* by Gunabhiram Barooah, is particularly representative for being one of the early examples of the historical memory of the emerging Assamese intelligentsia and as the beginning of a continuous tradition of nationalist narratives from Assam that were underscored by their agendas for power.

The text begins by acknowledging the modernity of the term 'Assam': 'the boundaries that have been determined now did not exist earlier either … there is no mention of Assam in the Mahabharata and the Kalikapurana. The term "Assam" is a derivation from the term Ahom for the dynasty that ruled the region of Upper Assam' (Barooah 1876: 7). It then dates the determining of the boundaries of the region to the sixteenth century when 'the river Karatoya was determined as the boundary between the Ahom kingdom and the Mughal territory of Bengal, prior to which the boundaries of Assam were constantly changing' (ibid.). In the introduction of another text, Lakhinandan Bora's *Asamor Sankhshep Itihas*, the author similarly recognises the possibility of the borders of Assam not being historically immutable and consistent (Bora 1875: 4).

This historicisation of the boundaries of Assam succumbed however, to the dialectic in which the new province admitted to its new borders while producing a national subject with an unruptured past. That the attempt to resolve this tension necessitated a reification and ahistoricising of Assam, was evident in several texts from nineteenth century Assam which appealed to ideas of a continuous past and space. The *Asam Buranji* exemplifies this predicament of the nineteenth century nationalist historian. The text lays out the geographical space that the author identifies as the historical reality of the modern province of Assam: 'the country in the northeastern corner of Bharatvarsha … most parts of which were within the limits of the ancient kingdom of Kamarupa. Apart from the present province of Assam, the region of Jalpaiguri and Rangpur in Bengal and the kingdom of Cooch Behar were also within the boundaries of the kingdom of Kamrup' (Barooah 1876: 13).[4] Within this pre-determined political territory, Assam's sovereignty over the neighbouring provinces and tributary chieftainships was represented as undisputed through history. The kingdom of Kamarupa was therefore also the territory of national culture with strong claims to an Aryan past for despite the ancient realm having been ruled by several non-Aryan rulers, 'it was the worship of Vedic goddesses including the Debi which was prevalent' (Barooah 1876: 14). 'This country is ancient … from ancient times it has been the abode of rishis and the centre of civilisation and prosperity', says the *Asam Buranji*.

Also being laid down were the boundaries of a national culture and its accompanying ideas of civilisational separations and hierarchies. In the decades preceding the formation of the province of Assam, the colonial state's application of a unified political authority in a region of previously more fluid territorialities and sovereignties systematically dismantled the pre-existing ties between forest and hill polities, and settled areas. The rules of colonial governmentality in northeastern India relied on notions of ethnicity that distinguished the tribal people who were governed by customary law from those governed by general laws, as in the plains (Baruah 2008: 15). 'Phrases such as "abode proper" and the "backward and degraded type" point to the peculiar logic of colonial racial and ethnic classification: a fixing of tribes to their supposed natural habitats' (ibid.). These categories were reproduced in the region which came to form the colonial district of Goalpara where large parts of the chieftainships like that of Bijni and Sidli were marked out as 'protected forest reserves', furthering the creation of 'inner frontiers' (Guha 1999: 8). The disassociation of the local chieftains and zamindars from the now relatively powerless communities living in the hills whose sovereignty and independence has earlier co-existed with theirs and also sustained their authority, interrupted processes of local practices of space. The subsequent hardening of lines between the hills and the plains produced demarcated social and political spaces for the former that located them definitively outside of the plains.

Producing some of the early examples of the 'hill–plain binary' in this part of colonial India were the civilisation narratives of histories from Assam which tended to be located at most times within the framework of the spatial imagination of the colonial state. In a textbook written for the primary schools of Assam in the mid-nineteenth century, the author's fairly candid reading of the relationship between civilisation and topography that underscored the civilisational superiority of the plains by their sedentary life, elaborated upon the differences between the Mikirs, the Garos and other hill communities, with the population of the plains: 'There are differences between the people of different countries. There are the civilised and the uncivilised. The people of this country, and the Mikirs, the Garos and other hill people are not the same. They are uncivilised and we are superior to them in all respects. Some of them do not know how to cultivate ... they lead nomadic lives. They build their houses with bark which are very uncomfortable to live in. Most of them are naked and do

not know the art of weaving or of cooking' (Phukan 1875: 23).
The *Asam Buranji* similarly described the Koch inhabitants of
Goalpara as 'a community which had sections living in the forests'
and was hence 'uncivilised'. The Daflas similarly were 'very cruel
and violent', while 'the Bhuts [or the inhabitants of Bhutan hills]
were the more civilized'. Of all these communities, the Ahoms
were those 'sharing the closest similarities with our people ...
[as] they did not live in the hills anymore' (Barooah 1876: 25).
The relationship between the forested hills and the surrounding
areas was represented as a fundamentally antagonistic one, periodic raids being seen as the most dramatic expression of this
antagonism (ibid.: 26).

The task of producing past realms of permanent and indivisible
territoriality was not left to historical consciousness alone. Rather,
if the enthusiastic descriptions of the achievements of the rulers of
kingdom of Kamarupa are in any indication, historical narratives
frequently intertwined with the mythical and the legendary to
produce pasts of the region that relied on the *Puranas* as a resource
of significance (ibid.: 7). Figures of glorious mythical kings of
Kamarupa were evoked in the *Asam Buranji*, which became part of
a dynastic sequence that ended with the rule of the Koch dynasty
in the seventeenth century (ibid.: 31). The text begins with the dynasties of the mythical kings of the kingdom of Kamarupa: 'In the
beginning there was Mahiranga Danab, and then Narakasura and
Bhagadattta. After Naraka's dynasty, the Kshatriyas, then the
Brahmaputras, then the Baro Bhuyans and then the Muslims ruled
over Assam' (ibid.). In the tradition of what Partha Chatterjee
calls 'Puranic history' (Chatterjee 1993: 85), Gunabhiram Barooah
explains dynastic changes in terms of divine intervention. Thus,
Narakasura of the Asura dynasty was 'a powerful king who died
at the hands of Krishna for his misdeeds' (Barooah 1876: 8). The
narrative then continues with the 'righteous rule of Bhagadatta,
the son of Naraka, who fought bravely for the Pandavas and
dharma with his elephants in the *Mahabharata*' (ibid.: 9).

By the early decades of the twentieth century the context for the
production of a shared historical memory of the region came to
be provided by the national space of 'Assam'. Events and person-
alities that could enhance this memory were indispensable for
Assamese historiography from this period. In the manner of other
dominant historical narratives, these histories too subscribed to

the rigors of the positivism as the means of retrieving the past. Significantly however, while the existence of a tradition of history writing was accepted as an indicator of the degree of civilisation and rationality, Assamese historiography did not begin with a lament for the absence of historical consciousness among the people of the region.[5] The emphasis instead was on a pre-colonial historical consciousness stretching into colonial modernity, on 'traditions of writing history in Asam Desh ... [that was] revived after a brief break that was caused by the Burmese invasions in the end of the eighteenth century' (ibid.: 8).

Critical evidence cited to indicate the presence of the historical mode in Assam's past were that of the *Buranjis*, political chronicles from the Ahom period. By the first half of the twentieth century, several of these texts had been 'recovered', translated and published by individuals frequently commissioned by the colonial state and by institutions set up to promote the formal study of history in Assam, including the Department of Historical and Antiquarian Studies in Guwahati.[6] Several officials of the colonial state participated in these projects of 'recovery' of 'indigenous traditions of history writing' from the late nineteenth century onwards. Edward Gait, the Director of Ethnography during this period, published a detailed *Report on the Progress of Historical Research in Assam* in 1897 in which he listed the 'several Ahom *Buranjis* discovered in the houses of several people' (Gait 1897: 3). Introducing them as 'descriptions of the Ahom rulers and their reigns', Gait classified the *Buranjis* as historical texts, as opposed to genealogies which he categorised as 'quasi historical writings' (ibid.). In the introduction to his *A History of Assam*, (Gait 1905) Gait identified the *Buranjis* as early forms of rational history writing from the region's pre-colonial past and asserted that they could be treated as historical records and were generally very trustworthy (ibid.: 11). 'The inhabitants of other parts of India had no idea of history. On the other hand, the Ahom conquerors of Assam were endowed with the historical faculty in a very high degree', suggested Gait. He went on to attribute the Ahoms historical sense to 'their priests and leading families [who] possessed *Buranjis* which were periodically brought up to date' (ibid.: 10).

Gait was much lauded by nationalist historians for his efforts to trace the historical mode of constructing the past in pre-colonial Assam. In his editor's introduction to one such published

Buranji, Hemchandra Goswami details the efforts of the Chief Commissioner of Assam in 1894, Sir Charles Lyall, for the preservation of these *Buranjis* 'which had not yet been destroyed': 'He [Lyall] had sanctioned some funds for the purpose ... the Secretary of the Treasury, Sir Edward Gait, was commissioned to begin historical research in Assam. As a result of his research and investigations, 6 *Buranjis* written in the Ahom language and 11 *Buranjis* written in the Assamese language were found. This text is one of those 11 texts' (Goswami 1922: 1).

The association of the *Buranjis* in the writings of Goswami and other nationalists from Assam with a culture that was historical, allowed for them to be deployed as resources that could be appropriated into a tradition of 'history writing from Assam'. This gave the nascent Assamese nation both a history and a tradition of writing it.[7] The idea of a 'true historical account' only reiterated this hegemonic hold of historicity. 'The ancient Hindus had a different notion of what is history' wrote Hem Chandra Goswami. 'They used the word *itihaas* in a very broad sense to include *Dharma, Artha, Kama*, and *Moksa*. They depended on divine intervention in the final results. They did not consider the listing of names of rulers as a matter of national pride' (ibid.: 2). This was contrasted with the tradition of writing *Buranjis* from the Ahom period which, it was argued, 'was based on scientific methods [and where] the truth was of utmost importance' (Ibid.: 3). Goswami suggested that 'the prevalence of truth in these *Buranjis* could be verified from the fact that the information provided in several *Buranjis* tally. The information could be verified further with dates on stone tablets and copper plates' (Ibid.). Archaeological remains were thus incorporated into the map of Assam as Lakshminath Bezbaroa argued that 'after Huien Tsang's departure and till the middle of the twelfth century we have no accounts of Assam. With the help of inscriptions on rock faces we can now throw light on this period' (Bezbaroa 1911: 95).

The repeated exhortations to the Assamese people to discover their past were located therefore in the idea that a region could be imagined within the realm of history.[8] The emphasis on a scientific rational history was at the core of attempts to 'recover the historical core' of epics and other mythical texts. Thus, proponents of 'professional history' and nationalists of repute such as Surya

Kumar Bhuyan stressed the need to recognise the authenticity and historicity of the characters in the epic, *Mahabharata*, as well as the possibility of its use as a source of scientific history.[9] 'Hidden below the layers of myths and legends that comprised of this epic', argued Bhuyan, is the 'original, historical text which forms a reliable source of the early history of the region'.[10] The break between myth and history in these writings however could hardly be exaggerated. Myths continued to be an essential part of the historical consciousness of the period with even 'real, objective history writing attaching validity to it'. Thus, *The Early History of Kamarupa* by Kanaklal Barooah claimed to present 'a connected history of the old kingdom known as Pragjyotisha or Kamarupa from the earliest times till the end of the sixteeth century' (Barooah 1933: 1). Mythical history makes its way into the narrative as the author tells us that 'about 1,000 years before the Christian era, the greater part of lower Bengal was probably under the sea while the greater part of northern Bengal was included within this kingdom. Allusions to the smaller kingdoms in Bengal then above the sea are rare in the Aryan records, but Pragjyotisha is mentioned in the Epics and the *Puranas*' (ibid.).[11]

In this negotiation between history writing and boundaries, standard nationalist elisions which either submerged or ignored alternative claims to the regions past played an important role. A significant appropriation was the history of the western borders of the province, including that of the region of Goalpara, into that of the ancient kingdom of Kamarupa: 'Goalpara was not only an integral part of Kamarupa but the centre of this ancient civilisation ... it was never an independent kingdom.'[12] In yet another example of the centrality that cultures of the periphery came to have in the project of Assamese nationalists, its proponents asserted that 'it is almost undisputed and has been suggested by scholars that Kamrup's capital in those times was either in the Goalpara district or in the region of Koch Bihar' (Bezbaroa: 1910c: 170). Boundaries of this ancient kingdom of Kamarupa were timeless and indivisible and changes were represented as 'losses' of territory. Within such history writing, rulers from this past with a strong cultural resonance in the contemporary could only appear as national heroes. The list of these heroes began with the mythical King Bhagadatta, 'who fought for the Kauravas' and is brought up to the medieval ruler Naranarayan, the Koch king who was claimed by Goalpara's historians (Bezbaroa 1910: 50). Naranarayan is described as 'one of modern Assam's three objects of pride', credited with a 'period of glorious revival and the restoration of territorial losses in the sixteenth century',[13] the other two being the temple of Kamakhya and the Vaishanva reformer, Sankardev.

The Narrative as Resistance

Underscoring powerfully the contingent and unstable character of these narratives of Assamese (as well as of Bengali) nationalisms, were the counter–perspectives from the western borders of the province. Unlike history writing from Assam, these alternative narratives comprised mostly of family histories and genealogies commissioned by local landlords, printed lectures delivered by them to political and cultural associations, and a scattered body of formal history texts and historical atlases. These were not the works of major historians, and it is difficult to see them as forming a continuous political tradition of history writing. Persistently resisting elisions by the nation and often produced in sites of discursive contestation with the latter, these writings from the margins were significant as illustrations of the historical memory of its inhabitants and of the complex trajectories of counter discourses in the region. This was reflected in the inevitable negotiations and appropriations that accompanied the unfolding of a distinct borderland linguistic and cultural identity in these writings, during the late nineteenth and the early decades of the twentieth century, primarily in Goalpara, but also in other parts of the borderland.

Of the early nineteenth century texts from the region that illustrate this idea of the narrative as history, the *Bijni Rajvamsha* is particularly important. The text was commissioned as a family history by the Raja of Bijni, Kumud Narain Bhoop, in the early 1870s. In the period after the collapse of Mughal rule in the late eighteenth century, Bijni was one of the most powerful chiefdoms in the region which later came to form the colonial district of Goalpara. It straddled the hills of the Eastern Duars and the plains below and in other areas shared its sovereignty with the rulers of Cooch Behar, Bhutan, Assam and Tibet. In the preface to the text, the author Tarini Prasad Sen attributed his work to the 'encouragement that he received from the Raja Bahadur' and from the Dewan of Bijni estate who provided him with the necessary papers to construct a genealogy of the kings of Bijni (Sen 1876: 1). The text recounts the history of the dynasties that ruled Bijni, constructed through a series of episodes that foregrounded events that maintained the trajectory of continuity regarding the origins of the present Bijni king. The genealogy of the Bijni kings provided the core narrative structure of the *Bijni Rajvamsha*, the text itself covering a period of more than 400 years beginning in the mid-fifteenth century.

In the manner of most nineteenth century *vamshavalis*, the *Bijni Rajvamsha* too, through a series of discursive maneuvers that involved repressions and appropriations, narrated the past by extending it into the present, in this case to help establish the rights of rulers. The concluding sections of the Bijni *vamshavali* accordingly, are largely in the form of an appeal to the colonial government to restore some amount of autonomy to the erstwhile Raja who had been settled as a zamindar of the Bijni estate in the district of Goalpara (ibid.: 123). Through much of the text, these claims of the Raja are sought to be constructed through a chronicling of events that enhanced the narrative of Bijni as a determinate region, with clear and fixed boundaries in the pre-colonial past, and as an area which included most parts of the colonial district of Goalpara. In the anachronistic narrative that Tarini Sen constructed, a clearly bounded political entity of Goalpara appeared to replace the non-bounded hierarchical political realm of the pre-colonial period.

The text begins with the author identifying the rulers of the Koch dynasty as the rulers of the region, whose descendants continued to rule Bijni in the late nineteenth century. This was followed by a description of the extent of the kingdom of the various Koch kings 'who ruled Bijni and the rest of Goalpara through the centuries ... Under the rule of the first most powerful ruler of this dynasty, the boundaries of the kingdom were extended to include the kingdom of Pragjyotisha in the east and Cooch Behar in the west' (ibid.: 104). The rule of Naranarayan and Chilarai who were among the most powerful kings of this dynasty during the sixteenth century, was succeeded by a period of rule under the Mughals, during which, the author asserted, 'Bijni maintained complete independence and paid only 85 *koris* annually to the

Emperor' (Sen 1876: 104). There are several pages of descriptions of the techniques of war used by the Koch King Jayanarayan to win the war 'on behalf of the Mughals against the Assamese'. The war ends with the Koch king taking over 'the fort of the Assam king and beheading several Assamese soldiers while the army of the Samrat [the Mughal Emperor] started blowing the victory bugle' (ibid.: 65). The *Rajvamsha* notes that 'as a token of gratitude for the help that he received from the Koch King Jayanarayan of Goalpara, Ram Singha, the Mughal general, praised him for his strategies and reinstated him as the king of Pragjyotishpur, the kingdom of his ancestors' (ibid.). The narrative goes on to describe the eventual submission of the Koches to the Mughals in the eighteenth century and the temporary reduction of their status to that of tributaries. The story ends with an emphasis on the tradition of freedom enjoyed by the ruler of Bijni, expressions of loyalty to the colonial government and an appeal to include the territories that were historically a part of the kingdom within the permanently settled estate of Bijni (ibid.: 107).

This historical narration is significant as much for its silences as for its appropriations. The Mughal–Ahom wars of the seventeenth century and the subsequent retreat of the Mughal army from Ahom territory is a familiar theme in the construction of Assamese cultural nationalism. In the history told by the *Bijni Rajvamsha*, however, this is clearly a competing narrative that needs to be silenced if the resources of local history are to be mobilised to create new cultural communities. Reclaiming the spatial strategies of the colonial state and of nationalism, including that of the territorialisation of sovereignty in order to construct politically charged places, the local elite was obviously setting out to claim for the region a past that had not been distorted by Assamese historiography. The *Bijni Rajvamsha* and some of the other genealogies and local histories appear to tell another story within the same past. The space of their histories was informed by certitudes of the political boundaries of the region of Goalpara that were similar to those in the histories from Assam. They simultaneously pointed however to the discrepancies and ambiguities involved in the creation of a new past for the region of Assam.

To begin with, reflecting the new political reality of the sixteenth century which saw the emergence of regional chiefdoms such as those of the Koch kings at the political peripheries of the Ahom kingdom, the text appears to suggest that the cultural closures suggested in it are either absent or far less definite than those present in the civilisational narratives of the nationalist historiography from Assam. Underpinning this as well as other texts from Goalpara and other parts of the borderland was a more fluid and negotiable relationship between topography and civilisation, one that was less insistent about civilisational boundaries between settled and forest communities. In its story about the mythical origins of the Koch dynasty, for instance, the *Bijni Rajvamsha* focuses on one of the popular legends in the region of Goalpara and Assam — the rebuilding of the Hindu temple of Kamakhya by the Koch king, Naranarayan, in the sixteenth century (Sen 1876: 20).

There were evidently several versions of the legend in the late nineteenth century when this text was being written. The version in the *Bijni Rajvamsha* tells us the story of how Naranarayan, while out hunting in the forests with his brother Chilarai and his followers, wandered off by himself and lost his way. He then discovered the site of the abandoned temple of Kamakhya in the middle of the forested hills (ibid.). From the same legend, the *Bijni Rajvamsha* then describes in the episode in which Naranarayan is transformed into a devotee of the goddess Kamakhya, and the subsequent renovation of the temple during his reign[14] as well as during the rule of the later Koch kings. The evident emphasis in the text is on tracing the movement of the Koch community from the ecological and political peripheries to the 'centre' and henceforth, the story in the legend is that of a settled bounded Hindu kingdom. It includes the representation of the Koch king, Naranarayan, as the chief of a forest polity and his subsequent transition into the ruler of a vast settled kingdom that included large parts of colonial Assam as well.

In the representation of the relationship between the forest and the Koch rulers, however, is a portrayal of a complementary rather than an oppositional relationship between the hilly forests and the settlements in the plains below. There are several references to the legend in other texts from both Goalpara and Assam during this period. In those from Assam, the earlier part of the legend is invariably left out and the story tends to begin with the renovation of the Kamakhya temple by Naranarayan.

In another text from Goalpara, Biswa Singha, the founder of the Koch dynasty, is described as the chief of a community of itinerant Koch hunters (Barooah 1882: 22). The legend tells of the difficulties encountered by Biswa Singha while worshipping the goddess and attributes them to his ignorance of the accepted forms of rituals (ibid.: 25). These difficulties were eventually resolved, and Biswa Singha's family, particularly his son Naranarayan, was then associated with the worship and the renovation of the most important Hindu temple in the region. The inclusion of this part of the legend into the text suggests an acceptance (or memory) of both the incorporation of new groups into the fold of the Hindu community and their transition to a more settled way of life.

The frontiers of difference are visible, but less so than in the histories from Assam during the same period. Rather than create a binary of settled–itinerant groups, the genealogies and family histories commissioned by the zamindars and history texts published independently by sections of Goalpara's intelligentsia, tell a story of other societal trajectories and places. They suggested therefore, new ways of responding to the imposition of hard categories by colonial knowledge and to associated historical claims, including an acknowledgement of the plurality of identities and the impossibility of making them co-extensive with nineteenth century boundaries.

With the connection between history writing and the national subject becoming more explicit and pronounced from the beginning of the twentieth century, it was inevitable that the transitionality and ambiguities of the nineteenth century be replaced by the certitudes of the twentieth. The mobilisation of the idea of a 'Goalparia' during this period demanded a representation of a regional cultural identity that would marginalise its historical others in the very act of forging this identity. Of the various representational practices that secured this identity between the region and its people, the production of a historical memory in the different interactive registers of formal and popular histories is of interest here.

We begin by looking at a series of historical atlases of the region of Goalpara that were published in the early decades of the twentieth century. There were at least five such atlases published during this period. Unlike the genealogies of the nineteenth century these were not commissioned by local zamindars but were published independently by local authors, frequently through the Hitsadhini Press in Dhubri. The focus here is on one such text, which was fairly representative of the others, *The Historical Atlas of Goalpara*, published in 1904. The author stated in the introduction to the text that the book was meant for 'scholarly use' and that its information differed from that being taught in the schools in Goalpara (Barua 1905: 3). The maps in the atlas were not confined to those of the region of Goalpara from the colonial period. Rather, based almost purely on the historical memory of the local elite, the series proceeded to construct an entire scheme of what was represented to be the region's history.

The author's construction of these maps is informed by a know-ledge of modern geography, for he apologises for maps of which the 'boundary line may not be mathematically accurate, although they are as correct as available information allows ... while the indefinite or unascertainable boundary lines of the district [had] been deliberately dropped' (ibid.: 5). The earliest map is of what the author identifies as the unified region of 'Goalpara in the Puranic period'. The note accompanying the map tells us that according to the *Kalikapurana*, the *Bishnu Purana* and the *Mahabharata*, Goalpara formed part of a large kingdom, which consisted of the hills of Bhutan, the district of Rangpur in Bengal, the region of Cooch Behar and parts of the western Brahmaputra Valley (ibid.). The second map is a construction of the kingdom of Bhaskarvarman who was a contemporary of the King Harshavardhana and the extent of his kingdom is marked out as 1,700 miles. This is followed by a map of the historical kingdom of Kamatapur and another of the establishment of the Koch dynasty by Biswa Singha in the sixteenth century. The last few maps are representations of the invasions of the region by the Nawabs of Bengal and the Mughal army and of the territories of the new colonial district of Goalpara (ibid.: 15).

Several themes emerge from these maps. The entire set taken together speaks of a reorganisation and redistribution of space by the local elite to construct a particular scheme of regional history. That these maps were not confined to the new political entity that was the colonial district of Goalpara, is also of significance. Instead, the atlas includes maps of the other parts of the borderland as well, in an evident allusion to a period of multiple overlordships and sovereignties. Thus although the historical sequence built tells a story of the emergence and growth of a historically unified region of a borderland that the elites called 'Goalpara'. Goalpara here is also a euphemism for a borderland space. The several invasions of the king of Gaur and of the Ahoms, who ruled neighbouring Assam, are projected as minor ruptures in this story of continuity. The maps locate the political history of Assam very firmly outside this story. A map depicting 'invasions by foreigners' was invariably followed by another of a consolidated and enlarged kingdom (Barua 1905: 23–29).

In the accompanying notes with the maps is also an acknowledgement of linear, fixed borders as a recent product of colonial technologies of rule. In a note accompanying the Puranic map of the mythical kingdom of Pragjyotisha, the author concedes that the boundaries of the region during that period 'changed all the time ... they extended during the rule of the powerful kings and shrank during the rule of the weak rulers' (ibid.: 15). But the establishment of the rule of Bhaskarvarman dated back to the seventh century AD is recognised as marking the beginning of the historical period, one of unchanging boundaries. The atlas questioned the singularity of the Assamese nationalist narrative in other ways as well. The maps of the Puranic period, and of the kingdom of Pragjyotisha, gave the region a sense of continuity over time and civilisation. They thus made the idea of a classical past for Assam, an uncertain one.

Accompanying the discourse of the invention of antiquity in the maps was a body of lectures and publications of local political associations that successfully deployed another inherited colonial spatial strategy — the historicising of geography to transform a place into a more politically charged space. Conveying an urgent need to reclaim the region's past, they reproach and lament the absence of a historical consciousness among the people of the region. This perceived sense of lack was an important underpinning of the movement for the separation of the district of Goalpara from Assam during the early decades of the twentieth century. 'What could have happened to make us forget our ancient glory and pride? If we have indeed forgotten the glorious chapters in our region's history, then come, let us recollect them today!' exhorted Gaurinath Shastri in his presidential address to the Goalpara District Association (Shastri 1928: 3).

The emphasis on the need to have a history of one's own, distinct from that of Bengal and Assam, forms a part of the introductory sections of some of the formal history texts from the region as well. That Goalpara's intelligentsia and other sections of the local elite should have felt orphaned in the absence of a long tradition of history writing from the region indicated also their refusal to locate their writings within the medieval tradition of *Buranji* writing, unlike the mainstream histories from Assam. 'We have an identity that is independent of both Assam and Bengal. These differences have persisted since time immemorial ... our iden-tity is located in our region and our history reflects this', stated Prabhat Chandra Baruah (Baruah 1928: 13).

The practice of history writing therefore needed to interpret the past in a way that was contingent with the expressions of a collective Goalparia and a greater borderland identity. The maps in the historical atlases were a part of this political tradition of writing history. In the political discourse from Goalpara in the early decades of the twentieth century, there was a clearer identification of both a historically unaltered political realm of Goalpara and of its imagined national community. While acknowledging the limits of a rational construction of the ancient past of Goalpara, history writing reinforced the unambiguous sovereignty of the region that was projected in these maps. Thus historians agreed that the beginning of the historical period could be dated to the seventh century AD, as the maps had represented (ibid.: 8). The identification of a permanent political realm, it was conceded in all the writings, could be traced to the beginnings of the Kamatapur kingdom. This again was a reaffirmation of the historical sequence represented in the maps.

From this period onwards, the history of the district of Goalpara collapses into the history of a 'frontier kingdom', a borderland space located outside the narrative of the mainstream history of Assam.[15] 'The history of our district is the history of an independent frontier kingdom', stated the historian K. M. Dhar. 'Together with Jalpaiguri and Rangpur in northern Bengal and the region of Koch Behar, it formed part of the Kamatapur kingdom which was ruled by several dynasties through history, particularly from the seventh century onwards. This independent kingdom later spread eastwards to encompass Assam and westwards up to Munger' (Dhar 1911: 9). In the evoking of the period of the medieval kingdom of Kamatapur as the 'golden past' can be read a critique by the local elite of the construction of colonial governmentality and of the violence of its borders. That these lines of difference ignored the shared civilisational imaginings of the region was a matter of much concern as well, for within the historical writings from Goalpara, the fixing of the boundaries of the modern district translated into a discourse of loss, of territories of the frontier kingdom and of its civilisational spread that encompassed parts of northern and eastern Bengal and the Bhutan foothills (Baruah 1928: 13).

A 'discovery' of texts argued to have been produced in the region in the pre-colonial period, followed. Of the works that were edited and published by the local elite during this period, the 'recovery' of the *Kabindra Mahabharata,* was of considerable significance. The text was edited and published by the Dewan of the zamindari estate of Gauripur, Gaurinath Shastri. Shastri begins his introduction by alluding to the various controversies that had emerged over the question of correctly identifying the original composer of the text, the language and the region of its composition. The fact that there were several versions of the original text by the early twentieth century did not make his task any easier. The introduction details the story for the search for the *Kabindra Mahabharata,* the manuscript of which, 'was to be found in the region of Goalpara and Rangpur in Bengal since very early times' (Shastri 1930: 1). The author traces his search back to a community of people called the *Padkirtaniyas* who he claimed, 'lived in the region of Khuntaghat in Goalpara and sang parts of this *Mahabharata'*. He then writes about how the text continues to live in the collective memory of the people living in areas around Goalpara and finally traces a copy of the text in the archives of the zamindar of Gauripur (ibid.).

The text is therefore located squarely within the history of the region. Shastri identifies its author as Kabindra Patra, a qanungo under the Mughals who was later recognised as the zamindar of Gauripur through a sanad. Kabindra Patra, the editor tells us, composed the text at the 'behest of Paragal Khan, who was an official of Alauddin Khan, who ruled over the region of Goalpara ... each section of the text thus ends with a stanza in praise of Paragal's bravery and courage' (ibid.: 5). Shastri dated the composition of the text to the sixteenth century and identified its language as Rajbanshi, the language spoken in the region of Goalpara and parts of northern Bengal (ibid.: 8). The publishing of the *Kabindra Mahabharata* and its eventual location within the tradition of history writing in Goalpara performed therefore, the function of identifying the political community around which the idea of the region was to be mobilised.

Shastri's introductory notes firmly lays out the alternative traditions of modern historiography within which the *Kabindra Mahabharata* was to be located. The historical authenticity of the text, accordingly, is sought not in the available conventional formal texts of history from Assam but in the *Social History of Kamarupa*, much critiqued in Assamese nationalist historiography as 'a false history with an incorrect representation of the facts'.[16] With the text as an incipient narrative, resistant to the homogenising narrative of neighbouring nationalisms, its author writes a history of the pre-colonial by drawing upon another such alternative and repressed product of local historical memory, the *Darrangrajar Vamshavali*. A family history and genealogy of the Koch dynasty, and claimed by Goalpara's intelligentsia as the subject of their history, the 1913 edition of the *Darrangrajar Vamshavali* already bore the marks of strategic appropriation by the modern Assamese nation. In the introduction to the text, one of Assam's nationalist historians described the Koch kings as having played an important role in Assam's past and 'expressed the hope that the book would help to restore the old happy relations between Goalpara and Assam' (Goswami 1917: xviii).

Goalpara's counter histories, although subsequently suppressed to make way for the claims of an emerging modern Assam, constituted more than a form of scholarly resistance. The spatial history of this region and the violence of its transformation into a colonial borderland demanded that the historical narrative be reinstated as a strategic tool of representation against various erasures by dominant narratives and not allowed the comfort of political ambivalence. In their act of destabilising dominant discourses and reclaiming political space, these counter–histories successfully performed the political function of the historical narrative, that of producing and maintaining cohesion for the historical subject that was the nation or region. That these histories continued to be produced despite their exclusion from the local school curriculum only further underscores their relevance as strategic discourses. And yet, while making claims for an alternate past, the production of this historical memory for the region frequently reproduced the very same subsuming structures of the nationalist narratives that they had sought to contest. There was a flattening of the complex dynamics of local spatial practices and identities and this submerged the histories of smaller polities such as Bijni and Sidli which were now seen as part of the emerging story of the region.[17] These erasures once again transformed the project of history writing into a continuous process of displacement, characterised by appropriations within appropriations, gesturing towards the always existent unstable discourses at the margins.

Of Elephant Catchers and Connected Pasts

While the govermentality of the colonial state makes a condition of total transgression impossible, therefore, there were sites of resistance that destabilised its narrative and this chapter has tried to recover some of them. This section extends this conversation to include a discussion of realms of collective experience, social memory and oral traditions in the region that had become a colonial borderland. It discusses the contested terrain of the first half of the twentieth century in which certain representations came to form part of the historical memory of the region, as well as critical spatial strategies for a traditional elite desperate to reinvent itself. The context is the early twentieth century debates around the bans on elephant catching which had come to be associated with 'lost' pre-colonial connected spaces for the zamindars and local powers of Goalpara.

Of the several issues that the scholarship on memory studies debates, it is the dimension of memory as constructed and contested, deeply implicated in the production of power and of social identity that is of interest here. 'The historical memory of archaic totalisations does not always disappear, and as this memory is periodically re-enacted, it often provides potent material along with which to mobilise the new community' (Duara 1995: 56). The oral literature and songs from the region of Goalpara and of northern and eastern Bengal, and the published collections and commentaries on the same from the first half of the twentieth century, would appear to offer several examples of the mobilising abilities of historical memory. Here the dual nature of oral literature that it is 'traditional, yet it lives through variation' (Blackburn and Ramanujan 1986: 11) comes into play. The songs from Goalpara and the regions around it demonstrate little in terms of innovative themes in their content during this period. Their fixity however lends an authority and tradition to them that in turn strongly foregrounds the element of continuity from the pre-colonial. When posited against colonialism's discourse of change, this fixity of form, combined with memory, could produce enduring ideas of borderland identities such as that of the 'Goalparia'.

To begin with, as the commentaries accompanying some published collections of songs from the region indicate, the oral traditions tend to locate themselves within a geographical area that overlaps quite precisely with the region of concern in this book. In *'Prantobashir Jhuli'*, the introductory essay in a collection of Nihar Baruah's writings by the same name (Barua 2000) its author locates them firmly within the frontier or the *Pranto* — 'the frontier of Assam, Cooch Behar, the Garo Hills and the kingdom of Bhutan ... it is the frontier of every place and its people are the inhabitants of a frontier (the Prantobashi)' (ibid.: 1). The daughter of Prabhat Chandra Barua, the zamindar of the estate of Gauripur in Goalpara, Barua wrote consistently on different aspects of local culture through the 1930s and the 1940s, gathering together some of the most popular songs in the region, along with her commentaries on them between 1925–26.

Several of these commentaries, along with her other writings, which were published in the Bengali periodical *Desh*, attempted to foreground the significance of commonalities in the speech practices of Goalpara, Cooch Behar, Mymensingh, Rangpur and Jalpaiguri with variations presented as masking an underlying cultural unity (ibid.: 56). 'The folk songs sung in this region are products of this frontier area and the Rangpur district', wrote Barua. The commonalities across the region in the themes, forms, images and analogies of the different genres of songs such as the *bhauwaiya*, the *biyer gaan* and the *sonaray*, underscored in various other collections of these songs, would appear to substantiate such claims. The form and music of the songs of love and longing from Goalpara — the *bhauwaiya*, for instance — have enough resonance with the *bhatiali* songs of Eastern Bengal to be sometimes mistaken for the latter (Datta 1995: 65) while the context for the Sonaray songs was similarly shared, provided by the dense tiger–inhabited forests of Cooch Behar, Rangpur, Goalpara, the Garo Hills, and the foothills of Bhutan.[18] There are similar suggestions of reflections of shared cultural histories across the region in Dineshchandra Sen's collection of popular ballads from Mymensingh: 'The songs are generally sung in that indigenous mode of music which is called "bhatiyal". It is the favourite mode of the rustics, especially the boatmen. Its plaintive appeal has a peculiar power. In the vast expanse of the East Bengal rivers, in the blue tinted Brahmaputra ... in the foaming Padma, the boatmen yield to the irresistible fascination of their favourite bhatial raag' (Sen 1923: xciv).

Boatmen and their songs, music and literature that 'travel' and are mobile and refuse to conform to static borders — all of these suggest another way of thinking about cultural difference and hierarchy, and thus by extension, are critiques of notions of stable, bounded essences. The *bhatial* songs reflected continuities in modes of circulation between the pre-colonial and the colonial periods, the routes of songs frequently overlapping with the trade routes that crisscrossed the region. That mobility was a cultural resource of significance for the region was made most apparent in another rich genre of music, the mahout and moishal songs. With the Godadhor, Brahmaputra and many other smaller rivers flowing through it, the region of Goalpara had a thriving culture of dairy farming for which buffalos were reared in *bathans* or *khutis* by the moishals (Datta 1995: 183). The theme of longing is a central one in the 'moishal songs'. It draws from the long periods of absence that the peripetatic lives of the moishal entailed:

Leave the bathan, leave the bathan, O moishal,
  Do come back home. I shall sell my necklace
And raise a sum that will equal your wages.[19]

The description of the life of the mahout in the mahout songs, centred around the arduous operation of elephant–catching in the northern forests of Bhutan and in the Garo Hills and Goalpara, sets his life in a similarly undisguised opposition to the settled, cultivated world. The season of activity for the mahout began with the onset of winter, when he accompanied the *phandis* to the forest, and ended with the beginning of the rainy season and summer. Since agriculture too was similarly structured by seasons, it is likely that these songs may have had a resonance with many at that time. The cycle of activities of both the mahout and the moishal was therefore structured by seasons[20] (Barua 2000: 91) marked by long periods of separation from their families. The songs of longing and separation reflect this:

> O my mahout of the great tuskers,
> My woman's heart keeps yearning for you when you go away to Assam[21]

In the descriptions of a life set apart in unspoiled nature and marked by seasonal rhythms, was a strong spatial imagery of a world free of social norms, a realm of freedom. This space was reinforced by the relationship of dependence shared by the mahout and his elephant and the subject of most of the genre of mahout songs. In a well loved song from the region, the mahout sings to his elephant, 'Alas, O my beloved daughter of the elephants! You have no compassion to spare for a mahout'.[22] There are allusions to the tension between the norms of settled society and transgression of these by the mahout and his unsettled life in the songs of the woman left behind in Assam by her lover: 'If you go away, my mahout friend, will you come back again? You graze the elephant under the wild bamboo groves ... do tell me the truth, tell me where is your home?' (Datta 1995: 186). In most of the collections of popular songs from the region that this book has looked at (Barua 2000; Datta 1982, 1985; Sen 1923) the return of the mahout to the forest is represented as a return from a constrained social order to an archaic, untouched way of life, (Barua 2000: 80) to a 'world which knows no differences in community, caste or region and recognises none of the ordinary rules of settled social life. It is a world in which the natural leader is the one who has proved to be the most dexterous and courageous in catching elephants' (ibid.: 92).

Non-static cultural forms were critical then in shaping the trajectories of the culture of this borderland, creating in the process fragmented spaces, quite unlike the bounded spaces produced by the ideology of colonialism and nationalism which were more about closures than about mobility. The oral narratives suggest that the dynamics of local spatial practices involved a negotiation not only with the totalising narratives of Assamese and Bengali nationalisms but also with the hegemonic discourse of 'stability' as against the fluid and the liminal. As a historian of another borderland puts it, popular music, 'rich in allusion and in simultaneity of meaning … constitutes its own heterotopic space, and within that space, we are able to imagine ourselves in motion, in mutating and plural relations with others and act accordingly' (Stokes 1998: 264).

But the moishal and mahout songs are also about people who continued to inhabit fluid worlds with other spatial imaginations, resisting the colonial state's obsessive spatial project of fixity. The world of the mahout and his elephant reflected an entire way of life that was gradually disappearing or being marginalised by the first decades of the twentieth century. A reconstruction of the everyday life of these people thus often required collectors such as Nihar Barua to take the narrative back into the early nineteenth century, 'when this region was covered in forests and wild elephant grass, for the essence of their life stories is connected to this history' (Barua 2000: 77). The several sedenterisation schemes of the state had regulated and repressed the ways of nomadic and semi-nomadic groups, confining them to the margins of an increasingly settled agrarian order. The privileging of a settled way of life over a more mobile way of being was also predicated on the advancement of ideas of civilisational separations and oppositional relationships between cultures with mobility being 'looked upon by colonial rulers as potentially subversive and to be limited as far as possible, if not altogether suppressed' (Markovits, Pouchepadass and Subrahmanyam 2003: 8).

In this borderland, these ideologies were singularly exemplified in the late nineteenth century colonial discourses around the prohibition of elephant catching, a measure that severely curbed the peripatetic lives of its inhabitants (particularly of certain groups such as the Hajongs and the Garos). The initial official intervention in this long continuing local practice was explained as an 'interference (that) arose from the knowledge that there were no permanent haunts of wild elephants within zamindari lands, that the natural habitats of these animals were in the Garo Hills and the Eastern Duars, and the zamindars made a pretence of granting of licences to Purneah catchers and others to hunt ostensibly within zamindari lands, but actually to catch elephants in the Government estates of the Garo Hills and the Eastern Duars'.[23] Attributing this to the changing practicalities of the colonial administration while acknowledging that 'elephant catching was a privilege, though not proven through documents, was conceded to the zamindars and never formally taken away',[24] the colonial state asked the local elite 'to produce evidence, documentary or other, in support of their claims ... with sufficient proof of the limits within which they had been exercised'.[25] The restrictions on elephant catching, it was argued, were necessary because of the 'entrance of elephant catchers into the Duars and the Garo Hills ... without licence [as] there [were] no permanent haunts of wild elephants within zamindari lands'.[26]

The extension of the Elephant Preservation Act of 1879 into this part of colonial India, 'forbidding and making criminal the unlicensed capture of elephants'[27] had as its stated objective, the prevention of 'a wasteful system of hunting the elephants'.[28] The actual implications of the Act however were rather different, with its many provisions underscoring the disciplinary project of the colonial state. The mere entry of elephant catchers into the Duars and the Garo Hills, 'with all appliances for catching elephants (was) cognizable by the police without the actual capture of wild elephants' as an offence that could invite conviction under Section 447 of the Indian Penal Code.[29] As instructions went out to the police to keep a look out on all parties of elephant catchers entering Goalpara, with the requirement that they report their movements every week to the nearest thana,[30] officials had to acknowledge that elephant catchers could now 'only follow their vocation by trespassing on Government lands, and appropriating Government property'.[31]

The mahout songs, their retrieval and their popularity in the early decades of the twentieth century and their emergence as sites that held the most familiar imagery of the region — moishals, mahouts, elephants, the Godadhor river — were therefore not about fluid ways of life alone. As powerful reiterations of the dramatic, irreversible changes that colonialism had effected on local culture, these songs were transformed into what Pierre Nora terms 'realms of memory' with 'a capacity for metamorphosis ... the recycling of knowledge through associations and new symbolic representations' and a sign of society's need to represent what ostensibly no longer exists (Nora 1996: 12–13). As the collective experience of society, the act of remembering then becomes one that constructs social identities, in this case the stereotypical images of a cultural world that was 'Goalparia'.[32] This world was often defined in opposition to the social codes of a (settled) Assamese society with the mahout from Goalpara as its romantic hero, whose transgressions were both celebrated and condemned.[33]

Understanding collective memory however, is also about the exploration of the processes of invention and appropriation that determine the subjects of popular representation (Confino 1997). In other words, the ability to decide what images and objects were to form part of the collective consciousness, to be transmitted across successive generations, depended crucially upon one's position of belonging to influential groups in society. This politics of memory ensured therefore that totalising representations of society remained deeply subjective, riven through by the social exigencies of the powerful. In the context of Goalpara, a condition that would have determined these representations would have been the concerns of the traditional elite over the loss of their privilege of elephant catching and hunting. Colonial restrictions on elephant catching by zamindars in the late nineteenth century[34] had evoked strong protests from the zamindars of all the estates, who argued that the *Dooar Hatishala*[35] was a privilege enjoyed by them from Mughal times, and later in the colonial period, with the consent of the state. In their replies to questions from officials, zamindars asserted their 'immemorial right and ownership to all moveable and immoveable, trees and animals which may exist in the land in their possession'.[36] The granting of pottahs to catch elephants, they pointed out, formed a key part of zamindari income in an area which was thinly inhabited and cultivated.[37] Despite the arguments put forward about the practical uses of the animal,[38] the Elephant Preservation Act of 1879 accepted that 'the zamindars cherish this right, not so much for the pecuniary profit thence derived as because they fancy it increases their social importance'.[39] And the Act sought to curtail the same, as was evident in the following response of the state to the legal representative of the zamindars:

Even where Government claims this right, it is not in its capacity as the owner of the soil, but as the sovereign and representative of the former rulers who always claimed and reinforced this right ... it has indeed been urged broadly that the rights to elephants as royal beasts is one of the attributes of sovereignty, at any rate in North India, and that no private right, adverse to that of the government can without express grant by the ruling power be recognised ... whereas in the countries formerly subject to the rulers of Assam, this right was continuously asserted by the sovereign, this argument seems valid ... [T]he right to capture elephants is one of the attributes of sovereignty in Bengal and Assam.[40]

Elephant catching in this context could then become a metaphor for a changing order and for Goalpara's zamindars, the selection and publishing of collections of mahout songs, a response to a perceived sense of loss of history and to the disappearance of certain living traditions. This response also had the added quality of subverting official narratives. It is perhaps no coincidence therefore, that one of the early collectors of oral narratives and songs from the region was Nihar Barua. In the manner of other contemporary 'collectors' of popular literature, Barua describes her collection as a search for the true repositories of the life in this *pranto*, the rural peasants and those who lived on the margins of civilisation, such as the mahouts, the phandis and the moishals (Barua 2000: 14).[41] The mahout and the moishal, in particular, emerge as the most complete representatives of local society, the 'least contaminated by foreign influence and [the] most in touch with the nation's recent past' (Burke 1992: 297). Both are represented as 'resourceful and independent', and as opposed to the upper classes, characterised by their 'endless courage, physical strength, and the possession of all qualities desired in a man ... he does not fear the tiger even' (Barua 2000: 78). The material and cultural distance between the traditional elite and the class to which the mahouts belonged in these representations would have been sufficient for the elites to attribute exotic qualities to their lives. The songs and the stories of their lives were therefore 'discovered' and narrated by a people whose knowledge was likely to have been a borrowed one.

What becomes important then, is why a particular past is being remembered and by whom, not just how a past is being constructed (Confino 1997: 1387). The use of select images by the elite from indigenous cultural reserves to retrieve narratives of community that people could identify with historically, made the act of remembering one that was essentially grounded in relationships of power. In the second decade of the twentieth century, this was evident in Goalpara during the movement for the politicisation of a borderland cultural collective which needed its own nationalistic tropes to resist marginality. Predictably, in its ability through acts of anachronism to transfer images, objects, spaces, values and emotions, from the present times into the past, oral literature worked as one such crucially important trope.

✳

Notes

1. Letter from J. E. Webster, Chief Secretary to the Chief Commissioner of Assam to the Secretary to the Government of India, 12 March 1919, Shillong, Ninth Despatch on Indian Constitutional Reforms, Q/IDC/46, OIOC, London.
2. There is a rich scholarship on historical narratives and their production of identities and categories in colonial India. For a recent exposition of the same, see Prachi Deshpande's (2007) analysis of the construction of a historical memory of the Maratha past.
3. I borrow Prachi Deshpande's use of the term with which she refers to 'visions of the past that are enthusiastically invoked by the broader population of a society, produced through frequent debate, and generated through scholarly writings as well a variety of forms (designated) as "popular histories"' (Deshpande 2007: 6).
4. There are similar descriptions of the geographical entity that was Assam in other texts from the late nineteenth century.
5. For instance, there is none of the reproach for the absence of 'a proper history' which reflected an awareness of the region's past and selfhood that characterises nationalist histories from Bengal from this period. For comments on this sense of a lack, see Chatterjee (1993); Kaviraj (1993); and Nandy (1995).
6. This was the first such initiative by the colonial government in India to set up a department of historical research.
7. 'Assam has a tradition of history writing from the 13th century onwards. It was considered a matter of shame for people of this country not to be learned in the history of the region' (Goswami 1922).

8. 'We alone have to retrieve the history of our community and of our country, Assam. Only those *jatis* or communities which have succeeded in this have been recognised as civilized and educated', exhorted Kanaklal Barooah in his 'Presidential address to the History Session of the Assam Sahitya Sabha' (Talukdar 1973: 27).

9. S. K. Bhuyan, 'Address to the History Session of the Assam Sahitya Sabha', 1926 (Hazarika and Goswami 1961: 45).

10. Ibid.

11. There are several similar examples of the use of mythical history to invoke notions of a unified past, some of them from Assam's more established historians. 'We must go beyond the boundaries of conventional history for the earliest mention of Assam. A properly organised state existed in this region long before the struggle between the Brahminists and the Buddhists and is illustrated in the Mahabharata. In those remote times, Assam had a powerful voice in the affairs of the subcontinent' (S. K. Bhuyan, 'Address to the History Session of the Assam Sahitya Sabha', 1926 in Hazarika and Goswami 1961: 46).

12. Ibid., p. 26.

13. Ibid., p. 30.

14. According to another popular legend from both Assam and Goalpara, the stone statues inside the temple of Kamakhya are those of the Koch King Naranarayan and his brother Chilarai.

15. 'Prior to even the rise of the kingdom of Kamatapur in the 13th century, this frontier area was under the rule of Gaureshwar. We can term this region as a "frontier". It was neither Assam not Bengal', argued K. M. Dhar in his work (Dhar 1911: 9).

16. Rajani Kumar Padmapati, 'President's address to the fourth history session of the Assam Sahitya Sabha', 1930 (Hazarika and Goswami 1961: 58).

17. 'But in practice, the distinction between the localization of meaning and the way a narrative shapes the real is sometimes hard to sustain because the same historical actor who disperses the meaning of the event may also return it to a centralising historical narrative' (Duara 1995: 80).

18. These songs were composed for Sonaray, the tiger–god, who was the local deity evoked to protect the villagers from wild animals, particularly the tiger, much like Dakhinray of the Sunderbans, and were sung during the Sonaray Puja in the month of Pos.

19. Or the poignant '*Chariya na jaan, mur moishal bondhu re*' (Don't leave me behind, O my beloved moishal).

20. Barua, 'The daughter of the elephant and the story and songs of the mahout' (Barua 2000: 91).
21. '*O mor dotal hatir mahut re, shedin mahut Asham jai narir mon mor jhuria jai re'*.
22. '*O mor hai hastir kanya re, khaniku daya nai mahuter lagiya re'*. There are many narratives of the story of 'the daughter of the elephant' in Goalparia oral literature. According to one such narrative, this 'daughter' was the neglected wife of a Brahmin, rescued from her plight by a herd of elephants during a flood who then crowned her their queen.
23. Letter from A. C. Campbell, Officiating Deputy Commissioner of Goalpara, to the Secretary to the Chief Commissioner of Assam, 20 January 1879, Home Department: Proceedings of the Chief Commissioner of Assam, March 1879, OIOC, London.
24. Letter from the Deputy Commissioner of Goalpara and the Secretary to the Chief Commissioner of Assam, 20 January, 1879 Home Political Proceedings, No. 29, OIOC, London.
25. Letter from the Secretary to the Chief Commissioner of Assam to the Deputy Commissioner of Goalpara, 28 January 1879, Home Political Proceedings, No. 30, OIOC, London.
26. Ibid.
27. Regulation No. 1 of 1880: Extension of The Elephants Preservation Act of 1879 to certain districts administered by the Chief Commissionership of Assam, Letter No. 8 from the Government of India (Fort William), 18 February 1880, Home, Revenue and Agricultural Department: Judicial, OIOC, London.
28. Letter from A. Eden, Secretary to the Government of Bengal, Judicial Department, to E. C. Bayley, Secretary to the Government of India, 21 February 1870, Home Department: Proceedings of the Chief Commissioner of Assam, OIOC, London.
29. Letter from A. C. Campbell, Officiating Deputy Commissioner of Goalpara, to the Secretary to the Chief Commissioner of Assam, 20 January 1879, Home Department: Proceedings of the Chief Commissioner of Assam, March 1879, OIOC, London.
30. Letter from A. C. Campbell, Officiating Deputy Commissioner of Goalpara to the Secretary to the Chief Commissioner of Assam, Shillong, 13 November 1876, Home Department: Proceedings of the Chief Commissioner of Assam, November 1876, OIOC, London.
31. Letter from T. J. Murray, Assistant Secretary to the Chief Commissioner of Assam to the Deputy Commissioner of Goalpara, 29 November 1876, Home Department: Proceedings of the Chief Commissioner of Assam, November 1876, OIOC, London.

32. The synonyms with nationalism are hard to miss, where the publishing of collections of oral literature and songs have often been considered as a necessary condition for the emergence of nationalism. See Burke 1978; Fernandez 1966; Blackburn and Ramanujan 1986. In Bengal this trend was reflected in appeals to the urban *bhadralok* to re-establish links with rural life and a gathering together of popular literature, songs and fairy tales, best exemplified in Sen (1923).

33. In the post-colonial period, these images of Goalpara have been recreated in the popular imagination of the Assamese people through the songs of Pratima Pandey and Bhupen Hazarika's rendering of the *'Gouripuria Gabhoru Dekhilu, Hati Dhoriboloi Goi ...'* (I saw this beautiful maiden from Gouripur, when on my way to catch elephants).

34. Legislation which prohibited elephant catching in the region included the Regulation Act of 1876 which banned 'hunting of elephants without a written license within the Garo Hills', the Forest Act of 1878 and the Elephant Preservation Act of 1879 which extended the terms of the 1876 Act. (Extract from the Deputy Commissioner of Garo Hills' Letter no. 499, 18 September 1880, to the Secretary to the Chief Commissioner of Assam, Home Political Proceedings, April 1881, No. 5, OIOC, London.

35. Duar Hatishala was a traditional right claimed by the zamindars of the region to hunt or catch elephants within their estates and one that was much contested by the colonial state.

36. Replies of the zamindars of Goalpara, to official queries regarding their right to catch elephants in their estates in the correspondence between the Deputy Commissioner of Goalpara and the Secretary to the Chief Commissioner of Assam, 20 January 1879, Home Political Proceedings, No. 29, OIOC, London.

37. Ibid.

38. The reply of the Gauripur zamindar in the correspondence between the Deputy Commissioner of Goalpara and the Secretary to the Chief Commissioner of Assam, 20 January 1879, Home Political Proceedings, No. 29, OIOC, London.

39. 'The ordinary law regulating the position of ferae is not strictly applicable to wild elephants — no other animal of the forest is susceptible to being tamed and utilised as it can be. It has always been considered a most invaluable auxiliary for military movements and the preservation of the species for State purposes justifies special legislation' (Ibid.).

40. Correspondence between the Deputy Commissioner of the Garo Hills and the Secretary to the Chief Commissioner of Assam, 27 January 1881, Home Political Proceedings, No. 7, OIOC, London.

41. Letter from the Secretary to the Chief Commissioner of Assam to the Legal Remambrancer, Calcutta, Home Proceedings, Revenue and Agriculture, July 1880, No. 5, OIOC, London.
42. 'She sought to capture the poetry that lay hidden in the speech of the ordinary man' (Baruah 2000: 9). In a similar trajectory of the discovery of the national self in Bengal, Dineshchandra Sen described the composers of the Mymensingh ballads as 'materially different from and opposed to, the dogmas of the Renaissance Brahmins' (Sen 1923: 26).

6

✿

Conclusion

The state is consolidating on a world scale. It weighs down on society (on all societies) in full force ...The state crushes time by reducing differences to repetitions or circularities ... This modern state promotes and imposes itself as the stable centre — definitively — of (national) societies and spaces. As both the end and the meaning of history, it flattens the social and cultural spheres. It enforces a logic that puts to end conflicts and contradictions. It neutralises whatever resists it by castration or crushing. Is this social entropy? (Lefebvre 1991: 23)

In northeastern India and its neighbourhood, where 'the modern state, in both its colonial and its independent guises, has had the resources to realize a project of rule that was a mere glint in the eye of its pre-colonial ancestor: namely to bring non-state spaces and people to heel' (Scott 2009: 4), writing spatial histories of borderlands allows for a reconceptualising of social space through an interrogation of otherwise apparently pervasive 'heartland' practices. A historiography of spaces, such as this book seeks to develop, contests and reconfigures state–centred post-colonial national histories, pushing history writing well beyond the nation. Through an exploration of the many interconnections between the discursive and political–economy aspects of spatial production and reorganisation over time, the book restores historicity to the category of the 'borderland'. In the process, it also offers an escape from some prevalent tired oppositional binaries (colonial/pre-colonial, civilised/wild, memory/history, written/oral, mobile/settled, hill/plain, core/margins) and their accompanying stereotypical representations, speaking instead to an emerging new and critical historical research on the region.

Writing histories of borderland spaces then makes a strong case for foregrounding of ideas of multiplicity and the contingent in the hope of returning the practices of the marginal and the suppressed. The book grounded these concerns in the specific context of what became the western borderlands of northeastern India, in the nineteenth and early decades of the twentieth century. It centred issues of space, but located abstract propositions in a historical analysis of the transformation of locales and local communities in the region.

The first two chapters and some of the third, very broadly, was about the making of a colonial borderland, the erasure of pre-colonial social and economic connections and of local ideas of space, place, power and cultural difference. The pre-colonial told the story of trajectories of state formation during the Mughal imperium, particularly of the negotiated character of state-making that had to speak to the existing plurality of ideas of space, nature and sovereignty, of a more liquid landscape that had mobility as an element of significance as in the various itinerant practices of the elephant catcher, the buffalo herder and the shifting cultivator. Not the comfortable narrative of a golden past, however, heterogeneity in ideas of power and space marked this world, as communities straddled settled agrarian life with itinerant practices, blurring lines between the hills and the plains, the fixed and the mobile. And within this more fluid landscape than the one that was to succeed it, structures of pre-colonial violence were pre-eminent as well, with several instances of sustained peasant rebellions against extractive regimes of revenue collection and land taxation. The pre-colonial period was equally about differently structured pasts with realms of overlapping sovereignties of local chieftains, zamindars, mercenaries, the Bhutan monarch and the Dalai Lama and their connected histories. These gave way to spatially delimited units of colonialism of the late nineteenth century, profoundly altering local social and spatial relationships.

Colonialism's most visible manifestations in these parts were, predictably, in conflicts over livelihoods and lifestyles. The imposition of an uniform notion of the sedentary cultivator as the ideal productive subject and the accompanying trajectory of change that included wasteland reclamation, the introduction of tenurial settlements and the encouragement of migration from other regions to enable the peasantisation that had been set in motion, have been the subject of several local histories, not just of this region but of other parts of colonial India as well. Where the book added to, but went critically beyond the available frameworks of economic history, however, was in analysing how transformations in the local economy enabled access to institutions such as colonial legality, thus offering insights into linkages between 'pure' economic practices and processes of colonial state–making in the region. The resultant fixing of ideas of space and power, it has been argued, could increasingly have only one predominant imagination of a relationship with nature and space — that of the sedentary cultivator with his land. For the new peasant proprietor cultivating the valleys of the Godadhor and the Brahmaputra, this enabled a neat collapse between nationalism and the land, an important basis for his growing sense of being part of a larger collective and his participation in the associational and agitational politics that marked the early twentieth century.

Within the colonial state's new political units in this part of eastern India, markets and trading practices, previously part of an extended social and political landscape and now deprived of their cultural underpinnings, became the new sites of confrontation between the local and colonial notions of space, territory and authority. Exemplifying colonialism's redefining of space in all its starkness was the reorientation of regional trading connections in the early twentieth century. From being a site for thriving commercial and cultural exchange between the northern polities of Bhutan and Tibet, and Assam and Bengal, Goalpara, within the space of a few decades of colonial rule, was transformed into a hinterland of goods for the Bengal market and a borderland economy.

A pre-colonial connected history of a liminal space was being rewritten as a confined history of a fragmented marginal region. Add to this the various closures and flattening of complex social relationships that effectively set in motion processes that identified the ethnic inhabitants of mountainous regions in northeastern India as the 'other' of a resurgent Indian civilisation and colonialism's impact begins to fall into perspective. In the spatial history of the region, this is the stage when the district of Goalpara becomes part of a colonial borderland, an 'in between' space between the now two 'core' provinces of Bengal and

Assam that does not get definitively absorbed into either of these 'civilisational spaces'. The imagining of nationalism excludes people and places both temporally and spatially and so was it with the Assamese and Bengali nationalist imaginings towards the end of the nineteenth and in the beginning of the twentieth century. 'Goalpara' in these narratives gradually comes to constitute the frontiers of Assamese, and to an extent Bengali, identity, the focus on its still shifting boundaries and identities ensuring that it had only a minimal role in the discursive terrain of nationalist politics. In short, the region becomes a good example of 'places that fell off the map' and through the cracks of the imagined history of nationalisms.

A borderland is therefore more than a political 'earthquake', the sudden product of the movement of 'political tectonic plates' that 'create fissures known as international borders' (van Schendel 2005: 2).[1] Instead, its making can be a process with a pre-history that spans a few centuries. The book has argued that the spatial history of the western borderlands of northeastern India would have to include the complex maze of different imaginations of power and space in the pre-colonial, connections and networks of mobility that involved Bhutan and Tibet, their transformation through the practices of the colonial state and of various core nationalisms but also by those of the inhabitants of the borderland who reenacted the historical memory of pre-colonial connections to forge new borderland collectivities, as in the mobilisation for a Goalparia identity in the early decades of the last century. This was the subject of the later chapters of the book, as they explored the complex ways in which colonial governmentality unravelled in practices of speech, historical memory, map making and the Census.

In the period that followed, the 1930s and the 1940s, the movement for a Goalparia identity became increasingly fragmented, its proponents preferring to identify with collectivities forged around notions of ethnicity, religion and class. Although this period falls outside the chronological bracket of this book, it in no way indicates any closure in the story of the spatial history of the region. It is only appropriate therefore that the book closes with a brief discussion of what happened after, if only to reiterate its argument about the tenacious hold of the colonial spatial order on the post-colonial and the practices of inclusion and exclusion that this generated.

The new solidarities that emerged in the 1930s and the 1940s in Goalpara and elsewhere in Assam, sharpened themselves on the anvil of nationalisms, 'Indian' and 'Assamese', retaining however, the ability to subvert even in the act of apparent surrender. Negotiating with issues of caste mobility and community identity was the Rajbanshi movement, which under the formal banner of the Kshatriya Samiti and the leadership of Panchanan Barma, mobilised people across the districts of Rangpur, Goalpara, Cooch Behar, Jalpaiguri and Dinajpur (Basu 2003: 71). As a period of Assam's fraught relationship with its immigrants began, cultivators who had migrated from eastern Bengal earlier in the century found new leaders within their community. The most popular of them all, Maulana Bhasani, founded the Goalpara District Praja Sanmilan at Ghagmari, near Dhubri, to avowedly protect the rights of the immigrant tenants that included not just a reduction in rents but also the right to have Bengali as the medium of instruction 'for all Bengali children of the Brahmaputra Valley in all primary and secondary schools' (Guha 1977: 249). In his report of 1938 on the response, or lack of it, to the debate over the Line System[2] from his district, the Deputy Commissioner of Goalpara had attributed this to 'the district being contiguous to Bengal, the language of the bulk of the people more akin to Bengali than Assamese and [hence] the indigenous people ... could easily accommodate themselves to the immigrants' ways and modes of life and ... the inherent hatred which local people entertain against the immigrants [was] non-existent'.[3]

These were hardly claims that could be made for the rest of society in the Brahmaputra Valley, where the immigrant from eastern Bengal had come to steadily represent the 'other' of the Assamese national subject. There is much in the writings from the time that could be cited as evidence of such representations but the protection of the 'easy going Assamese [who] could not put up a fight against the virile Mymensinghia'[4] were among the three reasons initially given by the state for setting up the Line System itself. The process of the freezing of the migrant and the 'indigenous Assamese', 'the domicile' and the 'native', as categories of cultural difference was apparent in the later debates over the proposed abolition of the Line System. Official reports from the time are accordingly suffused with constructions of the immigrant as 'the troublesome neighbour ... obsessed with far greater greed for land than the native of the Province...[and] often driven to commit offences and disturb the peace and tranquility of the Province'.[5] As the new Assamese nation redrew its several boundaries and identified its strategies of exclusion, it laid down the place for the 'immigrants' within this newly constituted space:

> the problem of the domicile was not a superficial one. If it can be grafted into the national life, it works for vigour and strength but if it grows like weeds, wild and untrimmed, then the whole soil is ... unfit for any cultivation. Justice to the domiciled communities must be done but not before one knows clearly who they are (Phukan 1939).[6]

The immigrants responded with their own set of representations to constitute the nation as is evident in the following exposition from the Assam Domiciled and Settlers' Association: '[the domiciles] managed to merge themselves into the life of Assam, and their "Bengaliness", mingling with the local values, helped to create a new people. This interchange of values, this co-mingling of blood, is as true in the life of Assam as of every province in India'.[7] The story of migration, its accompanying demographic shifts and the congealing of identities along lines of indigenous/migrant or insider/outsider only intensified in the subsequent decades as waves of immigrants fanned out in a process that James Scott in his recent work has evocatively termed the 'Last Enclosure movement in Southeast Asia' (Scott 2009: 4).[8]

Significant though these conversations are, they are but pointers to the several other 'reiterative and declarative tendencies' (Oinam 2009: 171) through which the discourses of exclusion and inclusion operate in the region. The history of spatial organisation did not stop with the end of British colonial rule as the postcolonial politics of ethnicity in the region continued to reproduce much of the colonial spatial imagination, ignoring the connections of earlier times that shaped local spatial practices: 'The ethno–territorial frame that colonial officials used to create boundaries between administrative units and to devise rules of exclusion, continue to shape notions of entitlement and the aspirations of ethnic groups — as articulated by political organizations speaking on their behalf'(Baruah 2009: 9). This is an ideological continuity of immense significance, as it frames the critical discourse around territoriality and indigeneity that has been at the core of the demands by various tribal groups for exclusive ethnic homelands in northeastern India. Entrenched in the colonial categories of hill–plain binaries that assigned ethnic groups to fixed territorial spaces (and discussed elsewhere in this book), the contemporary politics of territoriality and indigeneity, Sanjib Baruah argues, 'have become an exercise in defending the fences and walls that the colonial rulers have erected … are dissonant with existing local spatial practices … and have produced recurrent challenges to equal rights including episodes of ethnic violence and displacement, and a permanent crisis of citizenship' (Baruah 2008: 16).

In the seething multiplicity of practices and identities that have contested and transformed power and space in the western borderland of northeastern India in the late and post-colonial period however, were many examples of multiple voices that were not always appropriated by the nation; refusing to be silenced by state programmes of homogenising spatiality, they executed in turn various representations of the nation and of its spaces. Though a rather tentative thesis in need of more critical probing, it can be argued that the movement for a separate state of Kamatapur is a powerful instance from the post-colonial afterlives of the borders that has refused to limit itself to the dominant grid of territorial nationalism and hence of the colonial spatial ideology as well. The demand was articulated as early as 1954, when a proposal before the State Reorganisation Commission asked for the formation of a Kamatapur State consisting of Goalpara, Garo Hills, Cooch Behar, Darjeeling and Jalpaiguri.[9] The Commission turned it down, on the grounds that 'a new state, which may well mean that only one set of problems is exchanged for another, is not in our opinion, an appropriate remedy for the grievances of the minorities, if any',[10] drawing forced parallels here with the demand for a state of Purbachal that claimed to address the perceived marginalisation of the Bengali–speaking population of Assam after the Partition of Sylhet. The proposal for Kamatapur was about the protection of community identity, in this case of the Koch and Rajbanshi people, but equally importantly, about resistance from the borderlands to the exclusionary discourses of the state and of nation–building in the 1950s. That this demand transformed into a militant cross-border separatist movement for a Kamatapuri homeland that included districts from India and Bangladesh only reaffirms that such movements can be understood better by locating them within a long duree spatial history of the region, beyond imaginations caught in static national spaces. The narrative of the various connected spaces 'becoming a borderland' then takes on the edge of a critical history that reaffirms the significance of lost historical connections in post-colonial histories of the nation. The boundaries of this proposed Kamtapur overlap quite considerably with the 'frontier kingdom' that Goalpara's historians had written about and that this book discussed: northern Bangladesh, the Bhutan foothills, northern West Bengal and the Goalpara district of western Assam. This does not make them peripheral survivals of a pre-modern past of the nation. Instead these are movements forged in encounters with colonial modernity whose political claims thrive on the historical memory of earlier connections, which, even when erased, return as specters to haunt the contemporary histories of the nation. While historicising these contemporary appropriations of memories of the past, it is important to recognise that the demands for a separate state are also reiterations of the impossibility of writing histories that are determined by the anachronistic impulses of the modern nation state. To not recognise this is to commit the fallacy of perpetuating the nation's persistent structures of dominance.

Speaking to the growing genre of local histories as the absent present of colonialism and nationalism at the 'core', histories of borderlands evoke therefore, practices of the margins that routinely represent nationalism as a relational identity. In the context of northeastern India, these practices underline the historical and the contingent, as in the ways in which the 'northeast' comes to be constituted as various spaces: a 'pre-colonial frontier', 'a colonial borderland', the 'eastern borders of the postcolonial nation' or 'not as the periphery of India but as the centre of a thriving and integrated economic space linking two dynamic regions with a network of highways, railways, pipelines, transmission lines crisscrossing the region' (Sikri 2004 quoted in Baruah 2009:1). Beyond the specificities of the regional frame, however, these practices can problematise the very act of writing histories not just in Zomia but in all borderlands places that constitute 'a world of peripheries', their historical account 'sharply at odds with the official story most civilizations tell themselves' (Scott 2009: 3).

Transgressions of the nation's spaces, ironically, however, are predicated on the very recognition of national territoriality. Efforts to write more inclusive histories that see previously marginalised practices of the borderland as the conceptual starting point instead of those of the 'cores', based as they are on 'ways of imagining power and space different from the "heartland" practices' (van Schendel

2005: 5) can be in a danger of reproducing the very frameworks of dominance that they seek to resist. Stories of crossings of national borders can simultaneously freeze the 'borderland of the nation' into another 'core' with its own set of margins. A way out of this predicament, to return an argument from the Introduction of this book, is to continue imagining spaces in motion, in all their connections and flexibility, outside of the civilisational frames and boundaries of the nation–state that threaten to capture them. This is not to deny the presence of the fixed but to recognise the often obscured fluidity and the contingent as critical defining elements in history.

✻

Notes

1. 'The Bengal borderland was born with such suddenness that nobody actually knew its location till several days later' (van Schendel 2005: 2).
2. A measure adopted by the colonial state in 1920 which involved the drawing of a line across districts with a large migrant population from Bengal in order to separate their settlements from those of the native Assamese.
3. Report of the Deputy Commissioner, Goalpara, on the immigrant question in that district, Report of the Line System Committee 1938, Shillong.
4. Ibid.
5. Report of the Line System Committee, Shillong, 1938, Chapter II.
6. Phukan was then the President of the Jorhat Town Mouza, Congress Committee.
7. 'Social Composition of the Assamese People', Report from the Annual Conference of the Assam Domiciled and Settler's Association, 1940, Political History of Assam, State Archives, Guwahati.
8. Scott explains this enclosure movement thus: 'Seen from the state centre, this enclosure movement, is, in part, an effort to integrate and monetise the people, lands, and resources of the periphery so that they become … auditable contributors to the gross national product and to foreign exchange' (Scott 2009: 4).
9. Report of the State Reorganisation Commission 1955:184; I am grateful to Professor Sajal Nag for this reference.
10 Report of the State Reorganisation Commission 1955: 191.

Glossary

Abwabs	Cesses
Adhiars	Sharecropper entitled to half a share of the produce
Aghur	Precious, fragrant wood
Amlas	Clerks or ministerial officers
Annas	1/16 of a rupee
Bathan/Khuti	Enclosure for cattle
Begar	Forced labour
Bhati	Literally, downstream but also southern Assam and eastern and southern Bengal
Bhatias	People from bhati
Bigha	A measure of land, about 1/3 of an acre
Burkandezes	Mercenary soldiers and retainers
Char/chapori	Flood plains
Chowkis	Toll houses
Chukanidars	Tenure holder, below a jotedar
Chulunta Masool	Tax levied on timber floating down rivers
Cowries	Shells used as a medium of exchange
Dar-chukanidar	Tenure holder below a chukanidar
Desiya Bhasa	Local term for the language of Goalpara
Diwan	Zamindari officer concerned with finance
Dhing	Uprising, rebellion
Faujdar	Head of the police court
Fauzdari/Fauzdarry	Revenue on land held by faujdar
Gharuwari Paiks	Auxilliary footmen
Haats	Weekly markets
Jauna	A robe
Jote/jotedar	Cultivable land/holder of a jote directly from the state or the zamindar
Jhum	Shifting/swidden cultivation
Kabuliat	A deed recording the acceptance of the terms of the patta
Khas	Government land or estates
Khazana	Treasure
Khedda	Stockade trap for the capture of elephants
Lakhiraj	Rent free privileged tenure

Mahout	Elephant driver
Maunds	A measurement of weight, about 82 lbs
Mauzadars	Official in charge of the assessment of land revenue of the village
Moishal	A person employed to look after buffaloes
Munsif	Lower rank judge dealing mainly with revenue cases
Narayani Rupees	The currency of the state of Cooch Behar
Nirikh	Rate, a market price
Paat	Jute (Bengali)
Paikars	Itinerant merchants
Pargana	Subordinate unit in revenue administration
Payal Pattas	Perpetual leases granted by jotedars to cultivators in order to reclaim wastelands
Phandi	Elephant catcher
Pillos	Officials of the Bhutan monarchy
Pottahs/Patta	Lease/tenancy/ownership documentation of land
Pucca	Brick built
Puthis	Printed or handwritten texts
Qanungo	Revenue officer
Sairat	Non-agricultural taxes
Salami	Capitation fee usually paid at first assumption of tenancy or for clearing fresh land
Sanad	A deed/charter granted by a ruler
Soubahs	Deputy commissioner under orders of the Pillo
Thulijat	Tax levied on timber stacked on the banks of rivers
Tehsildar	Revenue official
Taluk	An administrative division
Vamshavalis	Family histories

Bibliography

PRIMARY SOURCES

Archival Sources

State Archives, Guwahati

Assam Police Abstract of Intelligence, 1914–1947.
Assam Secretariat Files: Revenue A and B, Confidential and Education 1890–1938.
Board of Revenue Papers 1781–1793, 1859–1872.
Chief Commissioner's Files, 1861–1916.
Colonisation of Wastelands Papers, 1878–1898.
Goalpara Papers, 1863–1881.
Government of Bengal Files: Revenue 1847–1875.
Papers of the Assam Domiciled and Settler's Association, PHA.
Papers of the Assam Sanrakshini Sabha, PHA.
Papers of the Goalpara Zamindar's Association, PHA.
The Political History of Assam Collection, 1916–1932.

Department of Historical and Antiquarian Studies, Guwahati

Maniram Barua, Buranji Vivek Ratna, 1838, Mss. 272, Transcript: 108.

Dhubri Collectorate, Dhubri

Magistrate's Records, 1910–1920.

National Library Annexe, Calcutta

Review of the Progress of Education in Assam, 1892–1932.

Oriental and India Office Collections (currently Asian and African Studies Collections), The British Library, London

Bengal Political and Secret Department Files: various years beginning 1816.
Board's Collection, 1776–1836.
Home Department, 1874–1905.
Linguistic Survey of India, Collection IV, Correspondence with the Government of Assam S/1/4/1.
Ninth Despatch on Indian Constitutional Reforms, Q/IDC/46, 1919.
Proceedings of the Assam Legislative Council, 1906–1947.
Proceedings of the Assam Legislative Assembly, 1937–1947.
Public and Judicial Department, 1869–1931.
Revenue Department, 1884–1931.

Unpublished Manuscripts and Private Papers

Asian and African Studies (formerly Oriental and India Office Collections), The British Library, London

Extracts from the Journal of Buchanan, including maps of Assam.
George Grierson Papers.
H. H. Risley Papers, 1901–1911, Vol. 9.
Letters from Major James Rennell, with one sketch map.
Papers of Captain Jenkins.
Papers of Henry Cotton.
Papers of Herbert Lewin.
Paper of John Ghrose.
Papers of John Haughton.
Papers of William Herschel.
The Bogle Papers.
The Buchanan Hamilton Manuscripts.
The Buchanan Hamilton Papers.
The Macnabb Collection.
Translation of the letter from Charles Cornwallis regarding the appointment of Hugh Baille as Resident of Goalpara.

Newspapers and Periodicals

All India Reporter, 1916–1936.
Amrit Bazar Patrika, 1925–1929.
Asam Bandhu, 1885–1886.
Asamiya, 1918–1947.
Assam Bandhav, 1908–1909.
Assam Sahitya Sabha Patrika, 1943–1955.
Assam Tribune, 1916–1925.
Awahan, 1929–1940.
Banhi, 1910–1928.
Bijuli, 1892–1893.
Jonaki, 1889–1902.
Journal of the Asiatic Society of Bengal, select issues.
Mou, 1886–1887.
Probashi, 1926–1940.
Rangpur Sahitya Parishad Patrika, 1906–1924.
The Orunodoi, 1846–1868.
Usha, 1907–1908.

Published Sources

Government Records, Reports, Census and Papers of Organisations

Administrative Report on the Frontier Tribes of Assam, 1911–1942.
Annual Report on the Progress of Education in Assam, 1874–1947.
Annual Report for Assam, 1894–1944.
Annual Report on the Frontier Tribes of Assam, 1915–1931.
Annual Report on the Trade between Assam and Adjoining Foreign Countries, 1877–78, Shillong, 1878.
Assam Gazette, Vol. VI, Guwahati, 1948.
Barpeta Hitsadhini Sabha Proceedings, Barpeta, 1897.
Bengal District Records: Rangpur, Vol. 1, 1770–1779, Calcutta, 1914.
Bengal District Records: Rangpur, Vol. 4, 1779–1785, Calcutta, 1921.
Bengal District Records: Rangpur, Vol. 6, 1786–1787, Calcutta, 1928.
Bengal Provincial Banking Enquiry Committee Report, 1929–1930, Vol. 1, Calcutta, 1930.

Census of India, 1891, Assam, Shillong, 1892.

Census of India, 1901, Assam, Shillong, 1902.

Census of India 1911, Assam, Shillong, 1912.

Census of India 1921, Assam, Shillong, 1923.

Census of India 1921, Bengal, Volume V, Part I, Calcutta, 1923.

Census of India 1931, Assam, Shillong, 1932.

Cunningham's Report for the Calcutta University Commission, 1917.

Evidence taken in the Assam Royal Commission on Agriculture in India, Vol. V, Calcutta, 1927.

Evidence taken in the Assam Provincial Banking Enquiry Committee, 1929–1930, Shillong, 1930.

Franchise Committee Report and Evidence, 1918–1919.

General Report on Public Instruction in Assam, 1874–1930.

Indian Statutory Commission Vol. 15: Oral Evidence, Assam, 1929.

Political Missions to Bhutan, comprising the reports of Hon'ble Ashley Eden – 1864; Capt. R.B. Pemberton, 1837, 1838, with Dr. Griffiths's Journal and the account by Baboo Kishen Kanta Bose, Calcutta, 1865.

Progress Report of Forest Administration in the Province of Assam, 1874–1949.

Report on the Administration of Assam, 1876–1939.

Report on the Administration of Cooch Behar, 1911–1930.

Report on the Administration of the Court of Wards Estate in Assam, 1905–1946.

Report on the Administration of Eastern Bengal and Assam, 1906–1912.

Report on the Land Revenue Administration of Assam, 1901–1935.

Report of the Assam Provincial Banking Enquiry Committee, 1929–1930, Vol. 1, Shillong, 1930.

Report of the Assam Sahitya Sabha, Guwahati, 1955.

Report on the Census of Rangpur, 1891 in Census of India, 1891, Vol. 5, Bengal Districts, Calcutta, 1892.

Report of the Line System Committee, Vols. I and II, Shillong, 1938.

Reports of the Police of the Cooch Behar Division (Annual Crime Reports), 1866–1871, Calcutta.

Report and Proceedings of the Cooch Behar Pooneah Exhibition Mela, Cooch Behar, 1894.

Report of the State Reorganisation Commission, New Delhi, 1955.

Resolution on the Land Revenue Administration of Assam, 1927–1928, Shillong, 1928.

Some Memorials, Representations and Notes by the Zemindars and Raiyats of the District of Goalpara, from 1874 to the present time, Calcutta, 1925.

Statement of newspapers and periodicals published in Assam, Shillong, 1924.

The New Dispensation in Assam and Bengal, Shillong, 1929.

Uttar Banga Sahitya Sanmilan, Sixth Session, Calcutta, 1917.

Village Directory of the Presidency of Bengal, Cooch Behar, 1885.

Books and Articles

Agarwala, Anandachandra. 1926. *Goalparar Purani Bibaran*, Goalpara.

Allen, B. C. 1854. *An Account of the Kingdom of Assam*, Calcutta.

———. 1905. *Assam District Gazetteer, Vol. II, Goalpara*, Calcutta.

Anderson, J. D. 1896. 'Assamese and Bengali', *Calcutta Review*, July.

Anon. 1867. 'Ancient Assam', *Calcutta Review*, 23 (45).

Ascoli, F. D. 1917. *Final Report on the Survey and Settlement Operations in the District of Dacca*, Calcutta.

Assam Sahitya Sabha. 1960. *Assam's State Language*, Jorhat.

Barooah, Gunabhiram. 1876. *Asam Buranji*, Calcutta.

———. 1971 (1880). *Anandaram Dhekiyal Phukanar Jivan Caritra*, Guwahati.

Barooah, Kanaklal. 1933. *Early History of Kamarupa*, Shillong.

Barua, Nihar. 2000. *Prantobashir Jhuli, Goalparar Lokojibon U Gaan*, Calcutta.

Barua, Prabhat Chandra. 1928. *Nikhil Goalpara Jila Samiti, Abhyathana Samitir Sabhapatir Bhasan*, Dhubri.

———. 1926. *Nikhil Goalpara Jila Samitir Sabhapatir Bhasan*, Dhubri.

Barua, Vinanada Chandra. 1926. *Maharaj Naranarayan*, Calcutta.

Basu, N. N. 1926. *Social History of Kamarupa*, Vol. 2, Calcutta.

Bezbaroa, Devendranath. 1933. *Asamiya Bhasa Aru Sahityar Buranji*, Jorhat.

Bezbaroa, Lakshminath. 1910a. 'Asamor Gauripurot Bangla Sahitya Sabha', *Banhi*, 11: 348–56.

———. 1910b. 'Asamor Gauripurot Bangla Sahitya Sabha', *Banhi*, 12: 365–70.

———. 1910c. 'Puroni Asamor Jilingoni Eti, *Banhi*, 6: 167–73.

———. 1910d. 'Asomiya Bhasa Samparke Aru Keitaman Kotha', *Banhi*, 2: 43–52.

———. 1911. 'Asam', *Banhi*, 3: 93–131.

Bhuyan, S. K. 1924. *Anandaram Barua*, Calcutta.

———. (ed.). 1947. *The Annales of the Delhi Badshahate, Being a translation of the old Assamese chronicle, Padshah Buranji*, Guwahati.

———. (ed.). 1964. *Asamar Padya Buranji*, Guwahati.

———. 1974. *Tungkhungia Buranji or the History of Assam 1681–1826*, Guwahati.

Bora, Jnananath. 1928. *Asomot Bideshi*, Guwahati.

———. 1932. 'Kamrup aru Bharatvarsha', *Awahan*, 3: 252–63.

———. 1935. *Srihatta Bisched*, Calcutta.

———. 1945. *Natun Jagat*, Calcutta.

Bora, Lakhinanda. 1875. *Asamar Sankhshep Itihas*, Guwahati.

Bora, K. Soniram. 1918. *The Historical Atlas of Assam*, Guwahati.

Borah, M. I. (ed.). 1936. *Baharastan-I-Gayabi: A History of the Mughal Wars in Assam, Cooch Behar, Bengal, Bihar and Orissa during the Reigns of Jahangir and Shah Jahan, by Mirza Nathan*, Guwahati.

Bordoloi, Kumud Chandra (ed.). 1960. *Sadaraminar Atmajivani*, Guwahati.

Bordoloi, Rajanikant. 1925. *Presidential Address of the Eight Session of the Assam Sahitya Sabha*, Nowgaon.

Brown, Nathan. 1942 (1848). *Grammatical Notes on the Assamese Language*, Jorhat.

Butler, M. J. 1854. *Travels and Adventures in the Province of Assam*, London.

Carter, Herbert R. 1909. *Cordage Fibres: Their Cultivation, Extraction and Preparation for Market*, London.

Carter, Herbert R. 1921. *Technical Handbook*, London.

Chakravarty, Taranath. 1927. 'Goalparar Biruddhe ``Prantobasir'' Sarajantra', *Asamiya*, Vol. 17, 14 August 1927.

Choudhuri, Jatindra Mohan. (ed.). 1928. *Permanent Settlement and the Income Tax*, Calcutta.

Choudhuri, Pramatha. 1926. *Raiyter Katha*, Calcutta.

Chaudhuri, Deen Doyal. 1915. *Nripendra Smriti*, Pabna.

Chaudhuri, H. N. 1903. *The Cooch Behar State and its Land Revenue Settlements*, Cooch Behar.

Clarke, R. 1854. *The Regulations of the Government of Fort William in Bengal, 1793–1853, Vol. 2*, London.

Curzon, G. 1907. *Frontiers*, Oxford.

Dalton, Edward T. 1872. *Descriptive Ethnology of Bengal*, Calcutta.

Das, P. 1940. 'Asomot Census Bibhrat', *Awahan*, 2: 224–28.

Datta Barua, Harinarayan. 1924. *Asam Buranji*, Guwahati.

———. 1941. *Prachin Kamrupia Kayastha Samajar Itibritta*, Nalbari.

Dhar, K. M. 1911. *Purbabanga U Asamer Sankhipta Biboron*, Silchar.

Dhekiyal–Phukan, Anandaram. 1829. *Ain O Byabastha Sangraha: Notes on the Laws of Bengal, Vol. 1*, Calcutta.

Dhekiyal–Phukan, Anandaram. 1875 (1849). *Asamiya Larar Mitra*, Gunabhiram Barooah (ed.), Goalpara.

———. 1977. '*Observations on the Administration of the Province of Assam and A Few Remarks on the Assamese Language and on Vernacular Education in Assam*', in Maheswar Neog (ed.), *Anandaram Dhekiyal Phukan: Plea for Assam and the Assamese*, Jorhat.

Dhekiyal–Phukan, Holiram. 1962 (1820). *Asam Buranji*, Jatindramohan Bhattacharya (ed.), Guwahati.

Eardley–Wilmot, S. 1906. *Notes on the Tour in the Darrang, Kamrup, Garo Hills and Goalpara Forest Divisions of Assam in 1906*, Calcutta.

Eden, Ashley. 1865. *Report on the State of Bootan and the Progress of the Mission of 1863–1864*, Calcutta.

Finlow, Robert Steel. 1906. *The Extension of Jute Cultivation in Assam*, Calcutta.

Firminger, Walter K. (ed.). 1914. *Bengal District Records: Rangpur, Vol. 1, 1770–1779*, Calcutta.

France, B. C. 1916. *Final Report on the Survey and Settlement Operations in the Riparian Areas of the District of Pabna*, Calcutta.

Friel, R. 1914. *Assam District Gazetteers, Goalpara, Supplement to Vol. III*, Shillong.

Gait, E. A. 1897. *Report on the Progress of Historical Research in Assam*, Shillong.

Gait, E. A., B. C. Allen and H. F. Howard. 1905. *Gazetteer of Bengal and North East India*, Shillong.

Ganguli, Kali Charan.1930. *Final Report on the Survey and Settlement Operations in the Cooch Behar State, 1913–1927*, Cooch Behar.

Glazier, E. G. 1873a. *A Report on the District of Rungpore*, Calcutta.

———. 1873b. *Further Notes on the Rungpore Records, Vol. II*, Calcutta.

Gohain Baruah, Padmanath. 1916. *Lachit Barphukan*, Tejpur.

———. 1922. *Buranji Bodh*, Tejpur.

———. 1925. *Jiboni Sangraha*, Tejpur.

———. 1976 (1899). *Asamar Buranji*, Guwahati.

Goswami, Hemchandra. 1917. *Darrang Raj Vamshavali*, Calcutta.

———. (ed.). 1977 (1922). *Purani Asam Buranji*, Guwahati.

Goswami, Pratap Chandra. 1971. *Jiban Smriti aru Kamrupi Samaj*, Guwahati.

Grierson, G. A. (ed.). 1903. *Linguistic Survey of India, Vol. V, Indo-Aryan Family, Eastern Group, Part I: Specimens of the Bengali and Assamese Languages*, Calcutta.

Hai, Abdul. 1922. *Adarsha Krishak*, Mymensingh.

Hart, G. S. 1915. *Note on the Sal Forests in the Jalpaiguri, Buxa and the Goalpara Forest Divisions, to Which is Appended A Note on the Forests of the Duars by R. S. Troup*, Simla.

Hartley, A. C. 1940. *Final Report on the Survey and Settlement Operations in the District of Rangpur 1931–1938*, Alipore.

Hazarika, Atul Chandra. (ed.). 1988. *Bezbaroa Granthavali, Vol. II*, Guwahati.

Hazarika, Atul Chandra and Jatindranath Goswami. (eds). 1955. *Assam Sahitya Sabha Bhasanavali, Vol. I*, Jorhat.

———. (eds). 1957. *Assam Sahitya Sabha Bhasanavali, Vol. II*, Jorhat.

———. (eds). 1961. *Assam Sahitya Sabha Bhasanavali, Vol. III*, Jorhat.

Hirst, F. C. 1911. *Notes on the Clearing and Marking of Boundaries in Eastern Bengal and Assam*, Shillong.

———. 1914. *A Memoir upon the Maps of Bengal, Constructed from 1764 Onwards by Major James Rennell*, Calcutta.

———. 1921. *Report of on the Cooch Behar–Jalpaiguri Boundary*, Cooch Behar.

Hirst, F. C. and A. B. Smart. 1917. *A Brief History of the Surveys of Goalpara District*, Shillong.

Hodgson, B. G. 1849. *Essay on the Bodo, Koch and Dhimal Tribes*, Calcutta.

Home, A. L. 1898. *The Assam Forest Manual*, Simla.

Hunter, W. W. 1875. *A Statistical Account of Bengal, Mymensingh, Vol. 5*, London.

———. 1879. *A Statistical Account of Assam, Vols. I and II.* London.

Jenkins, F. 1868. *Diary and Notes of Captain F. Jenkins, Commissioner and Agent to the Governor General for Assam and the Northeastern Part of Rungpore, 1837–1841*, Calcutta.

Kakati, Bholanath. 1910. 'Asomiya Sujug', *Banhi*, 1: 31–35.

Kerr, Hem Chunder. 1874. *Report on the Cultivation of, and Trade in, Jute in Bengal, and on Indian Fibres.* Calcutta.

Laine, A. J. 1917a. *Account of the Land Tenure System of Goalpara*, Shillong.

———. 1917b. *Report on the Defects of the Rent Law in Goalpara District with Suggestions for its Amendment*, Shillong.

Maccosh, John. 1837. *Topography of Assam*, Calcutta.

Mackenzie, Alexander. 1884. *History of the Relations of the Government with the Hill Tribes of the North East Frontier of Bengal*, Calcutta.

———. 1917. 'Memorandum on the North East Frontier of Bengal', in F. C. Hirst and A. B. Smart (eds), *A Brief History of the Surveys of Goalpara District*, Shillong.

Mahanta, B. 1940. *Biplobi Khetiyok*, Guwahati.

Martin, Montgomery. 1976 (1838). *The History, Antiquities and Topography and Statistics of Eastern India, Vol. 5*, Rangpur and Assam, London.

Mills, A. J. M. 1854. *Report on the Province of Assam*, Calcutta.

Monahan, F. C. 1910. *Report of the Duars Committee*, Shillong.

Nathan, Mirza. 1936. *Baharistan-I-Ghayabi: A History of the Mughal Wars in Assam, Cooch Behar, Bengal, Bihar and Orissa during the Reigns of Jahangir and Shahjahan*, trans. and ed. M. I. Bora, Guwahati.

Pemberton, R. B. 1835. *Report on the Eastern Frontier of British India*, Calcutta.

———. 1903. *An Account of the Province of Assam and its Administration*, Calcutta.

Phukan, Nilmoni. 1935. 'Asam Jatiya Mahasabha', *Awahan*, 6: 593–603.

———. 1939. 'Notes on the Domicile Question', *Assam Tribune*, October 6, Guwahati.

Playne, Somerset. 1917. *Bengal and Assam, Behar and Orissa; Their History, People, Commerce and Industrial Resources*, London.

Rabha, Bishnu Prasad. 1931. 'Brihattar Asomor Kolpona', *Awahan*, 11: 14–27.

Rajkhowa, Benudhar. 1913. *Notes on the Sylhetee Dialect, showing its relation to Assam*, Sylhet.

Raychoudhury, S. C. 1907. 'Rongpurer Deshiyo Bhasa', *Sahitya Parishat Patrika*,12 (1): 16–19.

Robinson, W. 1841. *A Descriptive Account of Assam*, Calcutta.

Sachse, F. A. 1919a. *Final Report on the Survey and Settlement Operations in the District of Mymensingh, 1910–1917*, Calcutta.

———. 1919b. *Bengal District Gazetteers: Mymensingh*, Calcutta.

Sadaramin Barua, Harakanta. 1930. *Asam Buranji*, Guwahati.

Sanderson, G. P. 1878. *Thirteen Years among the Wild Beasts of India: Their Haunts and Habits from Personal Observation; With an Account of the Modes of Capturing and Taming Elephants*, London.

Sarma, Satyendranath. (ed.). 1986. *Ambikagiri Roychoudhuri Racanavali*, Guwahati.

Sen, Dinesh Chandra. 1911. *History of Bengali Language and Literature*, Calcutta.

———. 1923. *Eastern Bengal Ballads, Mymensingh*, Calcutta.

Sen, Tarini. 1876. *Bijni Rajvamsha*, Goalpara.

Shah, Abdul Hami. 1921. *Krishak Bilap*, Mymensingh.

Shastri, Gaurinath. 1928. `Nikhil Goalpara Jila Samitir Gauripur Adhibheshanar Sabhapatir Abhibhasan', Presidential Address to the All Goalpara District Association, Dhubri.

———. (ed.). 1930. *Kabindra Mahabharata*, Dhubri.

Talukdar, Nanda. (ed.). 1973. *Kanaklal Barooah Racanavali*, Guwahati.

Tamuli Phukan, Kasi Nath. 1905. *Asam Buranji*, Guwahati.

Ward, W. E. 1897. *Note on the Assam Land Revenue System*, Shillong.

Wise, James. 1883. *Notes on Races, Castes and Tribes of East Bengal*, London.

———. 1894. 'The Muhammadans of East Bengal', *Journal of the Asiatic Society of Bengal*, 63: 28–63.

SECONDARY SOURCES

Published

Adas, M. 1981. 'From Avoidance to Confrontation: Peasant Protest in Pre-colonial and Colonial South East Asia', *Comparative Studies in Society and History*, 23 (2): 217–47.

Agnew, John and Stuart Corbridge. 1995. *Mastering Space: Hegemony, Territory and International Political Economy*. London: Routledge.

Ahmed, Rafiuddin. 1981. *Bengal Muslims 1871–1906: A Quest for Identity*. Delhi: Oxford University Press.

Ahuja, Ravi. 1998. 'Labour Unsettled: Mobility and Protest in the Madras Region, 1750–1800', *Indian Economic and Social History Review*, 35 (4): 381–404.

Ali, Daud. (ed.). 1999. *Invoking the Past: The Uses of History in South Asia*. Delhi: Oxford University Press.

Amin, Shahid. 1995. *Event, Metaphor, Memory: Chauri Choura, 1922–1992*. Berkeley: University of California Press.

———. 2002. *Alternative Histories: A View from India*. Calcutta: Centre for Studies in Social Sciences (CSSSC).

Anderson, Benedict. 1983. *Imagined Communities: Reflections on the Origin and Spread of Nationalism*, London: Verso.

———. 1990. *Language and Power: Exploring Political Cultures in Indonesia*. Cornell: Cornell University Press.

———. 1992. *Long Distance Nationalism: World Capitalism and Rise of Identity Politics*. Amsterdam: Centre for Asian Studies.

Appadurai, Arjun. 1993. 'Number in the Colonial Imagination', in Carol A. Breckenridge and Peter van der Veer (eds), *Orientalism and the Post Colonial Predicament*, pp. 314–39. Pennsylvania: Pennsylvania University Press.

———. 1996. *Modernity at Large: Cultural Dimensions of Globalisation*. Minneapolis: University of Minnesota Press.

Arnold, David. 1996. *The Problem of Nature*. Oxford: Oxford University Press.

Asiwaju, A. (ed.). 1985. *Partitioned Africans: Ethnic Relations across Africa's International Boundaries, 1884–1984*. London: C. Hurst and Company.

Bandyopadhyay, Sekhar. 1997. *Caste, Protest and Identity in Colonial India: The Namasudras of Bengal, 1872–1947*. Richmond: Curzon Press.

———. 2004. *Caste, Culture and Hegemony, Social Domination in Colonial Bengal*. Delhi: Sage Publications.

Bandyopadhyay, Sekhar, Abhijit Dasgupta and Willem Van Schendel (eds.). 1984. *Bengal, Communities, Development and States*. Delhi: Manohar.

Banerjee, Prathama. 2006. *The Politics of Time*. Delhi: Oxford University Press.

Barman, Santo. 1994. *Zamindari System in Assam during British Rule: A Case Study of Goalpara District*. Delhi: Spectrum Publications.

Barman, Upendranath. 1970. *Rajbanshi Kshatriya Jatir Itihaash*, Jalpaiguri.

Barooah, Nirode K. 1970. *David Scott in North–East India 1803–1831: A Study in British Paternalism*. Delhi: Munshiram Manoharlal Publishers.

Barpujari, H. K. (ed.). 1992. *Comprehensive History of Assam, Vol. 4*. Guwahati: Publication Board Assam.

———. 1996. *Assam in the Days of the Company 1826–1858*. Shillong: North-Eastern Hill University.

Barrier, N. Gerald. 1981. *The Census in British India: New Perspectives*. New Delhi: Manohar.

Barth, Fredrick. 1969. *Ethnic Groups and Boundaries: The Social Organisation of Cultural Difference*. Boston: Little Brown.

Baruah, Sanjib. 1999. *India Against Itself*. Delhi: Oxford University Press.

———. 2005. *Durable Disorder*. Delhi: Oxford University Press.

———. 2008. 'Territoriality, Indigeneity and Rights in North-east India', *Economic and Political Weekly*, 43 (12–13): 15–19.

———. 2009. *Beyond Counter-insurgency: Breaking the Impasse in Northeast India*. Delhi: Oxford University Press.

Basu, Swaraj. 2003. *Dynamics of a Caste Movement*. Delhi: Manohar.

Baud, Michiel and Willem Van Schendel. 1997. 'Towards a Comparative History of Borderlands', *Journal of World History*, 8 (2): 267–75.

Bayly, Chris. 1983. *Rulers, Townsmen and Bazaars*. Delhi: Oxford University Press.

———. 1988. *Indian Society and the Making of the British Empire*. Cambridge: Cambridge University Press.

———. 1998. *Origins of Nationality in South Asia: Patriotism and Ethical Government in the Making of Modern India*. Delhi: Oxford University Press.

Bhadra, Gautam. 1984. 'Two Frontier Uprisings in Mughal India', in Ranajit Guha (ed.), *Subaltern Studies, Vol. II*, pp. 43–59. Delhi: Oxford University Press.

Bhattacharya, Neeladri. 1996. 'Remaking Custom: The Discourse and Practice of Colonial Codification', in R. Champakalakshmi and S. Gopal (eds), *Tradition, Dissent and Ideology: Essays in Honour of Romila Thapar*, pp. 20–51. Delhi: Oxford University Press.

———. 2001. 'Pastoralists in a Colonial World', in David Arnold and Ramachandra Guha (eds), *Nature, Culture, Imperialism*, pp. 49–86. Delhi: Oxford University Press.

Bhattacharya, Neeladri. 2003. 'Predicaments of Mobility: Frontier Traders in the Nineteenth Century', in Claude Markovits, Jacques Pouchepadass and Sanjay Subramanyam (eds), *Society and Circulation: Mobile People and Itinerant Cultures in South Asia 1750–1950*, pp. 163–215. Delhi: Permanent Black.

Bhuyan, S. K. 1928. *Early British Relations with Assam*. Guwahati: Assam Secretariat Press.

———. 1949. *Anglo–Assamese Relations: 1771–1826*. Guwahati: Lawyer's Book Stall.

Blackburn, S. H. and A. K. Ramanujan. (eds). 1986. *Another Harmony*. Berkeley: University of California Press.

Bose, Sugata. 1986. *Agrarian Bengal: Economy, Social Structure and Politics, 1919–1947*. Cambridge: Cambridge University Press.

Braudel, Fernand. 1972. *The Mediterranean and the Mediterranean World in the Age of Philip II, Vol. 1*. Galsgow: Fontana.

Breckenridge, Carol A. 1977. 'From Protector to Litigant', *Indian Economic and Social History Review*, 14: 75–106.

Breckenridge, Carol A. and Peter van der Veer. (eds). 1993. *Orientalism and the Post Colonial Predicament*. Pennsylvania: Pennsylvania University Press.

Breman, Jan. 1990. *The Shattered Image: Construction and Deconstruction of the Village in Colonial Asia*. Amsterdam: Centre for Asian Studies.

Breman, Jan and E. Valentine Daniel. 1992. 'The Making of a Coolie', in E. Valentine Daniel, Henry Bernstein and Tom Brass (eds), *Plantations, Proletarians and Peasants in Colonial Asia*, pp. 268–91. London: Frank Cass.

Brenda, E. F. Beck, Peter J. Claus, Praphulladatta Goswami, and Jawaharlal Handoo. (eds). 1987. *Folktales of India*. Chicago: University of Chicago Press.

Broomfield, J. H. 1968. *Elite Conflict in a Plural Society: Twentieth Century Bengal*. Berkeley: University of Berkley Press.

Burghart, Richard. 1984. 'The Formation of the Concept of the Nation State in Nepal', *Journal of Asian Studies*, 44 (1): 101–25.

———. 1993. 'A Quarrel in the Language Family: Agency and Representations of Speech in Mithila', *Modern Asian Studies*, 27 (4): 761–804.

Burke, Peter. 1978. *Popular Culture in Early Modern Europe*. London: Temple Smith.

———. 1992. 'We, the People: Popular Culture and Popular Identity in Modern Europe', in Scott Lash and Jonathan Friedman (eds), *Modernity and Identity*, pp. 293–308. Oxford: Blackwell.

Chakravarty, Dipesh. 1991. 'History as Critique and Critique of History', *Economic and Political Weekly*, 26 (37): 2162–166.

Chakravarty, Dipesh. 1992. 'Postcoloniality and the Artifice of History: Who speaks for "Indian" Pasts?', *Representations*, 37: 1–26.

Chandra, Sudhir. 1989. 'The Nation in the Making: Regional Identities in 19th Century Indian Language Literature', in P. C. Chatterjee (ed.), *Self Images, Identity and Nationality*, pp. 218–26. Shimla: Indian Institute for Advance Studies.

Chartier, Roger. 1987. The *Cultural Uses of Print in Early Modern France*, trans. Lydia G. Cochrane. Princeton: Princeton University Press.

Chatterjee, Joya. 1995. *Bengal Divided: Hindu Communalism and Partition, 1932–1947*. Cambridge: Cambridge University Press.

———. 1999. 'The Refashioning of a Frontier: The Radcliffe Line and Bengal's Border Landscape, 1947–1952', *Modern Asian Studies*, 33 (1): 185–242.

———. 2007. *Spoils of Partition, Bengal and India, 1947–1967*. Cambridge: Cambridge University Press.

Chatterjee, Kumkum. 1998. 'History as Self-Representation: The Recasting of a Political Tradition in Late Eighteenth-Century Eastern India', *Modern Asian Studies*, 32 (4): 913–48.

———. 1999. 'Discovering India: Travel, History and Identity in Late Nineteenth and Early Twentieth century India', in Daud Ali (ed.), *Invoking the Past: The Uses of History in South Asia*, pp. 192–227. Delhi: Oxford University Press.

Chatterjee, Partha. 1980. *Agrarian Relations and Politics in Bengal: Some Considerations on the Making of the Tenancy Act Amendment 1928*. Calcutta: Centre for Studies in Social Sciences.

Chatterjee, Partha. 1986. *Nationalist Thought and the Colonial World: A Derivative Discourse*. London: Zed Books.

———. 1993. *The Nation and Its Fragments: Colonial and Postcolonial Histories*. Princeton: Princeton University Press.

———. 1994. 'Claims of the Past: Genealogy of Modern Historiography in Bengal', in David Arnold and David Hardiman (eds), *Subaltern Studies VIII: Essays in Honour of Ranajit Guha*, pp. 1–49. Delhi: Oxford University Press.

———. (ed.). 1996. *Texts of Power: Emerging Disciplines in Colonial Bengal*. Calcutta: Samya.

———. 1997. 'Beyond the Nation? Or Within?', *Economic and Political Weekly*, 32 (1): 30–34.

Chatterjee, S. K. 1954. *The Place of Assam in the History and Civilisation of India*, Calcutta: Gauhati University.

———. 1974. *Kirita–jana–Kriti: The Indo-Mongoloids, Their Contribution to the History and Culture of India*. Calcutta: Asiatic Society of Bengal.

Choudhuri, Amanatullah Ahmad. 1936. *Kochbiharer Itihaas, Vol. 1*, Kochbihar.

Clifford, James. 1992. 'Traveling Cultures', in L. Grossberg, C. Nelson and P. Treichler (eds), *Cultural Studies*, pp. 96–112. London: Routledge.

Cohn, Bernard S. 1990a. 'Census and Objectification', in Bernard S. Cohn (ed.), *An Anthropologist Among Historians and Other Essays*, pp. 224–55. Delhi: Oxford University Press.

———. 1990b. 'Regions Subjective and Objective: Their Relation to the Study of Modern Indian History and Society', in B. S. Cohn (ed.), *An Anthropologist Among Historians and Other Essays*, pp. 100–36. Delhi: Oxford University Press.

———. 1997. 'Law and the Colonial State in India', in Bernard S. Cohn (ed.), *Colonialism and its Forms of Knowledge: The British in India*, pp. 57–76. Delhi: Oxford University Press.

Confino, Alon. 1997. 'Collective Memory and Cultural History: Problems of Method', *American Historical Review*, 102 (5): 1386–1403.

Cooper, Frederick and Ann Laura Stoler. (eds). 1997. *Tensions of Empire: Colonial Cultures in a Bourgeois World*. Berkeley: University of California Press.

Crane, Robert I. (ed.). 1967. 'Regions and Regionalism in South Asia: An Exploratory Study', Monograph No. 5, Duke University.

Daniel, E. Valentine. 1997. 'Three Dispositions Towards the Past: One Sinhala, Two Tamil', in H. L. Seneviratne (ed.), *Identity, Consciousness and the Past*, pp. 22–41. Delhi: Oxford University Press.

Das, Dhiren. 1998. *O Mor Hai Hastir Kanyare*. Dhubri: Nabin Prakashan.

Dasgupta, Keya. 1981. *The Formation of the Transport Network in an Export Oriented Economy: Brahmaputra Valley: 1839–1914*, Occasional paper No. 36. Calcutta: Centre for Studies in Social Sciences.

Dasgupta, Keya. 1986. *Wastelands Colonization Policy and the Settlement of Explantation Labour in the Brahmaputra Valley: A Study in Historical Perspective*, Occasional Paper No. 82. Calcutta: Centre for Studies in Social Sciences.

Dasgupta, Ranajit. 1992. *Economy, Society and Politics in Bengal: Jalpaiguri, 1869–1947*. Delhi: Oxford University Press.

Datta, Birendranath. 1982. *Goalparar Loko Sanskriti Aru Asomiya Sanskritiloi Iyar Obodan*. Dhubri: Assam College Teachers Association.

———. 1995. *A Study in the Folk Culture of the Goalpara Region of Assam*. Guwahati: Gauhati University.

De Haan, Arjan and Ben Rogaly. (eds). 2002. *Labour Mobility and Rural Society*. London: Frank Cass.

Deshpande, Prachi. 2004. 'Caste as Maratha: Social Categories, Colonial Policy and Identity in Early Twentieth Century Maharashtra', *Indian Economic and Social History Review*, 41 (1): 7–32.

———. 2007. *Creative Pasts: Historical Memory and Identity in Western India, 1700–1960*. New York: Columbia University Press.

Deshpande, Satish. 2000. 'Hegemonic Spatial Strategies: The Nation–Space and Hindu Communalism in Twentieth Century India', in Partha Chatterjee and Pradeep Jeganathan (eds), *Subaltern Studies XI*, pp. 167–212. Delhi: Oxford University Press.

Dirks, Nicholas B. 1982. 'The Pasts of a Palayakarar: The Ethnohistory of a South Indian Little King', *Journal of Asian Studies*, 41 (4): 655–83.

———. 1986. 'From Little King to Landlord: Property, Law and the Gift under the Madras Permanent Settlement', *Comparative Studies in Society and History*, 28 (2): 307–33.

———. 1987. *The Hollow Crown: Ethnohistory of a Small Kingdom*. Cambridge: Cambridge University Press.

———. 1990. 'History as a Sign of the Modern', *Public Culture*, 2 (2): 25–32.

———. (ed.). 1992. *Colonialism and Culture*. Ann Arbor: University of Michigan Press.

———. 2001. *Castes of Mind: Colonialism and the Making of Modern India*. Princeton: Princeton University Press.

Donnan, Hastings and T. M. Wilson. (eds). 1994. *Border Approaches: Anthropological Perspectives on Frontiers*. Lanham, MD: University Press of America.

Donnan, Hastings and Dieter Haller. 2000. 'Liminal No More: The Relevance of Borderland Studies', *Ethnologia Europea: The Journal of European Ethnology*, 30 (2): 7–22.

Dove, Michael R. 1994. '"Jungle" in Nature and Culture', in Ramachandra Guha (ed.), *Social Ecology*, pp. 90–115. Delhi: Oxford University Press.

Duara, Prasanjit. 1995. *Rescuing History from the Nation: Questioning Narratives of Modern China*. Chicago: University of Chicago Press.

Dutta, S. C. 1984. *The North East and the Mughals*. Delhi: D. K. Publishers.

Eaton, Richard M. 1993. *The Rise of Islam and the Bengal Frontier, 1204–1760*. Berkeley: University of California Press.

Embree, Ainslie. 1977. 'Frontiers into Boundaries: From the Traditional to the Modern State', in R. G. Fox (ed.), *Realm and Region in Traditional India*, pp. 253–80. Duke: Duke University Press.

Everitt, Alan. 1977. 'River and the World: Reflections on the Historical Origins of Regions and Pays', *Journal of Historical Geography*, 3 (1): 1–19.

Febvre, Lucien. 1973. 'Frontiere: The Word and the Concept', in Peter Burke (ed.), *A New Kind of History: From the Writings of Febvre*, pp. 208–18. London: Routledge and Kegan Paul.

Fernandez, J. W. 1966. 'Folklore as an Agent of Nationalism', in I. Wallerstein (ed.), *Social Change: The Colonial Situation*, pp. 585–91. New York: Wiley.

Finley, M. I. 1965. 'Myth, Memory and History', *History and Theory*, 5 (3): 281–302.

Fraser, Nancy. 1998. 'Social Justice in the Age of Identity Politics: Redistribution, Recognition, and Participation', in G. B. Peterson (ed.), *The Tanner Lectures on Human Values, Vol. 19*. Salt Lake City: University of Utah Press.

Freitag, Sandra B. 1989. *Collective Action and Community: Public Arenas and the Emergence of Communalism in North India*. Berkeley: University of California Press.

Frykenberg, Robert E. (ed.). 1969. *Land Control and Social Structure in Indian History*. Wisconsin: University of Wisconsin Press.

———. 1987. 'The Concept of the "Majority" as a Devilish Force in the Politics of Modern India: A Historiographic Comment', *Journal of the Commonwealth History and Comparative Politics*, 25 (3): 267–74.

Foucault, Michel. 1986. 'Of Other Spaces', *Diacritics*, 16 (1): 22–27.

Fox, Richard. 1971. *Kin, Clan, Raja and Rule: State–Hinterland Relations in pre-industrial India*. Berkeley: University of California Press.

———. 1977. *Realm and Region in Traditional India*. New Delhi: Vikas Publication.

Gardner, Katy and Filippo Osella. 2003. 'Migration, Modernity and Social Transformation in South Asia', *Contributions to Indian Sociology*, 37 (1&2): v–xxviii.

Ghosh, Dhruba and Dane Kennedy. (eds). 2006. *Decentering Empire: Britain, India and the Transcolonial World*. New Delhi: Orient Longman.

Gidwani, Vinay Krishna. 1992. 'Waste and the Permanent Settlement in Bengal', *Economic and Political Weekly*, 27 (4): 39–46.

Gordon, Stewart. 1988. 'Legitimacy and Loyalty in Some Successor States of the Eighteenth Century', in J. F. Richards (ed.), *Kinship and Authority in South Asia*, pp. 327–48. Delhi: Oxford University Press.

Gordon, Stewart. 1990. 'Burhanpur: Entrepot and Hinterland, 1650–1750', in Sanjay Subrahmanyam (ed.), *Merchants, Markets and the State in Early Modern India*, pp. 48–65. Delhi: Oxford University Press.

Goswami, Manu. 1998. 'From Swadeshi to Swaraj: Nation, Economy, Territory in Colonial South Asia, 1870 to 1907', *Comparative Studies in Society and History*, 40 (4): 609–36.

———. 2004. *Producing India*. New Delhi: Permanent Black.

Goswami, Prafulladatta. 1960. *Ballads and Tales of Assam*. Guwahati: Guwahati University.

Guha, Amalendu. 1974. 'East Bengal Immigrants and Bhasani in Assam Politics, 1928–1947', *Indian History Congress Proceedings*, pp. 348–65. Calcutta: The Indian History Congress.

———. 1977. *Planter Raj to Swaraj: Freedom Struggle and Electoral Politics in Assam 1826–1947*. Delhi: Indian Council of Historical Research.

———. 2000. *Jamidar Kalin Goalpara Jilar Artha Samajik Avastha*. Guwahati: Natun Sahitya Parishad.

Guha, Ramachandra. 2000. *The Unquiet Woods*. Berkeley: University of California Press.

Guha, Ranajit. 1956. 'A Report on an Investigation of the Gauripur Raj Estate Archives', in *Annual Report, Regional Record Survey Committee, West Bengal, 1955–56*, Calcutta.

———. 1963. *A Rule of Property for Bengal*. Paris: Mouton & Co.

———. 1983. *Elementary Aspects of Peasant Insurgency in Colonial India*. Delhi: Oxford University Press.

———. 1988. *An Indian Historiography of India; A Nineteenth Century Agenda and its Implications*. Calcutta: K. P. Bagchi and Co.

———. 1996. 'The Small Voice of History', in Shahid Amin and Dipesh Chakravarty (eds), *Subaltern Studies, Vol. XI*, pp. 1–12. Delhi: Oxford University Press.

———. 1997. *Dominance without Hegemony: History and Power in Colonial India*. Harvard: Harvard University Press.

Guha, Sumit. 1999. *Environment and Ethnicity in India 1200–1991*. Cambridge: Cambridge University Press.

Gutierrez-Jones, Carl. 1995. *Rethinking the Borderlands: Between Chicano Culture and Legal Discourse*. Berkeley: University of California Press.

Habib, Irfan. 1982. *An Atlas of the Mughal Empire*. Delhi: Oxford University Press.

———. 1999 (1963). *The Agrarian System of Mughal India*. New Delhi: Tulika.

Halbwachs, Maurice. 1980 (1950). *The Collective Memory*, trans. Francis J. Ditter, Jr. and Vida Yazdi Ditter. New York: Harper and Row.

Hall, Stuart. 1992. 'The Question of Cultural Identities', in Stuart Hall, David Held and Tony McGrew (eds), *Modernity and Its Futures: Understanding Modern Societies*, pp. 274–316. Cambridge: Polity Press.

Hazarika, Sanjoy. 2000. *Rites of Passage: Border Crossings, Imagined Homelands: India's East and Bangladesh.* New Delhi: Penguin Books.

Hill, Jonathan D. (ed.). 1984. *Rethinking History and Myth: Indigenous South American Perspectives on the Past.* Illinois: University of Illinois.

Hirschman, Charles. 1987. 'The Meaning and Measurement of Ethnicity in Malaysia: An Analysis of Census Classifications', *Journal of Asian Studies,* 46 (3): 555–82.

Hobsbawm, Eric and Terrence Ranger. (eds). 1983. *The Invention of Tradition.* Cambridge: Cambridge University Press.

Inden, Ronald. 1990. 'Orientalist Constructions of India', *Modern Asian Studies,* 20 (3): 401–6.

Jafri, S. Z. H. 1990. 'Rural Bureaucracy in Cooch Behar and Assam under the Mughals: Archival Evidence', *Indian History Congress Proceedings, 49th Session,* pp. 277–87. Delhi: The Indian History Congress.

Jalal, Ayesha. 2002. 'Negotiating Colonial Modernity and Cultural Difference: Indian Muslim Conceptions of Community and Nation, 1878–1914', in Leila Tarazi Fawaz and C.A. Bayly (eds), *Modernity and Culture,* pp. 230–61. New York: Columbia University Press.

Kakati, Banikanta. 1941. *Assamese: Its Formation and Development.* Guwahati: Lawyer's Book Stall.

Kar, Bodhisattva. 2008. '"Tongue Has No Bone": Fixing the Assamese Language, c. 1800–c. 1930', *Studies in History,* 24 (1): 27–76.

Kar, M. 1975. 'Assam's Language Question in Retrospect', *Journal of the Indian School of Social Sciences,* 4 (2): 21–35.

Kaviraj, Narahari. 1972. *A Peasant Uprising in Bengal, 1783: The First Formidable Peasant Uprising against the Rule of the East India Company.* New Delhi: People's Publishing House.

Kaviraj, Sudipta. 1990. 'Writing, Speaking, Being: Language and the Historical Formation of Identities in India', in *Identity in History: South and South East Asia,* pp. 25–64. Heidelberg: The South Asia Institute, University of Heidelberg.

———. 1993. 'The Imaginary Institution of India', in Partha Chatterjee and David Arnold (eds), *Subaltern Studies, Vol. 7,* pp. 1–39. Delhi: Oxford University Press.

———. 1994. 'On the Construction of Colonial Power: Structure, Discourse and Hegemony', in Dagmar Engels and Shula Marks (eds), *Contesting Colonial Hegemony, State and Society in Africa and India,* pp.19–54. London: British Academic Press.

Khaderia, Nandita. 1990. 'Internal Trade and Market Network in the Brahmaputra Valley 1826–1873', *Indian Historical Review,* 17 (1–2): 152–73.

King, Christopher B. 1989. 'Forging a New Linguistic Identity: The Hindi Movement in Banaras 1868–1914', in Sandra B. Freitag (ed.), *Culture and Power in Banaras 1800–1914,* pp. 170–202. Berkeley: University of California Press.

King, Christopher B. 1994. *One Language, Two Scripts: The Hindi Movement in Nineteenth Century North India*. Bombay: Oxford University Press.

Kopytoff, Igor. (ed.). 1987. *The African Frontier: The Reproduction of Traditional African Societies*. Indianapolis: Indiana University Press.

Kulke, Hermann. 1993. *Kings and Cults: State Formation and Legitimation in India and Southeast Asia*. Delhi: Manohar.

Ladurie, E. LeRoy. 1979. *The Territory of the Historian*, trans. Ben Reynolds and Sian Reynolds. Chicago: University of Chicago Press.

Lattimore, Owen. 1962. *Studies in Frontier History*. London: Oxford University Press.

Lefebvre, Henri. 1991. *The Production of Space*, trans. Donald Nicholson Smith. Oxford: Blackwell.

Lelyveld, David. 1993. 'The Fate of Hindustani: Colonial Knowledge and the Project of a National Language', in Carol A. Breckenridge and Peter van der Veer (eds), *Orientalism and the Postcolonial Predicament*, pp. 189–214. Pennsylvania: University of Pennsylvania Press.

Loomba, Ania. 1998. *Colonialism/Postcolonialism*. London: Routledge.

Ludden, David. 1994. 'History Outside Civilisation and the Mobility of South Asia', *South Asia*, 17 (1): 1–23.

———. 2002. 'Spectres of Agrarian Territory in Southern India', *Indian Economic and Social History Review*, 39 (1 and 2): 233–57.

———. 2005. 'Where is Assam? Using Geographical History to Locate Current Social Realities', *Himal South Asia*, November, Kathmandu.

Markovits, Claude, Jacques Pouchepadass and Sanjay Subrahmanyam. (eds). 2003. *Society and Circulation, Mobile People and Itinerant Cultures in South Asia 1750–1950*. Delhi: Permanent Black.

Marshall, P. J. 1987. *The New Cambridge History of India, II, 2, Bengal: The British Bridgehead, Eastern India 1740–1828*. Cambridge: Cambridge University Press.

Mayaram, Shail. 2004. *Against History, Against State: Counter Perspectives from the Margins*. New Delhi: Permanent Black.

McLane, John. 1993. *Land and Local Kingship in 18th Century Bengal*. Cambridge: Cambridge University Press.

Misra, Sanghamitra. 2005. 'Changing Frontiers and Spaces', *Studies in History*, 21 (2): 215–46.

———. 2006. 'Redrawing Frontiers: Language, Resistance and the Imagining of a Goalparia People', *The Indian Economic and Social History Review*, 43 (2): 199–225.

———. 2008. 'Law, Migration and New Subjectivities: Reconstructing the Colonial Project in an Eastern Borderland', *Indian Economic and Social History Review*, 44 (4): 425–61.

Misra, Tilottoma. 1987. *Literature and Society in Assam: A Study of the Assamese Renaissance 1826–1926*. Guwahati: Omsons Publications.

Misra, Udayon. 2005. 'Assam', in Mayumi Murayama, Kyoko Inoue and Sanjoy Hazarika (eds), *Subregional Relations in the Eastern South Asia, with Special Reference to India's North Eastern Region*, Joint Research Programme Series No.133. Tokyo: Institute of Development Economics.

Morris-Suzuki, Tessa. 1996. 'The Frontiers of Japanese Identity', in Stein Tonnesson and Hans Antlov (eds), *Asian Forms of the Nation*, pp. 42–66. Richmond: Curzon Press.

Mukherjee, Radhakamal. 1938. *Changing Face of Bengal: A Study in Riverine Economy*. Calcutta: The University Press.

Nagazato, Nariaka. 1994. *Agrarian System of Eastern Bengal 1870–1910*. Calcutta: K. P. Bagchi and Company.

Nandy, Ashis. 1995. 'History's Forgotten Doubles', *History and Theory*, 34 (2): 44–66.

Naregal, Veena. 2001. 'Figuring the Political as Pedagogy: Colonial Intellectuals, Mediation and Modernity in Western India', *Studies in History*, 17 (1): 17–55.

Nath, Dwijen. 1977. *Goalparar Diary*, Kokrajhar.

Neog, Hariprasad. 1968. *Pramathanath Chakravarty*, Jorhat.

Nora, Pierre. 1996. 'Between Memory and History', in *Rethinking the French Past, Realms of Memory, Volume 1: Conflicts and Divisions*. New York: Columbia University Press.

Nugent, Paul and A. I. Asiwaju. (eds). 1996. *African Boundaries, Barriers, Conduits and Opportunities*. London: Pinter.

Oinam, Bhagat. 2009. 'Preparing for a Cohesive Northeast: Problems of Discourse', in Sanjib Baruah (ed.), *Beyond Counter-insurgency: Breaking the Impasse in Northeast India*, pp. 170–80. Delhi: Oxford University Press.

Omvedt, Gail. 1980. 'Migration in Colonial India: The Articulation of Feudalism and Capitalism by the Colonial State', *The Journal of Peasant Studies*, 7 (2): 185–212.

Panda, Chitta. 1996. *The Decline of the Bengal Zamindars: Midanpore, 1870–1920*. Delhi: Oxford University Press.

Perlin, Frank. 1983. 'Proto-industrialisation and the Pre-colonial South Asia', *Past and Present*, 98: 30–95.

———. 1994. 'Changes in the Production and Circulation of Money in the Seventeenth and the Eighteenth Century India: An Essay on Monetisation before Colonial Occupation', in Sanjay Subrahmanyam (ed.), *Money and Market in India 1100–1700*, pp. 276–308. Delhi: Oxford University Press.

Pinch, William R. 1996. *Peasant and Monks in British India*. Berkeley: University of California Press.

Pouchepadass, Jacques. 1974. 'Local Leaders and the Intelligentsia in the Champaran Satyagraha (1917): A Study in Peasant Mobilisation', *Contributions to Indian Sociology*, 8: 67–87.

Prescott, J. R.V. 1987. *Boundaries and Frontiers*. London: Unwin Hyman.

Raj, Kapil. 2003. 'Circulation and the Emergence of Modern Mapping: Great Britain and Early Colonial India, 1764–1820', in Sanjay Subrahmanyam (ed.), *Society and Circulation: Mobile People and Itinerant Cultures in South Asia 1750–1950*, pp. 23–55. Delhi: Permanent Black.

Ramanujan, A. K. and Brenda Beck. 1981. 'Social Categories and their Transformations', in Peter Claus and D. P. Pattanayak (eds), *Indian Folklore*. Mysore: Central Institute of Indian Languages.

Rampini, R. F. and J. H. Kerr. 1907. *The Bengal Tenancy Act*. Calcutta: S. K. Lahiri.

Rao, A. (ed.). 1986. *The Other Nomads: Peripatetic Minorities in Cross Cultural Perspective*. Cologne: Bohlau Verlag.

Ray, Rajat. 1984. *Social Conflict and Political Unrest in Bengal, 1875–1927*. Delhi: Oxford University Press.

Ray, Ratnalekha. 1979. *Change in Bengal Agrarian Society, 1765–1850*. Delhi: Manohar.

Ray, Subhajyoti. 2002. *Transformations on the Bengal Frontier: Jalpaiguri, 1765–1948*. London: Routledge Curzon.

Robb, Peter. (ed.). 1992. *Rural India: Land, Power and Society under British Rule*. Delhi: Oxford University Press.

———. 1993. 'Ideas in Agrarian Society: Some Observations on the British and Nineteenth Century Bihar', in David Arnold and Peter Robb (eds), *Institutions and Ideologies. Essays in South Asian History*, pp. 201–23. Richmond: Curzon Press.

———. 1997a. 'The Colonial State and the Construction of Indian identity: An Example on the Northeast Frontier in the 1880s', *Modern Asian Studies*, 31 (2): 245–83.

———. 1997b. *Ancient Rights and Future Comfort: Bihar, the Bengal Tenancy Act of 1885 and British Rule in India*. Richmond: Curzon Press.

Rogaly, Ben. 2003. 'Seasonal Migration and Shifting Ethnic Identity in Contemporary West Bengal', *Contributions to Indian Sociology*, 37 (1/2): 281–310.

Rose, Leo E. 1977. *The Politics of Bhutan*. London: Cornell University Press.

Royle, Edward. (ed.). 1998. *Issues of Regional Identity*. New York: Manchester University Press.

Ryley, J. Horton. (ed.). 1899. *Ralph Fitch: England's Pioneer to India and Burma*. London: T. F. Unwin.

Sahlins, Peter. 1989. *Boundaries: The Making of France and Spain in the Pyrenees*. Berkeley: University of California Press.

Saikia, Arupjyoti. 2005. *Jungles, Reserves, Wildlife: A History of Forests in Assam*. Guwahati: Wildlife Areas Development and Welfare Trust.

Saikia, Rajen. 2000. *Social and Economic History of Assam, 1853–1921*. New Delhi: Manohar.

Saikia, Yasmin. 2005. *Assam and India: Fragmented Memories, Cultural Identity, and the Tai–Ahom Struggle*. Delhi: Permanent Black.

Sanyal, Charu. 1965. *The Rajbanshis of North Bengal: A Study of a Hindu Social Group*. Calcutta: The Asiatic Society.

———. 1973. *The Meches and Totos: Two Sub-Himalayan Tribes of North Bengal*. Darjeeling: University of North Bengal.

Sarkar, Sumit. 1998. *Writing Social History*. New Delhi: Oxford University Press.

———. 1999. 'Post-modernism and the Writing of History', *Studies in History*, 15 (2): 293–322.

Schmitt, Carl. 2006. *The* Nomos *of the Earth in the International Law of the Jus Publicum Europaeum*, trans. G. L. Ulmen. New York: Telos Press.

Scott, James. 2009. *The Art of Not Being Governed: An Anarchist History of Upland Southeast Asia*. New Haven: Yale University Press.

Sen, Ashok, Partha Chatterjee and Saugata Mukherjee. 1982. *Three Studies on the Agrarian Structure in Bengal, 1850–1947*. Calcutta: Centre for Studies in Social Sciences.

Sen, Sudipta. 1998. *Empire of Free Trade: The East India Company and the Making of the Colonial Marketplace*. Pennsylvania: University of Pennsylvania Press.

Singh, Chetan. 1995. 'Forests, Pastoralists and Agrarian Society in Mughal India', in David Arnold and Ramachandra Guha (eds), *Nature, Culture, Imperialism*, pp. 21–49. Delhi: Oxford University Press.

———. 1998. *Natural Premises: Ecology and Peasant Life in the Western Himalayas 1800–1950*. Delhi: Oxford University Press.

Singh, Nagendra. 1978. *Bhutan: A Kingdom in the Himalayas*. New Delhi: Thompson Press.

Sivaramakrishnan, K. 1996. 'British Imperium and Forested Zones of Anomaly in Bengal, 1767–1833', *The Indian Economic and Social History Review*, 33 (3): 243–82.

———. 1999. *Modern Forests: Statemaking and Environmental Change in Colonial Eastern India*. California: Stanford University Press.

Skaria, Ajay. 1997. 'Shades of Wildness: Tribe, Caste and Gender in Western India', *The Journal of Asian Studies*, 56 (3): 726–45.

———. 1999. *Hybrid Histories: Forests, Frontiers and Wildness in Western India*. Oxford: Oxford University Press.

Skinner, G. William. 1964–1965. 'Marketing and the Social Structure in Rural China', *Journal of Asian Studies*, 24: 3–43.

Stokes, Martin. 1998. 'Imagining "the South": Hybridity, Heterotopia and Arabesk on the Turkish–Syrian Border', in Thomas M. Wilson and Hastings Donnan (eds), *Border Identities*, pp. 263–89. Cambridge: Cambridge University Press.

Subrahmanyam, Sanjay. 1997. 'Connected Histories: Notes towards a Reconfiguration of Early Modern Eurasia', *Modern Asian Studies*, 31 (3): 735–62.

———. 2005. *Explorations in Connected History: From the Tagus to the Ganges*. Delhi: Oxford University Press.

Tambs-Lyche, Harald. 1997. *Power, Profit and Poetry: Traditional Society in Kathiawar, Western India*. Delhi: Manohar.

Tonnesson, Stein and Hans Antlov. (eds). 1996. *Asian Forms of the Nation*. Richmond: Curzon.

van Schendel, Willem. 1992. 'The Invention of the "Jummas": State Formation and Ethnicity in South Eastern Bangladesh', *Modern Asian Studies*, 26 (1): 95–128.

———. 2002a. 'Geographies of Knowing, Geographies of Ignorance: Jumping Scale in Southeast Asia', *Environment and Planning D: Society and Space*, 20 (6): 647–88.

———. 2002b. 'Stateless in South Asia: The Making of the India–Bangladesh Enclaves', *The Journal of Asian Studies*, 61 (1): 115–47.

———. 2005. *The Bengal Borderland*. London: Anthem Press.

Veer, Peter van der. 1997. *Religious Nationalism: Hindus and Muslims in India*. Delhi: Oxford University Press.

Veer, Peter van der and Hartmut Lehmann. (eds). 1999. *Nation and Religion: Perspectives on Europe and Asia*. New Jersey: Princeton University Press.

Washbrook, David. 1981. 'Law, State, and Agrarian Society in Colonial India', *Modern Asian Studies*, 15 (3): 649–721.

———. 1988. 'Progress and Problems: South Asian Economic and Social History, c.1720–1860', *Modern Asian Studies*, 22 (1): 57–96.

———. 1991. 'To Each a Language of His Own: Language, Culture and Society in Colonial India', in David Wasbrook and Penelope Corfield (eds), *Language, History and Class*, pp. 179–203. Oxford: Basil Blackwell.

Weiner, Myron. 1983. 'The Political Demography of Assam's Anti–Immigrant Movement', *Population and Development Review*, 9 (2): 279–92.

West, W. Gordon. 1965 (1938). *The Geography Behind History*. London: Nelson.

Wilson, Jon E. 2005. '"A Thousand Countries to Go To": Peasants and Rulers in Late Eighteenth Century Bengal', *Past and Present*, 189 (1): 81–109.

Wilson, Thomas M. and Donnan Hastings. (eds). 1998. *Border Identities: Nation and the State at International Frontiers*. Cambridge: Cambridge University Press.

Winichakul, Thongchai. 1994. *Siam Mapped: A History of the Geo Body of a Nation*. Honolulu: University of Hawaii Press.

Yang, Anand A. (ed.). 1985. *Crime and Criminality in British India.* Arizona: University of Arizona Press.

———. 1989. *The Limited Raj: Agrarian Relations in Colonial India, Saran District, 1793–1920.* Berkeley: University of California Press.

———. 1998. *Bazaar India: Markets, Society and the Colonial State in Gangetic Bihar.* Berkeley: University of California Press.

Zbavitel, Dusan. 1963. *Bengal Folk Ballads from Mymensingh.* Calcutta: University of Calcutta Press.

Unpublished Ph.D. Dissertations and Papers

Kumar, Avinash. 2003. 'Defining the Disciplines: Hindi History versus Hindi Literature, 1900–1940'. Paper presented at the 'South Asia Seminar', School of Oriental and African Studies, 11 March, London.

Mohapatra, Pragati. 1997. 'The Making of a Cultural Identity: Language, Literature and Gender in Orissa in Late Nineteenth and Early Twentieth Centuries'. Unpublished Ph.D. thesis, School of Oriental and African Studies.

Pande, Vasudha. 1999. 'The Making of Modern Kumaon circa 1815–1930'. Unpublished Ph.D. thesis, University of Delhi.

About the Author

Sanghamitra Misra teaches at the Department of History, University of Delhi, India.

Index

For Product Safety Concerns and Information please contact our EU
representative GPSR@taylorandfrancis.com
Taylor & Francis Verlag GmbH, Kaufingerstraße 24, 80331 München, Germany